SCENES AND MACHINES
ON THE ENGLISH STAGE
DURING THE RENAISSANCE

SCENES AND MACHINES ON THE ENGLISH STAGE DURING THE RENAISSANCE

A CLASSICAL REVIVAL

BY

LILY B. CAMPBELL

BARNES AND NOBLE, INC. · NEW YORK

PUBLISHERS · BOOKSELLERS · SINCE 1873

221435

Published in 1923 by the
Cambridge University Press

Reprinted by Barnes & Noble, Inc.
by Special Arrangement with the Cambridge University Press

PRINTED IN THE UNITED STATES OF AMERICA

TO THE READER

THIS book was written in the belief that the building of theaters in the Renaissance was as much influenced by the revived knowledge of classical theory and precedent as was the writing of the plays to be presented in them. The fount from which flowed this authority in architecture was Vitruvius, Serlio being its most influential expounder and adapter. Obviously there were experienced craftsmen able and willing to apply their accustomed skills to new adventures in theatrical construction and dramatic presentation. What was new in these adventures seems to me to be the emphasis laid on four matters:

1. Public and private theaters were clearly distinguished, public theaters being amphitheaters built in round or oval shapes, private indoor theaters being rectangular.

2. Scenes and machines were considered an essential part of the architect's business.

3. The stage setting was to be determined more by dramatic genre than by consideration of geography or place of action.

4. The new scenery provided artists their supreme opportunity to display the wonders of perspective.

Since the recognition of dramatic genre is a distinguishing mark of Renaissance drama, and the introduction of perspective differentiates Renaissance painting from the Primitive, the history of drama and of painting needs to be viewed in close alliance with the history of the theater itself. Furthermore, since there were both private and public theaters in England as elsewhere, it is desirable to stress the fact in trying to reconstruct an Elizabethan playhouse.

L.B.C.

v

PREFACE

SUITABLY to acknowledge the various obligations
incurred in the preparation of this study of the
origins of modern stage spectacle seems wellnigh impossible. Specific instances of indebtedness I have tried
to indicate in the foot-notes. But there remain to be
acknowledged those more general obligations, which,
while less definite, have been even more important in
determining the results of my work. The study was
undertaken as a dissertation for the Ph.D. degree at the
University of Chicago, and from the outset I had the
great privilege of the counsel and advice of Professor
J. M. Manly, who with Professor C. R. Baskervill
read the entire study, section by section, as it was
written. To them both and to Professor Myra Reynolds,
who was responsible for much of my initial interest in
the history of the theatre, I owe my sincere gratitude.

Most of my work has been done in the University of
Chicago Libraries, and to the librarians of these libraries
I am indebted for the courtesy and helpfulness which
made possible the securing of books necessary to
scattered investigation. To the Art Institute of Chicago
and particularly to the Burnham Architectural Library
of the Art Institute, I am indebted for access to most of
the works cited in the earlier chapters of this study; to
the librarian of the Burnham Library, Miss Marian
Cummings, I am indebted for help too extensive and
too varied to be adequately indicated. The librarians
of the Chicago Public Library, the Newberry Library,

and the John Crerar Library of Chicago, and of the New York Public Library and the Avery Architectural Library of Columbia University have also given courteous help. To the University of Columbia Library, the Library of Congress, the Boston Public Library, and the Harvard University Library I am indebted for the loan of necessary books.

To the Master of Peterhouse, Sir A. W. Ward, who read my work in manuscript, I am specially indebted. But my greatest obligation is to Professor Manly, to whom I owe both my interest in research and the training that has made possible whatever is sound in my work.

L. B. C.

Los Angeles,
California, 1923.

CONTENTS

		PAGE
TO THE READER	. . . .	v
PREFACE	. . . .	vii
INTRODUCTION.	. . . . . .	I

PART I

THE CLASSICAL REVIVAL OF STAGE DECORATION IN ITALY

CHAP.
I.	THE INFLUENCE OF VITRUVIUS ON THE SCENIC REPRESENTATION OF THE DRAMA	9
II.	THE RE-DISCOVERY OF THE ART OF PERSPECTIVE IN SCENES	28
III.	THE ADOPTING OF THE PERSPECTIVE SCENE IN DRAMATIC PRODUCTIONS . .	43
IV.	MACHINES	59
V.	THE THEORY OF THE DRAMA . . .	66

PART II

STAGE DECORATION IN ENGLAND DURING THE SIXTEENTH CENTURY

VI.	EARLY CLASSICAL INFLUENCES IN ENGLAND	73
VII.	DRAMATIC REPRESENTATIONS IN THE GRAMMAR SCHOOLS, UNIVERSITIES AND INNS OF COURT	83
VIII.	DRAMATIC REPRESENTATIONS AT COURT	99
IX.	SCENERY IN THE PUBLIC THEATRES . .	116
X.	DRAMATIC CRITICISM	122

PART III

STAGE DECORATION IN ENGLAND
1600–1650

CHAP.   PAGE

XI. PROGRESS IN THE THEORY OF ARCHI-
TECTURE AND PERSPECTIVE . . . 145

XII. THE WORK OF INIGO JONES AND HIS CON-
TEMPORARIES IN ENGLAND . . . 161

XIII. SPECTACLE IN THE THEATRES . . . 195

PART IV

STAGE DECORATION IN ENGLAND
AFTER THE RESTORATION

XIV. THE INCORPORATION OF SCENES IN THE
PUBLIC THEATRES 217

XV. THE JUSTIFICATION OF DRAMATIC SPEC-
TACLE 253

XVI. THE INFLUENCE OF OPERA ON DRAMATIC
GENRE 257

XVII. "DISCOVERIES" 272

XVIII. MOVABLE SCENES AND THE UNITY OF
PLACE 278

XIX. CONCLUSIONS 290

INDEX 295

LIST OF ILLUSTRATIONS

TEXT-FIGURES

PAGE

1. THE GREEK THEATRE, from the Jocundus Edition of Vitruvius, 1513 20

2. THE ROMAN THEATRE, from the Jocundus Edition of Vitruvius, 1513 21

3. BARBARO'S INTERPRETATION OF THE ROMAN THEATRE, from Conte Montenari, *Del Teatro Olympico*, 1749 . . . 25

4. THE "COMICALL" SCENE, from Serlio, *The Second Book of Architecture* (English Translation), 1611 . . . 36

5. THE "TRAGICALL" SCENE, from Serlio, *The Second Book of Architecture* (English Translation), 1611 . . . 37

6. THE "SATIRICALL" SCENE, from Serlio, *The Second Book of Architecture* (English Translation), 1611 . . . 38

7. PLAN OF THE OLYMPIC THEATRE, from Conte Montenari, *Del Teatro Olympico*, 1749 58

8. THE METHODS OF SHIFTING STAGE SCENERY, from Sabbatini, *Pratica di fabricar Scene e Machine ne' Teatri*, 1638 . 155

9. From Sabbatini, *Pratica di fabricar Scene e Machine ne' Teatri*, 1638 158

10. DESIGN BY INIGO JONES FOR THE STAGING OF THE MASQUE *SALMACIDA SPOLIA*, from Reyher's reproduction from Lansdowne MS. 1171 181

11. THE THEATRE AT PARMA, from George Saunders, *A Treatise on Theatres*, 1790 196

12. THE TEATRO DI FANO OF TORELLI, from the *Pianta e Spaccato del Nuovo Teatro d'Imola*, Architettura del Cavalier Cosimo Morelli, 1780 216

13. JOHN WEBB'S PLAN OF THE RUTLAND HOUSE STAGE FOR *THE SIEGE OF RHODES*, reproduced with the kind permission of Mr W. G. Keith and the *Burlington Magazine* 224

14. SECTION OF RUTLAND HOUSE STAGE, SHOWING BACK AND FRONT STAGE, reproduced with the kind permission of Mr W. G. Keith and the *Burlington Magazine* . . 225

15. From Andrea Pozzo, *Prospettiva de' Pittori ed Architetti*, 1693 248

PLATES

TO FACE PAGE

I.   PROFILE AND GROUND PLAN OF SERLIO'S THEATRE, from
     Serlio, *The Five Books of Architecture* (English Transla-
     tion), 1611   34

II. ILLUSTRATION FROM LEONARDO SALVIATI, *IL GRANCHIO*,
     1566, reproduced through the courtesy of Professor
     J. M. Manly   42

III. THE STAGE OF THE OLYMPIC THEATRE, from Conte
     Montenari, *Del Teatro Olympico*, 1749   .   .   .   54

IV. INIGO JONES'S PLAN, showing the arrangement of the stage
     and hall on the occasion of the presentation of *Florimène*,
     1635   178

V.   THEATRE PLAN DISCOVERED BY W. G. KEITH IN INIGO
     JONES'S COPY OF PALLADIO, reproduced with the kind per-
     mission of Mr W. G. Keith and the *Burlington Magazine*   204

VI, VII. PLANS 80, 81, 82, from the original drawings by
     Sir Christopher Wren, reproduced by kind permission
     of the Warden and Fellows of All Souls College, Oxford,
     and by courtesy of the *Architectural Record* .   .   .   242

VIII. A "DISCOVERY" AS REPRESENTED BY ONE OF THE "SCULP-
     TURES" IN *THE EMPRESS OF MOROCCO*, reproduced
     through the courtesy of Professor F. C. Brown   .   .   276

SCENES AND MACHINES ON THE ENGLISH STAGE DURING THE RENAISSANCE: A Classical Revival

INTRODUCTION

IT seems inevitable that any discussion of the use of scenery on the English stage should take its rise in the Malone-Steevens controversy forever on exhibit in the Boswell edition of Malone's *Shakespeare* (1821), where in the third volume, as notes to Malone's *Historical Account of the Rise and Progress of the English Stage*[1], are recorded the comments of Steevens. The fundamental question there considered was whether scenery (a *scene* being defined by Malone as "a painting in perspective on a cloth fastened to a wooden frame or roller")[2] was known on the English stage before the Restoration. Malone showed "how little the imaginations of the audience were assisted by scenical deception," and how much necessity Shakespeare had to "call on them 'to piece out imperfections with their thoughts.'" Steevens reached other conclusions on the basis of practically the same evidence.

The evidence and the conclusions of Malone and Steevens were endlessly reviewed and debated throughout the century. The question they tried to answer continued to be the question to which an answer was sought, and the point of view assumed by Malone of scenery

[1] Cf. pp. 81 *sq*.
[2] Collier in *The History of English Dramatic Poetry to the Time of Shakespeare* and *Annals of the Stage to the Restoration* (1871), vol. III, p. 170, commented on this definition of Malone's as too strict and argued that the definition of a *scene* need not be otherwise restricted, "provided it was a painting in perspective, and movable with the change of place represented in the play."

C S   1

as an aid to dramatic illusion was the accepted and un-
questioned point of view throughout the century. In
1886, an unusually careful survey of the matter made
by Joseph Knight in his edition of *Roscius Anglicanus*
concluded:

> In the performance of *The Siege of Rhodes* at Rutland
> House, stage scenery was for the first time used. Scenery of a
> sufficiently elaborate kind had been employed in different
> countries in the representations of the Miracle plays....In the
> time of Shakespeare and Ben Jonson, as evidence conclusively
> proves, expensive scenery was provided for masques. So far as
> regards a stage-play, it was first used by Davenant[1].

Likewise R. W. Lowe in his *Life of Thomas Betterton*,
published in 1891, commented on the scenery used in
operas and certain plays after the Restoration as the
outcome of the elaborate mechanism used by Inigo
Jones and others in the presentation of the court masques
of the first half of the century[2].

Since 1900, however, a new and more scientific attitude has developed toward the whole question. New
sorts of evidence have been carefully sought and as
carefully considered. The evidence of the Elizabethan
plays has been studied exhaustively, and the work of
Reynolds[3], Neuendorff[4], and Albright[5] has tended to
establish on the basis of the evidence so gained the
general principles upon which Elizabethan plays were
presented and consequently to establish also the type
of theatre and stage constructed for their presentation.
The work of Monsieur Feuillerat in transcribing and

---

[1] Cf. pp. xix, xx.   [2] Cf. chap. II.
[3] G. F. Reynolds, *Some Principles of Elizabethan Staging*. Reprinted from *Modern Philology* (1905). Also articles in *Modern Philology* for 1907–8, 1911, 1914.
[4] B. Neuendorff, *Die englische Volksbühne im Zeitalter Shakespeares
nach dem Bühnenanweisungen* (1910).
[5] Victor E. Albright, *The Shakespearian Stage* (1909).

editing the records of the Office of the Revels[1] and that of Professor Adams in gathering together the records of documents relating to the Office of the Revels during its administration by Sir Henry Herbert[2] have made available for the consideration of the student of the subject much invaluable material. The work of Greg[3] and Wallace[4] and other scholars[5] has made possible also the reconsideration of the early theatres in Adams's *Shakespearean Playhouses*[6]. The significance of the court presentation of plays has become apparent through the work of Chambers[7] and Feuillerat[8] and Graves[9]. A

[1] Albert Feuillerat, ed., *Documents relating to the Office of the Revels in the time of Elizabeth* (1908). Also *Documents relating to the Revels at Court in the time of King Edward VI and Queen Mary* (1914); *Materialien zur Kunde des älteren englischen Dramas*. The editor's comments on the results of his study in connection with the first of these works is contained in his *Le Bureau des Menus-Plaisirs (Office of the Revels) et la Mise en Scène à la cour d'Elizabeth* (1910).

[2] Joseph Quincy Adams, ed., *The Dramatic Records of Sir Henry Herbert, Master of the Revels, 1623–1673* (1917).

[3] W. W. Greg, ed., *Henslowe's Diary* (1904–1908). Also *Henslowe Papers* (1907).

[4] C. W. Wallace, especially *The Children of the Chapel at Blackfriars, 1597–1603* (1908), and *The Evolution of the English Drama up to Shakespeare* (1912).

[5] The work of Mrs C. C. Stopes should be particularly noted because of its many indirect contributions to the study of methods of staging plays during the reigns of Henry VIII and Elizabeth. Cf. especially *William Hunnis and the Revels of the Chapel Royal* (1910), *Burbage and Shakespeare's Stage* (1913), and *Shakespeare's Environment* (1914). An article by the same author on "Elizabethan Stage Scenery," in the *Fortnightly Review*, June 1907, indicates the acceptance of the long-established point of view in regard to the relation of scenery and dramatic illusion.

[6] Joseph Quincy Adams, *Shakespearean Playhouses* (1917).

[7] E. K. Chambers, "Court Performances before Queen Elizabeth," *Modern Language Review* (1906), and "Court Performances before James I," *ibid.* (1907). [8] Cf. note 1, above.

[9] T. A. Graves, *The Court and the London Theatres during the Reign of Elizabeth* (1913).

knowledge of the technique attained in the use of scenery before the Restoration has come through the investigations of the court masques made by Brotanek[1] and Reyher[2]. The records of the university drama gathered by Professor Boas[3], the study of early English classical tragedy made by Professor Cunliffe[4], and the study by Professor Bond of plays from the Italian[5] have given the student of the stage much necessary material. Mr W. J. Lawrence's constant search for new material and for new interpretations of old material, witnessed by the multitude of his writings on the subject[6], has borne fruit in the work of every student of the sixteenth and seventeenth century theatre. The careful studies of Davenant's contribution to stagecraft made by Professor Tupper[7] and by Mr W. G. Keith[8] have also been illuminating. And the massing of material by Professor Thorndike[9] and Professor Odell[10] has made much scattered material easily accessible.

Gradually, therefore, there has become available to the student of the scenic development of the English theatre a mass of evidence as well as a body of considered opinion in regard to the significance of the evidence. The material with which the student is now usually concerned is, in general, of four sorts: (1) con-

[1] R. Brotanek, *Die englischen Maskenspiele* (1902).
[2] P. Reyher, *Les Masques Anglais* (1909).
[3] F. S. Boas, *University Drama in the Tudor Age* (1914).
[4] J. W. Cunliffe, *Early English Classical Tragedy* (1912).
[5] R. W. Bond, *Early Plays from the Italian* (1911).
[6] Cf. particularly *The Elizabethan Playhouse* (1912). Second series (1913).
[7] J. W. Tupper, ed., *Love and Honour* and *The Siege of Rhodes* of Sir William Davenant (1909).
[8] "The Designs for the first Movable Scenery on the English Public Stage," *Burlington Magazine*, April 1914. Other articles by Mr Keith are considered elsewhere.
[9] A. H. Thorndike, *Shakespeare's Theatre* (1916).
[10] G. C. D. Odell, *Shakespeare from Betterton to Irving* (1920).

temporary English evidence as to stage conditions, including the evidence of the plays themselves; (2) the testimony of late seventeenth century writers as to conditions that had existed on the stage before the wars; (3) the comments of foreigners on the comparative development of the English stage; (4) documents bearing on the cost of the production of plays. Yet the question to be answered by this mass of evidence has remained fundamentally the same which Malone and Steevens debated, the question of the use of scenery on the English stage before the Restoration. Likewise the point of view assumed by Malone has remained practically fixed, a point of view which regards scenery as a gradual accretion of the drama, the result of a purposive attempt to create and develop the illusion of reality as an aid to dramatic effect[1].

Yet material of a fifth sort exists in great abundance, and it is in the hope that I can at least point out the significance of this material that I have undertaken this study. This material is that relating to a definite theory of stage decoration which grew up as the result of classical researches by the early scholars of Italy in-

[1] Possible exceptions to this statement are found in the articles of Mr Keith published in *The Builder* for 1913 and 1914, and in the *Burlington Magazine* for 1917, as well as in Professor Tupper's introductory study in his edition of *The Siege of Rhodes*. In his *Builder* articles Mr Keith says that the history of scene-painting properly begins with the history of modern perspective. He notes various Italian artists of the Renaissance who were interested in the matter of scene-painting, and he infers the influence of Italy on England in the matter of stage decoration as an influence exerted by Serlio and other Italian artists on Inigo Jones. The *Burlington Magazine* article on "A Theatre Project" is a most important study of the influence of the Olympic Theatre on Jones and Webb. Professor Tupper comments on the scenery for *The Siege of Rhodes* as "an extension of the old method of indicating the place by posting its name over a door," so that it may be regarded as illustrative of the action. Further acknowledgment of my indebtedness to these two writers will be found elsewhere in this study.

terested in the revival of the classical drama, and also by the artists of the Italian Renaissance in its second period interested in rediscovering the ancient laws of proportion and perspective.

Necessarily such a study assumes a point of view different from that which has characterized other studies. To prove the change of point of view justifiable, however, I hope to be able to show (1) that on the basis of classical authority scenery was from the beginning of the revival of the classical drama in Italy regarded as an accepted part of dramatic production; (2) that on the foundation of classical authority there was gradually built up a definite theory of the use, construction, and arrangement of scenery and spectacular devices; (3) that the classical influence and the resulting theories and practices of stagecraft found their way into England before the Restoration for the most part directly from Italy, but after the Restoration by way of both Italy and France; (4) that the scenic development of the stage inspired by classical authority found its natural culmination in the excessive and detailed formalism of the late seventeenth century in the so-called period of classicism.

PART I

THE CLASSICAL REVIVAL OF
STAGE DECORATION IN ITALY

CHAPTER I

THE INFLUENCE OF VITRUVIUS ON THE SCENIC REPRESENTATION OF THE DRAMA

STUDENTS are coming more and more to recognize the continuity of dramatic history both in England and on the Continent. That the influence of the old Roman drama never died completely out, in Italy at least, is becoming increasingly apparent[1]. Yet the fact remains that the rediscovery of the Greek and Roman classics and the introduction of printing with movable type, which made possible the wider diffusion of these rediscovered writings of the ancients, did bring to the drama a distinctly new impetus, just as they brought to all science and all art what has come to be called the Renaissance. That from Italy, where it had its rise, the Renaissance spread to the rest of western Europe and to England is too well known to need restatement save that it is necessary to point out the fact that the arts which attended the production of the drama followed the general lines of Renaissance progress. The same stages of advancement were manifest in the development of the art of scenic decoration of the drama that were manifest in the development of the drama and of all art. Always men desired first to possess in full their heritage from the past, to reproduce the past in their present. This period of possession was followed by a period of imitation, of moulding new materials in old forms; and

[1] Cf. A. Chassang, *Des essais dramatiques imités de l'antiquité au xive et au xve siècle* (1852); Karl von Reinhardstöttner, *Plautus. Spätere Bearbeitungen Plautinischer Lustspiele* (1886); W. Cloetta, *Beiträge zur Litteratur-geschichte des Mittelalters und der Renaissance* (1890).

this in turn by a period of modification, which, as complete mastery of technique was attained through imitation, resulted in experimentation and finally in original creation.

Spingarn marks as one of the great stages of the progress of humanism the formation "of academies, in which the classics were studied and humanized, and which as a result produced a special cult of learning[1]." It is to these academies of the late fifteenth century in Italy that we must look if we are to find the beginnings of the theory of scenic production that flourished during the Renaissance. And particularly we must look to the Roman Academy which owed its origin to Julius Pomponius Laetus (1425–98), who had succeeded his teacher Laurentius Valla as perhaps the leading spirit among the humanists. His fanatic devotion to the customs and arts of old Rome has been often recorded. He even refused to study Greek because he feared that he might thus spoil his Latin style. He tilled a small plot of land according to the precepts of Varro and Columella. He delighted in Roman festivals. He and his followers assumed Latin names and as far as was possible projected the life of old Rome into their own time. In 1468 the Academy was suppressed by Paul II "on the ground of its political aims and its pagan spirit," and Pomponius and others suffered imprisonment and torture. But the Academy was revived under Sixtus IV (1471) and reached its greatest glory under Leo X[2].

Pope Sixtus IV appointed as cardinals his young

[1] J. E. Spingarn, *A History of Literary Criticism in the Renaissance* (1899), p. 125.

[2] For accounts of Pomponius Laetus and the Roman Academy, see, for instance, J. E. Sandys, *A History of Classical Scholarship* (1908), vol. II, pp. 92, 93; J. A. Symonds, *Revival of Learning*, pp. 359–66; J. Burckhardt, *The Civilisation of the Renaissance in Italy* (trans. 1914), pp. 279, 280; Chassang, *op. cit.* p. 129; G. Voigt, *Die Wiederbelebung des classischen Alterthums* (1893), vol. II, pp. 237 *sq.*

nephews Piero Riario and Giuliano della Rovere. On Piero Riario particularly he heaped wealth and power, and the young cardinal lived in a state of luxurious indulgence hitherto unheard of. He seems to have been much interested in the new glories of entertainment made possible through the researches of Pomponius Laetus, and in 1473 we hear of the plays given at great expense in honour of Eleanor of Aragon as she passed through Rome to Ferrara after her marriage with Duke Ercole d'Este. But the young cardinal died in 1474, and the pope, grieved for the loss of his favourite nephew, and continuing to follow his much-opposed policy of nepotism, shortly afterward appointed as cardinal, young Raffaelle Sansoni, a nephew of Piero Riario, who then at the request of the pope took the name of Raffaelle Riario. The identity of these two Cardinals Riario is often confused. But young Cardinal Raffaelle Riario continued to patronize the undertakings of the Roman Academy[1].

How early the Roman Academy took up the acting of Roman plays as one of its occupations is not definitely known—probably before its suppression in 1468. But under the patronage of Cardinal Raffaelle Riario the restoration of the theatre of the ancients became one of its chief interests. The young nobles acted the rôles under the instruction of their leader Pomponius Laetus. The theatre was usually a room in the palace of one of the cardinals. They revived the plays of the Roman dramatists, Plautus especially, and also wrote and acted other plays[2]. In 1484 *The History of the Emperor Con-*

---

[1] Cf. E. Müntz, *Histoire de l'art pendant la Renaissance* (1895), vol. II, pp. 55–8; Chassang, *op. cit.* pp. 129, 131; M. Creighton, *History of the Papacy during the Period of the Reformation* (1887–94), vol. III, p. 63.

[2] Cf. G. Tiraboschi, *Storia della Letteratura Italiana* (1809), vol. VI, p. 874; Chassang, *op. cit.* p. 131.

stantine was presented in the court of the pontifical palace, Pope Innocent VIII watching the performance from his window. It is conjectured that this may have been the tragedy of Sulpitius Verulamus which it is known was presented before the pope[1]. But it is impracticable to record in full the productions of this academy, the activities of which were suspended by the general disaster of the Fall of Rome in 1527.

As a matter of course, it was impossible that the revived Roman plays should be produced under Pomponius Laetus in any other way than that which classical authority decreed. The man who tilled the soil according to the precepts of the Romans must necessarily produce Roman plays in the Roman fashion[2]. And there was only one possible source of information in regard to the staging of plays in the early Roman theatres, the work of Vitruvius, which is said to be "the only formal utterance of an ancient artist on matters concerning his own craft which has come down to us[3]." The work had been known in manuscript since early in the century, and under the influence of the Roman Academy, Sulpitius Verulamus caused to be published in Rome, probably in 1486, the first edition of the *De Architectura*[4]. Sulpitius dedicated this edition to Cardinal Raffaelle Riario, and in his dedicatory letter he wrote:

Tu enim primus Tragoediae, quam nos juventutem excitandi gratia et agere et cantare primi hoc aevo docuimus; (nam ejus

---

[1] Cf. Chassang, *op. cit.* p. 134.

[2] Cf. Chassang, *op. cit.* p. 185: "Ainsi s'était fondé peu à peu en Italie le théâtre moderne. D'abord les érudits avaient étudié et imité les drames anciens, moins par amour de l'art dramatique, que parce que l'art dramatique était l'une des gloires de l'antiquité, et s'imposait à leur ardeur studieuse, au même titre que tout autre genre littéraire. Cela fit connaître le théâtre ancien, cela le fit comparer et préférer à celui du moyen âge."

[3] G. Baldwin Brown, "Vitruvius," in the *Burlington Magazine*, vol. XXVIII, p. 101.   [4] Cf. Sandys, *op. cit.* vol. II, p. 103.

actionem jam multis saeculis Roma non viderat) in medio foro
pulpitum ad quinque pedem altitudinem erectum pulcherrime
exornasti: eamdemque postquam in Hadriani mole Divo Inno-
centio spectante est acta, rursus intra tuos penates, tamquam in
media Circi cavea, toto consessu umbraculis tecto, admisso
populo, et pluribus tui ordinis spectatoribus honorifice excepisti.
Tu etiam primus picturatae scenae faciem, quum Pomponiani
Comoediam agerent, nostro saeculo ostendisti. Quare a te
quoque Theatrum novum tota Urbs magnis votis expectat.
Videt enim liberalitatem ingenii tui, qua ut uti possit, deus et
fortuna concessit, ec[1].

Thus we are given a picture of the scene, and we
know that at least to the Roman Academy Cardinal
Riario seemed to be the patron of the revived classical
drama who had made possible to them the presentation
of the drama with its appropriate decoration of the
painted scene. It is interesting to note too, that Sulpitius adds, "Quare a te quoque Theatrum novum tota
Urbs magnis votis expectat," for the study of Vitruvius
seems always to have carried in its wake projects for
new theatres constructed according to his plans.

But while these activities of the Roman Academy
were progressing, the drama was flourishing in equal
or greater magnificence in Ferrara under the patronage
of Duke Ercole d'Este, and as early as 1471 we hear
of a dramatic representation. In 1486 the *Menaechmi*
of Plautus was given, and in 1491, when it was again
given, we hear of scenery painted by Niccolo del Cogo[2].

---

[1] Quoted in Tiraboschi, *op. cit.* vol. vi, p. 874, note. Cf. Chassang,
op. cit. p. 131. Professor Cunliffe, *op. cit.* p. xxiv, notes that Sulpitius
"refers to a *scena picturata*, but as the play was acted under a tent, this
can hardly mean the introduction of painted scenery." That such a
deduction as to the necessary relation of painted scenery and a permanent theatre is not justified by the evidence of events throughout the
sixteenth century seems to me certain.

[2] In regard to the dramatic performances at Ferrara, see especially
Chassang, *op. cit.* pp. 142, 168–72; Julia C. Ady, *Beatrice d'Este*

But the greatest glories of the court of Ferrara came in the representation of Ariosto's comedies and in the theatre built for the production of Ariosto's work, a theatre planned and supervised by Ariosto himself. Unfortunately this theatre was built only to be burnt down the year before Ariosto's death (d. 1533), and all knowledge of its structure has apparently disappeared, though it has attracted the attention of scholars in the claim advanced concerning it, that it was the first permanent modern theatre on the Continent[1].

Likewise at Venice, Mantua, Milan, Urbino, Naples, Florence, and later, Vicenza, the drama flourished[2]. By 1500 there seem to have been numerous academies also, the chief business of which was the production of plays[3]. Every prince, indeed, had his theatre or his banqueting hall arranged for dramatic performances. And one of the chief antiquarian interests of the Renaissance was expressed in dramatic revivals. It was not until Palladio erected the famous Olympic Theatre at Vicenza late in the century that the ideas of theatre building fostered by the continued study of Vitruvius had their full fruition, but meanwhile the desire to re-

(1903), pp. 34–6; Cunliffe, *op. cit.* pp. xxx, xxxix. Professor Cunliffe says of the 1486 and the 1491 performances of the *Menaechmi* (p. xxxix) that in each case "the staging was that of the *sacre rappresentazione*, four or five houses or castles being provided, each with a door and window." In this interpretation, I believe, Professor Cunliffe fails to recognize the significance of the description of the stage and its conformity to the usual neo-classical stage to be described hereafter.

[1] Cf. Cunliffe, *op. cit.* p. xii; Symonds, *Italian Literature*, vol. 1, p. 499.

[2] The influence of one court on another is easily seen in Chassang's accounts of the interrelations of Rome, Ferrara, Mantua, and Milan especially. Paul Kristeller's *Andrea Mantegna* (English ed. by A. S. Strong, 1901) gives a particularly good account of the performances at Mantua.

[3] The academies are most fully described by Tiraboschi, but all accounts of the Renaissance contribute to our knowledge of them.

store the drama of antiquity to modern life had brought the modern drama into existence. And the ancient drama that was rediscovered for the moderns as well as the modern drama afterwards created was essentially an acted, visualized, scenic drama. This point cannot be too strongly emphasized; the revived drama was a spoken and not a read drama, a drama acted and adorned with all the spectacle possible of attainment. And this spectacular element of the dramatic presentation was as carefully planned by scholarly research as was any other phase of the presentation. The greatest artists of the Renaissance were called upon to paint the scenery for these dramatic representations. The names of the scenic artists include those of Mantegna, Peruzzi, Raffaello, the two Gengas, San Gallo, Ghirlandajo, Bigio, Francesca Indaco, Battista Franco, and many others. Müntz exclaims:

Egoïsme véritablement impardonnable chez les amateurs si éclairés de la Renaissance! Pour embellir leurs fêtes éphémères, ils n'hésitaient pas à confisquer un temps que les princes de l'art auraient pu consacrer à des œuvres durables[1].

Certainly the scenic production of the drama was taken as seriously as its oral production, and its scenic adornment was furthermore accepted apparently from the outset as an essential part of its production.

Thus it becomes of prime importance to ascertain just what were the underlying principles of the scenic representation of this drama of the Renaissance. And we must turn, as a matter of course, to the work of Vitruvius[2].

[1] Müntz, *op. cit.* vol. II, p. 55. It is necessary to remember, however, that some of the early scenes for theatres were in reality painted as mural decorations for the halls or theatres in which the dramas were produced rather than as scenes for the stage, the latter being usually referred to as *perspective scenes*. See below, pp. 45–47.

[2] *La Scenografia* by Giulio Ferrari (Milan, 1902) gives an account

It is necessary to note as a primary consideration the fact that Vitruvius classes the work of the scenic representation of the drama as part of the regular business of the architect. On the basis of the assignment of this work to the architect by Vitruvius we find even in the seventeenth century in England the production of the court masques under the charge of the Surveyor of the King's Works. And in this connection it must be remembered that according to Vitruvius the education of the architect must include training in drawing, geometry and optics, arithmetic, history, philosophy, music, medicine, laws, and astronomy. Therefore among the matters treated in the *De Architectura* are the zodiac (Book IX), the orders of architecture (Book IV), machines (Book X), and the manufacture and use of colours, as well as the construction of public and private buildings.

A considerable section of Book V of the *De Architectura*, which book deals with public buildings, is given over to the discussion of theatre building and to an analysis and comparison of the plans and principles of structure of the Greek and Roman theatres. As to the historical authority for the use of scenery and for the idea of scenery as painting in perspective, he said:

In the first place Agatharcus, in Athens, when Aeschylus was bringing out a tragedy, painted a scene, and left a commentary about it. This led Democritus and Anaxagoras to write on the same subject, showing how, given a center in a definite place, the lines should naturally correspond with due regard to the point of sight and the divergence of the visual rays, so that by this deception a faithful representation of the appearance of buildings might be given in painted scenery, and so that, though

of the possible indebtedness of the early Italian scenic artists to classical authorities, particularly Vitruvius and Pollux, but I did not have access to this work until after my own study was in the hands of the publishers. Detailed reference to it is, therefore, not made in these pages.

all is drawn on a vertical flat façade, some parts may seem to be withdrawing into the background, and others to be standing out in front[1].

In regard to the *scena* of the ancient theatre, Vitruvius explained in the passage perhaps more variously interpreted during the Renaissance than any other of the many disputed passages:

The "scaena" itself displays the following scheme. In the center are double doors decorated like those of a royal palace. At the right and left are the doors of the guest chambers[2]. Beyond[3] are spaces provided for decoration-places that the Greeks call περίακτοι, because in these places are triangular pieces of machinery which revolve, each having three decorated faces. When the play is to be changed, or when gods enter to the accompaniment of sudden claps of thunder, these may be revolved and present a face differently decorated. Beyond these places are the projecting wings which afford entrances to the stage, one from the forum, the other from abroad[4].

In regard to scenes Vitruvius wrote further:

There are three kinds of scenes, one called the tragic, second, the comic, third, the satyric. Their decorations are different and unlike each other in scheme. Tragic scenes are delineated with columns, pediments, statues, and other objects suited to Kings; comic scenes exhibit private dwellings, with balconies and views representing rows of windows, after the manner of ordinary dwellings; satyric scenes are decorated with trees, caverns, mountains, and other rustic objects delineated in landscape style[5].

[1] *The Ten Books of Architecture of Vitruvius* (trans. by M. H. Morgan, 1914), Bk VII, *Intro.* § 11.

[2] Translating *hospitalia*.   [3] Translating *secundum*.

[4] Bk V, chap. VI, § 8. Pollux in his *Onomasticon* laid greater stress on this matter of the significance of the stage entrances.

[5] Bk V, chap. VI, § 9. According to the text established by Rose, the last phrase of this description reads: *satyricae vero ornantur arboribus speluncis montibus reliquisque agrestibus rebus in topiarii speciem de-*

C S   2

Vitruvius also gave instruction concerning the construction and use of "machines," and he gave the definition of *machine* which throws much light on the use of the word in stage parlance during the sixteenth and seventeenth centuries:

A machine is a combination of timbers fastened together, chiefly efficacious in moving great weights. Such a machine is set in motion on scientific principles in circular rounds....

He added:

The difference between "machines" and "engines" is obviously this, that machines need more workmen and greater power to make them take effect....Engines, on the other hand, accomplish their purpose at the intelligent touch of a single workman[1]....

The preface to Book X, dealing with machines, justified the discussion partially on the ground that "every year both praetors and aediles have to provide machinery for the festivals." And in this statement he fortified one of the Renaissance conceptions of the giving of "shows" as one of the functions of the ruler. Also he referred to the "shows given by magistrates, whether of gladiators in the forum, or of plays on the stage."

Thus we see at their inception the characteristic Renaissance doctrines of the stage: (1) the classical authority for the use of scenery for plays; (2) the idea of scenery as necessarily involving painting in perspective; (3) the rules governing the construction and use of

---

formatis. This reading becomes important in later discussions of Vitruvius's meaning. It is worthy of notice, too, that in Bk VII, chap. v, where Vitruvius makes a plea for recognition of reality in painting and for appropriateness, he says of the ancients that "in their open rooms, such as exedrae, on account of size, they depicted the façades of scenes in the tragic, comic, or satyric style." This whole discussion in Bk VII, chap. v, might well have become the basis of certain Renaissance teachings on verisimilitude, but I do not believe that it was so interpreted.

[1] Bk X, chap. 1, §§ 1, 3.

stage entrances and exits; (4) the idea of changing scenes; (5) the use of thunder as an accessory of divinity; (6) the formal differentiation of scenery according to the *genre* of the drama to be presented; (7) the use of "machines" and "engines" as contributory to dramatic spectacle; and finally (8) the conception of public entertainment as a function of the ruler. The interpretation of these doctrines occupied the architects and the dramatists alike throughout the sixteenth and seventeenth centuries.

The unquestioning acceptance of Vitruvius which characterized the three hundred years after the first edition of the *De Architectura* is almost incomprehensible to the man of to-day who is accustomed to sit in judgment on every book that he reads, unless he recalls the same sort of acceptance of the value of the work that even yet characterizes a certain type of student of the Bible. During a period of the Renaissance Aristotle was accorded the same sort of authority in literary criticism, but never, I believe, to the extent that it was given in architecture to Vitruvius. Incipient rebels were silenced by the *ipse dixit* of his ultimate authority. Brief phrases were elaborated by the always bewildering process of exegesis until they seemed to offer definite pronouncements on every artistic subject. Chiefly under the influence of the various academies in Italy numerous editions of his work followed the first edition of 1486, a second edition appearing in Florence in 1496, and a third in Venice in 1497.

In 1511 appeared at Venice the edition by Jocundus (Fra Giocondo), and in 1513, 1522, and 1523, this same edition was republished at Florence. This edition was the first edition to use drawings to illustrate the words of Vitruvius. I have seen from this group only the 1513 edition (the Giunta edition), but the drawings of the theatres show how confusedly the editor was following the instructions of Vitruvius. It is important to note, however, that the drawings represented plans for rectangular theatres.

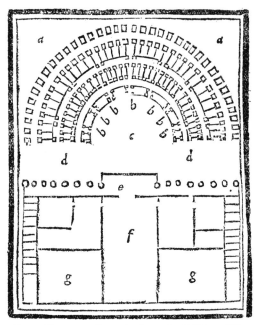

Fig. 1. The Greek Theatre. From the Jocundus Edition of Vitruvius, 1513

a, porticus theatri ; *b*, cunei ; *c*, orchestra ; *d*, proscenium ; *e*, pulpitum ; *f*, scena ; *g*, hospitalia

In 1521 there was published at Como the first translation of Vitruvius into a vulgar tongue[1], the Italian translation and annotations being the work of Caesar

---

[1] It is to be noted, however, that when, in 1514, Raffaello succeeded Bramante as architect of St Peter's, he was given as special adviser the old monk, Fra Giocondo, then about eighty years old. In order further to prepare himself for his task Raffaello had caused a special translation of Vitruvius to be made by Marco Fabio Calvi of Ravenna. Raffaello became so much interested that he proposed a restoration of old Rome. Cf. Sandys, *op. cit.* vol. ii, p. 121; Müntz, *Raphael* (trans. by W. Armstrong, 1882), pp. 547–9.

Caesariano. Vasari says that Caesariano was so unhappy over his failure to receive just recognition for his work on Vitruvius that he refused to do any more work as

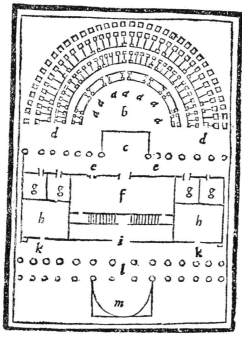

FIG. 2. THE ROMAN THEATRE. From the Jocundus Edition of Vitruvius, 1513

a, cunei ; *b*, orchestra ; *c*, pulpitum ; *d*, proscenium ; *e*, podium ; *f*, scena ; *g*, scenae membra ; *h*, hospitalia ; *i*, valvae regiae ; *k*, hospitaliorum valvae ; *l*, porticus post scena ; *m*, odeum

long as he lived. Yet his work seems to have had a lasting influence. A particularly interesting note in this edition is that concerning the making of thunder and lightning[1], which concludes by instancing the darkness

---

[1] Caesariano's note on Vitruvius's phrase, *con li tonitrui* (Bk V, chap. VII, § 8), reads: "cioe como sariano quelle canne acialmente compacte de le minore artigliarie quale dicemo li organeti: quali se impleno de la artificiosa puluere: con li interpositi botoni plumbei: & entro

and thunder that accompanied the passion of "nostro Signore Iesu Christo." It is worthy of comment that the classical and pagan theory of the use of thunder as an accompaniment of a divine appearance should here be given Christian and definitely religious signification by the instancing of the horrors of the scene of the crucifixion of Christ.

Editions of some Italian translation were issued in 1524 and 1535[1]. And in 1536 was published Caporali's Italian translation.

About this time an academy was formed in Rome under the patronage of Cardinal Ippolito dei Medici for the purpose of studying the works of Vitruvius. The academy was known as the *Accademia della Virtù*[2], and its members were pledged to actual work on a colossal task, which included the establishing of a corrected text of Vitruvius with the addition of variant readings, notes,

quilliuna tessera seu dato diferro si como etiam se imponemo in le altre canneae balote di maiore quantitate da trahere a longe in le disposite guerre como si sa notissimamente: queste canne si sono facte di ferro sono meliore che de altro metallo domodo siano ben consolidate & perforate: con le ferreae tribelle al modo: che hora si usano li sclopeti facti in la Germania: il che quando se incēdeno per scaricarle a la iactura: se incendeno luno & laltro: & uersandoli si discharichano con frequente strepito cōmo fano li tonitrui coelesti uel como sono le tenebre quale se sonamo la septimana de la passione del nostro Signore Iesu Christo: aut como li molini cō li quali se torge la seta: uel cō una corruinatione de saxi facta in oculto in epsi loci: & cosi per uarii modi si pono fare quisti coruinanti tonitrui & altre horendi moti quali emitariano uoce crepitante como paresse dal coelo le uoce quale deno uenire il di del iuditio de Dio."

[1] In general I have followed Gwilt in regard to the editions of Vitruvius. These two editions he regards as editions based on Caesariano's translation but without the notes.

[2] For accounts of this academy, cf. Tiraboschi, *op. cit.* vol. vii, pp. 146–8; Sandys, *op. cit.* vol. ii, p. 93; Müntz, *Histoire de l'art*, vol. iii, pp. 108, 109; Symonds, *Revival of Learning*, p. 366; Vasari, *The Lives of the Most Eminent Painters, Sculptors, and Architects* (trans. by S. Du C. De Vere, 1912–14), vol. viii, p. 237.

and illustrations. The academy purposed also to transcribe all the records remaining of Roman antiquity, including inscriptions from various sources as well as records of surviving works of art. Thus the programme was both philological and archaeological in character. Jacopo Barozzi of Vignuola (generally spoken of as Vignole or Vignola) worked under the direction of the academy, taking measurements of all the architectural remains of ancient Rome. *The Five Orders of Architecture* of Vignola remains as one of the permanent results of this work, being studied by all modern architects. The results of the work of the academy were, however, to bring results in many quarters.

The philological study of Vitruvius was brought particularly into prominence by the work of Philander, who in 1544, with the encouragement of Francis I of France, published his notes on Vitruvius. In 1550 these notes, together with the Latin text, were again published, and in 1552 and again in 1586 the edition of text and notes was republished. The De Laet edition published in 1649 at Amsterdam took as its basis this same edition, though it included notes and related matter from many other sources.

One of the most interesting contributions of Philander to the study of stage history is found in his note to Book V, chapter VI:

Quae disiungat proscenij pulpitum. Proscenium, auctore Diomed., est locus ante Scenam. *Quod omnes artifices in scenam dant operam.* Secus apud Graecos, apud quos cum reliqui artifices per Orchestram peragãt sua, soli Tragici & Comici suas in Scena praestant actiones. Est autem Scena ut Cassiodoro placet Variarũ libro quarto, frons Theatri, id est ea Theatri pars quae ab uno eius cornu ad alterum cum coopertura ducebatur, quòd fieret Theatrũ in hemicycli ferè formam. Ea aut uersilis fuit, quum subitò tota machinis quibusdam uerteretur & aliam picturae faciem ostenderet: aut ductilis, quum tractis tabulatis hac atq; illac species

picturae nudaretur interior. Auctor Seruius libro tertio Georg.[1]
sed libet Cassiodori uerba de origine Theatri adferre, sunt autem
ex Epistola ad Symmachum. Cùm agricultores (inquit) feriatis
diebus sacra diuersis numinibus per lucos uicósque celebrarent,
Athenienses primum agreste principium, in urbanum spectaculum collegerunt, Theatrum Graeco uocabulo, uisorium
nominantes, quòd eminus astantibus turba conueniens sine aliquo
impedimento uideatur. Frons autem Theatri, scena dicitur, ab
umbra luci densissima, ubi à pastoribus inchoante uerno, diuersis
sonis carmina cantabantur, hactenus Cassiodorus.

The early acceptance of the authority of Cassiodorus
in regard to the arrangement of the theatre and in regard
to the history of the origin of the theatre indicated in
this reference by Philander is significant. But the most
important contribution of the passage comes in the
recording of the fact that in addition to the turning
triangular prisms described by Vitruvius, the ancients
also used a method of effecting changes of scene by
withdrawing one scene to reveal another concealed
by it. The *scena versatilis* and the *scena ductilis* here
entered on classical authority the discussion of stagecraft.

A note of Philander on Book V, chapter VII, also is
of great interest to the historian of the stage, for in this
note the authority of Pollux is cited in regard to the
machines of the Greek theatre:

Ita vti mediae valuae ornatus habeant aulae regiç. Trium
ualuarum, media βασίλειον, aut οἶκος εὔδοξος, á Pol˙ ice

---

[1] Cf. Servius on Vergil, *Georg.* III, 24: "*Vel scaena ut versis* D, F.—
Apud maiores theatri gradus tantum fuerunt, nam scaena de lignis ad
tempus fiebat: unde hodieque consuetudo permansit, ut componantur
pegmata a ludorum theatralium editoribus scaena autem quae fiebat,
aut versatilis erat aut ductilis: versilis tunc erat, cum subito tota machinis
quibusdam convertebatur et aliam picturae faciem ostendebat; ductilis
tunc, cum tractis tabulatis hac atque illac species picturae nudabatur
interior: unde perite utrumque tetigit dicens 'versis discedat frontibus,'
singula singulis complectens sermonibus. quod Varro et Suetonius
commemorant."

dicitur. *Seu deorum aduĕtus cum tonitribus repentinis.* Quae ad hoc pertinent sunt tria uocabula apud Pollucem libro quarto cap. 19. θεολογεῖον, unde Dij è sublimi super scenam apparebant, κεκραυνοσκοπεῖον, alta versatilis machina instar speculae,

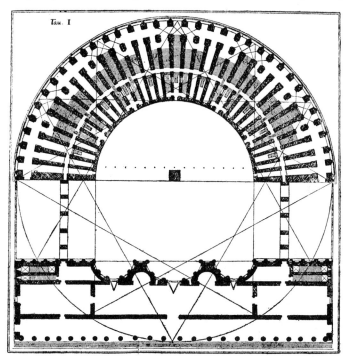

FIG. 3. BARBARO'S INTERPRETATION OF THE ROMAN THEATRE
From Conte Montenari, *Del Teatro Olympico,* 1749

ex qua fulmina Iupiter eiaculabatur, βροντεῖον, locus post Scenam, in quo utribus calculis confertis & per aera versatis, tonitrus similitudinem imitabantur. *Secundum ea loca versurae sunt procurrentes,* περίακτοι à Polluce uocantur[1].

Another famous translator and commentator was Daniello Barbaro, who is known to have worked with

---

[1] Cf. chap. IV below in regard to the Renaissance adaptations of the machines of the classical stage and in regard to the influence of Pollux in this connection.

Andrea Palladio in their common architectural studies. He published in 1556 an Italian translation of Vitruvius, and in 1567 an edition which included the Latin text with the Italian translation. This edition was republished in 1584, 1629, and 1641. Barbaro also made a most interesting contribution to the discussion of stage spectacle in his note on Book V, chapter VII:

Valvae mediae, quae medio cuneo è quinque Scenae attributis respondent, ab ornamentis & amplitudine, quam habebant, regiae dicebantur. Vtrimque aliae portae erant concharum modo, quas *Nichios* dicimus, ita pro fronte Scenae tres erant apertiones, ante quas in singulis machinae erant collocatae triangulares axibus versatiles, in singulis earum frontibus picturae erant secundum fabularum, quas agebant, opportunitatem. nam in una comica Scena, pro comoediis, in altera tragica pro tragoediis, in tertia satyris designabatur. Vertebantur illae facies, & ab illis machinis Dii loquebantur. Tonitrua in eorum aduentu fiebant, utribus, & pellibus corijs inflatis, calculisq; repletis, uel ictibus percussis, quos nos tamburros nominamus. Itaque decorum seruabant, Deos inuisibiles tantum audientes. Ita pro machina in Aiace Fl'gillifero Vlissi Minerua loquitur, & non uidetur, aitq; Vlisses uocem Deae per similem esse tyrrenicae aereae tubae, quae horrorem sonitu incutere solet. Hae machinae igitur conuertebantur, ideo graece periactus dicunt, dabantq; aditibus locum, vias referentes, unam á foro, alteram aliunde.

The discussion has never stopped as to whether the three sides of the triangular prisms corresponded in their decoration to the types of drama. The very interesting comment, however, "ab illis machinis Dii loquebantur" shows a distinct confusion in regard to the *deus ex machina*. It seems probable that Philander had the same idea in mind, though his notes are not quite definite on the subject.

In Germany a Latin edition of Vitruvius was published in 1543. But it was not until 1547 or 1548 that there was published at Nürnberg the German transla-

tion by Gualther Rivius, which was with the possible
exception of the Philander edition the edition in which
Vitruvius was best known in England until the 1673
edition of Perrault. The Rivius translation was reprinted
in 1575 and in 1614.

In France a translation of Vitruvius was published
in 1547 and was reprinted in 1572 and in 1618, the
translation being the work of J. Martin. The great edition of France did not come, however, until the 1673
carefully annotated and illustrated edition of Claude
Perrault, which was revised and republished in 1684.

No complete English translation appeared before the
eighteenth century, but there was published in London
in 1692

*An Abridgment of the Architecture of Vitruvius....*Illustrated.
...To which is added...the etymology...of the terms used in
Architecture. First done in French by Monsr Perrault...and
now Englished, with additions.

A Spanish translation was published in 1602. And
before the close of the seventeenth century there were
thus printed in Europe more than thirty editions of
Vitruvius besides countless works of commentary and
explanation based on his work.

CHAPTER II

THE RE-DISCOVERY OF THE ART OF
PERSPECTIVE IN SCENES

ALONG with the study of Vitruvius there was growing up throughout the period of the Renaissance
a theory of scientific perspective based primarily on a
careful study of the architectural remains of Roman antiquity and increasingly dependent on a knowledge of
geometry. To Brunelleschi is generally given the credit
for having been the first of the moderns to rediscover
perspective, and Vasari adds that though he "was ignorant of geometry, his good sense yet led him to just
drawing." Müntz comments that it is difficult to believe that Brunelleschi was not familiar with the work
of Vitruvius, which his compatriot Poggio had discovered in manuscript in St Gall in 1414[1]. However
this may be, Leon Battista Alberti was apparently the
first of the moderns to write a reasoned work on the
principles and practices of his art, comparing the Roman
theory with the practices evidenced in the remains of
old Rome still extant[2]. Among the other early writers
on perspective was Bramante of Milan, whose work appeared between 1440 and 1450. With him is often
confused Bramante of Urbino, who went early to Milan

[1] Cf. Müntz, *Hist. de l'art*, vol. I, p. 238; Symonds, *Revival of
Learning*, p. 137; Vasari, *op. cit.* vol. II, pp. 195 *sq.*; L. Scott, *Filippo
di Ser Brunelleschi* (1901); W. G. K. (W. G. Keith), "Notes on the
History of Stage Decoration," in *The Builder*, vol. CVII, p. 46. The date
is also given as 1416.

[2] Alberti's work was in three parts, *De Architectura*, *De Sculptura*,
and *De Pictura*. Chassang, *op. cit.* pp. 78 *sq.*, gives an interesting
account of Alberti's *Philodoxios*, written in imitation of a Latin comedy.

in order that he might see great works of art, and who there came under the influence of Caesar Caesariano, a geometrician and the first translator of Vitruvius[1]. Bramante is said by Serlio to have revived the art of perspective. His interest seems to have been the result of his study of antiquity, in the pursuit of which study he went to Rome and there measured all the buildings in the city and in the Campagna outside. Upon the basis of these investigations he came to a knowledge of proportion and to a just view of perspective.

In spite of these important beginnings the scientific theory of perspective may properly be said to begin with the work of Piero della Francesca dal Borgo a San Sepolcro (Piero dal Borgo). It was, of course, impossible that great advancement should be made in the study of perspective without a knowledge of geometry. Euclid had been translated into Latin and first printed in 1482 at Venice. In Vicenza another Latin edition was printed in 1491, and in Venice again other editions were printed in 1505 and in 1509. The first Greek text was not published until 1533[2]. Piero seems to have been a serious student of Euclid, and on the basis of his knowledge of geometry he built up generalized rules for perspective drawing[3].

Piero's work was studied by Baldassare Peruzzi, a great architect and a student of antiquity. Of his work in stage scenery I shall speak later. Peruzzi was also a student of Vitruvius and apparently intended editing an edition of Vitruvius. He had many drawings pre-

---

[1] See above, p. 20.

[2] Cf. Sandys, *op. cit.* vol. ii, p. 104, and *Index*.

[3] Vasari, *op. cit.* vol. iii, p. 17, gives an account of Piero in his old age growing blind and having his work stolen from him by a student, Fra Luca dal Borgo. There has been much discussion relative to this work and to the student who published it, a discussion reviewed by M. Poudra, *Histoire de la perspective ancienne et moderne* (1864), pp. 119 *sq.*, 131.

pared to illustrate the work of Vitruvius as well as many other drawings. Part of these drawings and notes were inherited by his pupil Sebastiano Serlio, who utilized them in the seven books of his *Architettura*, the second of which treats of perspective and was published in 1545.

In 1505 appeared the first book dealing exclusively with perspective, a treatise by Viator, illustrated by figures supposed to have been taken from Piero or Peruzzi[1]. And in 1525 appeared the work of Albert Dürer, of interest because of his invention of instruments to be used for perspective drawing.

The posthumous work[2] of Leonardo da Vinci (d. 1519) too gives us an idea of the consuming eagerness of the artists of this period to master the difficulties of perspective. "Perspective is to Painting," Leonardo said, "what the bridle is to a horse," and again,

Those who become enamoured of the practice of the art, without having previously applied to the diligent study of the scientific part of it, may be compared to mariners, who put to sea in a ship without rudder or compass, and therefore cannot be certain of arriving at the wished-for port[3].

It is from the work of Leonardo, too, that we learn of the early knowledge of the "aerial perspective," which was to become increasingly important in the creation of scenic effects. Because of the difference in the air, he said, it is easy to determine the distance of different objects, though they be drawn on the same line. Therefore, to create the sense of distance, it is necessary to imagine the air thick, and if one building is to appear to be five times as far off as another, it should be painted with colour to which has been added five times the amount of azure used in the colour for the other[4].

[1] Cf. Poudra, *op. cit.* p. 132.
[2] Cf. Leonardo da Vinci, *A Treatise on Painting* (trans. by J. F. Rigaud, 1892).
[3] *Ibid.* p. 37.   [4] *Ibid.* p. 125.

An edition of Euclid's treatise on optics added to the theory of perspective when it was published in 1557. Probably it was known earlier, since Serlio says that he will not speak of the philosophy of perspective since "learned Euclides writeth darkely thereof." A work on optics supposed to be by Ptolemy was likewise published at Venice in 1558[1].

In 1559 Daniello Barbaro published at Venice his *La Pratica della Perspectiva*, which like his edition of Vitruvius, seems at once to have been accepted as authoritative and to have taken precedence over all earlier works on the subject, save only that of Serlio. Barbaro quoted freely from Vitruvius and based his work on Vitruvian principles. He ridiculed the work of Piero dal Borgo but gave renewed emphasis to the necessity for a mathematical basis for the study and practice of perspective, and in the fourth section of the work discussed scenes and scene-painting. Poudra says, however, that he ignored the whole question of perspective-relief, which is the primary question for the scenic artist[2].

In 1583 was published *Le due Regole dell prospettive Pratica* of Vignola. Vignola reiterated much of what

[1] Cf. Poudra, *op. cit.* pp. 4 *sq.* Cf. also the article on Ptolemy in *Enc. Brit.* (eleventh edition). Euclid's work is based on the fundamental assumption that the rays proceed from the eye. The relation of this idea to perspective work is apparent, and the question was debated during the seventeenth century by many learned men. At the very end of the seventeenth century it was still deemed undesirable to look at stage scenery with two eyes, since the conflicting cones made by the rays emitted from the eyes were annoying.

[2] Cf. Poudra, *op. cit.* pp. 169 *sq.* It is well to note also that contemporary with the work of Barbaro was the work of J. Cousin, *Livre de la perspective*, published in 1560, the first French work on perspective, though the work of Serlio was translated into French in 1547 by J. Martin, the translator of Vitruvius. Du Cerceau's *Leçons de perspective positive* was published in Paris in 1576. From this time the literature of perspective grew in France as in Italy.

Vitruvius had said in regard to the stage scenery of the ancients and described the turning triangular prisms by which a change of scene was effected on stages he himself had seen[1].

Thus we see the materials of the art of stage decoration growing in an increasing knowledge of geometry, whereby results could be achieved surely and accurately, and in an increasing knowledge of the modification of colour and line necessary to achieve artistic results in perspective work.

The system of stage decoration developed as the result of the study of Vitruvius and the growing knowledge of scientific perspective is most fully explained in the important work of Serlio already mentioned. Indeed, it is from this work that we get our most detailed knowledge of the theory as well as of the practice of stagecraft during the sixteenth century. The first five books of the *Architettura* appeared between 1537 and 1547, the second book dealing with perspective appearing in 1545 and being published in Paris, where Serlio had been called to give assistance in the planning and building of the Louvre. The story of his disillusionment and his retirement has no place in this account, but it is necessary to note the significance of this work, the first on scenic decoration, as issued in Paris, though dealing with the practices and theories of the Italian masters. It is necessary, too, to recall the fact that Serlio was the pupil of Peruzzi and the heir of much of his artistic work[2]. "Descent by pupilship," to use a borrowed phrase, was the method by which the theory of dramatic spectacle was handed down. It is in this work of Serlio that we find most insistently emphasized the interdependence of architecture and perspective as

[1] Cf. Poudra, *op. cit.* pp. 175 *sq.*

[2] Cf. Vasari, *op. cit.* vol. v, p. 72; Müntz, *Hist. de l'art*, vol. iii, p. 298, note; or, indeed, any history of Renaissance architecture.

witnessed by the studies and achievements of his predecessors and masters, Bramante, Raffaello, Peruzzi,
Genga, and Giulio Romano.

The greater part of the book on perspective is given
over by Serlio to a description of scenography, which
here becomes identified with the art of painting and
arranging scenes on the stage[1]. Serlio is writing with
the banqueting hall of a prince chiefly in mind, and he
is, consequently, first concerned to make clear the
method of constructing the scaffold[2]. Such a hall as
this, he says, usually has a chamber built over it at one
end, and under this chamber the scaffold is to be
erected, its size and proportions to be determined by
the demands of the particular hall in which it is to be
built. He tells us how the rules of antiquity in regard
to the seating of the audience in a round theatre may
be modified to the requirements of such a hall, so that
this scaffold may yet remain clearly visible to all. The
scaffold or stage is built in two parts, the front part
raised as high as the level of a man's eyes and built
strongly and firmly and on a level. The second part is
raised by one-ninth of its depth above the first scaffold
and is built on an incline, so that the scenes, which are
arranged on this scaffold, may be the more easily seen.
The back wall of the stage is to be built at a distance
from the wall of the hall sufficient to make possible the
passing back and forth of the "personages" behind the
scenes without their being visible to the audience.

Serlio, like all his successors, gives confused directions
for the establishing of the horizon and the fixing of the

[1] The distinction between *sciography* and *scenography* gradually grew
up, but Vitruvius had made scenography show "the front and receding
side properly shadowed, the lines being drawn to their proper vanishing
points."

[2] The account of the theories of Serlio is based on the English translation of the *Five Books of Architecture* published in 1611.

lines upon which the "houses" or scenes are to be arranged. The principles of the triangular perspective in their application to scenic arrangements are emphasized, but Serlio seems to have contributed the idea of fixing the horizon outside the scene. He says, indeed, that it is to be placed back of the scene a distance equal to that of the depth of the second or "hanging" scaffold. The advantage thus gained of making the scene end in a line rather than a point and the consequent advantage of having the "houses" less subject to extreme foreshortening is evident even to the layman. But Serlio was extremely practical in effecting this arrangement, for he advised,

and for that men should breake the wall, if they would use all this Horizon in grosse, which may not be done, therefore I have alwayes made a small modell of wood and Paper just of the same bignes, and by the same modell set it downe in grosse, from piece to piece.

This idea of working by a model was one adopted in the Office of the Revels in England under Elizabeth, but whether it was adopted through the fear of the alternative necessity of breaking the wall to find the horizon I do not know. At any rate, it is clear that the greatest possible care was, according to Serlio, to be taken for the arrangement of the houses on the stage according to the rules of perspective as they were then understood.

The "houses" or scenes that Serlio describes were built with two sides, "as these must be built that men may see out of them on both sides." They were built on wooden frames covered with canvas and painted exactly to resemble real architectural creations. Architectural detail was emphasized. The houses were carefully foreshortened according to their arrangement on the stage, and the doors and windows and ornaments were sub-

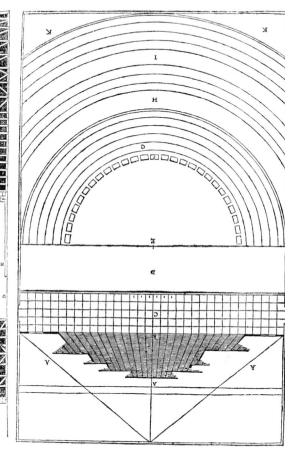

PLATE I

PROFILE AND GROUND PLAN OF SERLIO'S THEATRE

From Serlio, *The Five Books of Architecture* (English Translation, 1611)

C, first scaffold; *A—B*, second scaffold; *M*, wall of the hall; *P*, "the backe or upholding behind of the Scene"; *D*, "the post scene";
E, orchestra; *F*, places for the noblest persons; *G*, places for the noblest women; *H*, *I*, passages; *K*, places for others;
L, the line fixing the horizon

jected to the same careful foreshortening that determined their outline in general.

The back curtain and the flat scene were alike suggested as possibilities of perspective painting, for Serlio says that "in the Buildings which stand far backward the Painting worke must supplie the place by shadows without any bossing out." And he also advises, "But if you make any flat Buildings, they must stand somewhat farre inward, that you may not see them on the sides." In his own stage plan it is evident that the two scenes nearest the back did not have the second side.

Neither was Serlio neglectful of the demand for variety. In addition to an irregular sky line and variations of the outline of the houses attained by the use of cut-out and painted pieces of wood added to the houses as chimneys, cornices, etc., devices not unlike those of the later "relief" work were used. "An open Gallery or lodge through which you may see another house," "hangings over and shootings out at the ends," "houses which have great bearing out, like lodgings or Chambers for men," an arrangement of the "smalest houses before, that you may see other houses over or above them" are means advised specifically for effectiveness.

Great and glorious effects are thus to be achieved in scenes "built by Carpenters or Masons, skilful in Perspective Worke":

great Palaces, large Temples, and divers Houses, both neere and farre off; broad places filled with Houses, long streets crost with other wayes: tryumphant Arches, high Pillars or Colummes, Pyramides, Obeliscens, and a thousand fayre things and buildings, adorned with innumerable lights.

Taking his text from Vitruvius's directions for the three kinds of scenes, Serlio builds up an elaborate scheme of scenes designed according to dramatic types.

He speaks first of the "Comicall" scene, "whereof the Houses must be made as if they were for common or ordinarie people," and explains more fully that "the houses must be slight for Citizens, but specially there

Fig. 4.   The "Comicall" Scene

From Serlio, *The Second Book of Architecture* (English Translation), 1611

must not want a brawthell or bawdy house, and a great Inn, and a Church; such things of necessity to be there-in"—a text for the sociologist.

Houses for Tragedies must be made for great personages, for that actions of love, strange adventures, and cruell murthers, (as you reade in ancient and moderne tragedies) happen always in the houses of great Lords, Dukes, Princes, and Kings. Therefore in such cases you must make none but stately houses.

But it is in regard to "satiricall scenes" that Serlio becomes rhapsodic:

The Satiricall Scenes are to represent Satirs, wherein you must place all those things that be rude and rusticall,

FIG. 5. THE "TRAGICALL" SCENE
From Serlio, *The Second Book of Architecture* (English Translation), 1611

he says, but he amends this harsh dictum by adding that Vitruvius said

they should be made with Trees, Rootes, Herbs, Hils and Flowers, and with some countrey houses....And for that in our dayes these things were made in Winter, when there were but fewe greene Trees, Herbs and Flowres to be found; then you must make these things of Silke, which will be more commendable than the naturall things themselves.

Growing reminiscent concerning the glories of the court

of Urbino and the scenes there constructed by Genga, he exclaims:

Oh good Lord, what magnificence was there to be seene, for the great number of Trees and Fruits, with sundry Herbs and Flowres, all made of fine silke of divers collors. The water

FIG. 6. THE "SATIRICALL" SCENE
From Serlio, *The Second Book of Architecture* (English Translation), 1611

courses being adorned with Frogs, Snails, Tortuses, Toads, Adders, Snakes, and other beasts: Routes of Corrale, mother of Pearle, and other shels layd and thrust through betweene the stones, with so many severall and faire things, that if I should declare them all, I should not have time inough.

Since the use of coloured lights seemed never to pall on these early scenic enthusiasts, Serlio gives special and detailed instructions for their use. White and red wine are bottled, as well as various solutions of colours watered to the desired shade, and the bottles arranged on shelves placed back of the shaped openings in the houses through which they are to shine. A lamp is put back of the bottle, and in case a very bright light is desired, a torch is placed behind the bottle of "painted color," and a "bright Bason" placed behind the torch to act as a reflector.

An object may be made to burn, Serlio tells us, by wetting it thoroughly "with excellent good Aquavite; and setting it on fire with a candle it will burne all over." Thunder may be imitated by rolling "a great Bullit of a Cannon or of some other great Ordinance" in the chamber above the stage. The making of lightning is more intricate:

There must be a man placed behind the Scene or Scaffold in a high place with a boxe in his hand, the cover whereof must be full with holes, and in the middle of that place there shall be a burning candle placed, the boxe must be filled with powder of vernis or sulphire, and casting his hand with the box upwards the powder flying in the candle whill show as if it were lightning. But touching the beames of this lightning you must draw a piece of wire over the Scene, which must hang downewards, whereon you must put a squib covered over with pure gold or shining sattin which you will: and while the Bullit is rouling, you must shoote of some piece of Ordinance, and with the same giving fire to the squibs, it will worke the effect which is desired.

Much emphasis is put on the accessory effects of the stage. The morisco dances, one infers, were rather boisterous affairs, for the need of solidity and endurance in the stage is constantly emphasized. The clothing of men in the habits of beasts for these dances seems especially to have delighted Serlio. In describing the satyrical scenes, he says that the mermaids, monsters, and other stage beasts made by Genga "seemed in shew as if they went and stirred," a statement which would indicate the use of stuffed figures also. He recounts the opinions of some who paint figures of men and animals in the scenes, but he himself considers this practice as opposed to reality, though he admits the possible addition of painted figures, such as sleeping animals, which would not of necessity move during the time represented in the performance. This is the first appeal to the idea of verisimilitude in staging with which I am familiar.

The use of pasteboard figures on the stage has been noted as a custom even late in the eighteenth century[1], but Serlio gives us our first indication of the manner of their use:

The while that the scene is emptie of personages, then the workman must have certaine figures or formes ready of such greatness as the place where they must stand, will afford them to be, which must be made of paste board, cut out round and painted, signifying such things as you will, which Figures must leane against a rule or lath of wood, crosse over the scene where a gate, doore, or way is made, and there some one or other behind the doore must make the figures pass along, sometime in forme of Musitions with instruments, and some like singers; and behind the Scene some one must play on, upon certaine instruments and sing also; sometime you must make a number of foote men and horsemen going about with Trumpets, Phifes, and Drummes, at which time you must play with Drumbes, Trumpets, and Phifes, very softly behind, which will keep the peoples eyes occupied, and content them well.

Similarly planets and other objects of pasteboard may be made to pass along in the air by putting rings on the backs of the objects and slipping the rings over wire, then attaching pieces of black thread to the objects and

[1] Cf. Odell, *op. cit.* vol. i, p. 435.

having them pulled back and forth by some one behind the scenes who holds the other ends of the threads.

The description of "God descending downe from Heaven," of "the bright shining Moone ascending only with her hornes," of the sun rising, making his course around the world, and at the end of the play, going down "most artificially[1]" would lead us to suppose that other effects such as were introduced by "machines" must have been known.

Very definitely, too, Serlio sees dramatic productions as princely pleasures. There is a constant emphasis of the need "never to take care what it shall cost." The more such things cost, the more they are esteemed, he insists, "for they are things which stately and great persons doe, which are enemies to niggardliness."

Serlio's work is of supreme importance to the student of the stage because of its detailed and naïve descriptions. It was important in the history of the stage because it first formulated the practices of the best

[1] That there was a definite relation between the idea of the "artificial day" which was being advocated at this time as the manifestation of the unity of time and this sun rising at the beginning of the play and going down at its close "most artificially" seems certain. Cf. R. W. Bond, op. cit. pp. xlii, xliii. Professor Bond, however, seems to regard this rising and setting sun as movable scenery. The clearest description of the method of using an artificial sun of this sort is that given by Vasari in his account of "Bastiano da San Gallo, called Aristotile" (vol. viii, p. 10), where in the account of the nuptials of Duke Cosimo in 1539 he records: "He then arranged with much ingenuity a lantern of wood in the manner of an arch, behind all the buildings, with a sun one braccio high, in the form of a ball of crystal filled with distilled water, behind which were two lighted torches, which rendered the sky of the scenery and prospect-view so luminous, that it had the appearance of the real and natural sun. This sun, which had around it an ornament of golden rays that covered the curtain, was drawn little by little by means of a small windlass that was there, in such a manner that at the beginning of the performance the sun appeared to be rising, and then, having climbed to the centre of the arch, it so descended that at the end of the piece it was setting and sinking below the horizon."

craftsmen of its time. The inherent relationship of drama and spectacle; the scenes for comedy, tragedy, and satyrical drama; the emphasis on perspective; the devices for the descent of the gods and for simulating thunder and lightning; the architectural type of scenery; the emphasis on the princely character of dramatic spectacle, are echoes of a distinctly classical theory in Serlio. But it is significant that the satyric scene is much elaborated, that the detail of all the work has become important, that certain practices are judged upon the basis of their resemblance to reality. There is a distinct indication throughout Serlio's work that the rules of Vitruvius are becoming rationalized and that they are to find their justification in their conformity to the demands of verisimilitude.

That Serlio gained a great reputation as the successful artist of stage effects is evident, for we hear of the stage which he built in Vicenza for the Olympic Academy; and indeed, he himself speaks with unbounded enthusiasm of his own work on this stage. As for the effect of the *Architettura* on the Continent and in England, this tale is told in every record of the history of architecture. Yet his importance as the first spokesman for the new art of perspective in scenes must also be reckoned in any consideration of the history of architecture as well as in any account of the history of stagecraft.

PLATE II

ILLUSTRATION FROM LEONARDO SALVIATI, *IL GRANCHIO*, 1566
Reproduced through the courtesy of Professor J. M. Manly

CHAPTER III

THE ADOPTING OF THE PERSPECTIVE
SCENE IN DRAMATIC PRODUCTIONS

IT is significant that the theory of stage scenery and the artistic means of exemplifying that theory came alike from the antiquarian researches of the time. The study of Vitruvius and the search for an adequate method of representing objects in perspective in order to obtain the effects described by Vitruvius as resulting from the proper observance of perspective were perhaps the dominant interests of the artistic Renaissance. The theory and practice of stage decoration were thus from the outset dependent upon the interpretation of Vitruvius and the knowledge of perspective which was developing as a result of the impetus received from the study of the ancients.

It should, of course, have been remembered by early students of Vitruvius that he was giving instructions for a permanent theatre with a permanent and fixed stage and a permanent scene wall in which the entrances were fixed; whereas the early dramatic revivals took place on temporary stages, built with increasing frequency in the great halls of princely palaces. But the modifications necessitated by changed conditions seem to have been only gradually forced on the unwilling devotees of Vitruvius. Whatever they did, they did as though authorized by the Vitruvian formulae. But it must be remembered in this connection that the early editions of the *De Architectura* show how confused were the first interpretations of the Vitruvian theatre and particularly of the Vitruvian stage. It must be remembered also that Jocundus pictured a rectangular theatre.

It is, therefore, probable that the early court and academic theatres were arranged according to the demands of the Vitruvian theatre as these demands were then interpreted.

How early there was conceived the idea of the perspective scene as made up of the separate architectural units of the scene, built, painted, and arranged on the stage according to the demands of perspective, it seems impossible to assert, but that the *scena pictura* referred to by Sulpitius in 1486 was something new at the time it was presented is undoubtedly implied. Furthermore, the fact that the work of stage decoration was considered the work of the architect would make quite logical the idea of scenery as architecture in perspective. Of course, the necessity for a substitute for the scene wall as a place which provided entrances for the actors and also provided concealment for the actors when off the stage was also to be considered. But buildings on the stage were familiar in the sacred representations, and it is, therefore, impossible to determine whether the "houses" were used because they had become familiar in the sacred representations, or whether they were used as the architect's interpretation of scenery, or whether they were a conscious combination of scene wall and decoration. Probably all these considerations had something to do with the form of stage decoration adopted during the Renaissance. At any rate, we are sure that this method of scenic decoration was an innovation, as both Sulpitius and Vasari bear witness[1]. We know that scenery was regarded as an essential element in the representation of the drama of the ancients and consequently in the modern imitations of the classical drama. And we know also that the distinguishing characteristic of this stage scenery revived on classical authority was the observance of perspective. So much was this true

[1] See above, p. 13, and below, pp. 46, 47.

that whereas throughout the sixteenth century we find references to "scenes" which were used as decorations for the hall or auditorium or for the stage curtain, we find the scenery on the stage generally referred to as the "perspective scene."

Such references to scenes built for theatres have often brought confusion to the student of dramatic history, however, and it is well perhaps to notice three instances where such descriptions have been particularly confusing. Among the most frequently quoted documents of the stage is a letter of 1501 written by Sigismondo Cantelmo to Duke Ercole d'Este and describing the setting arranged for the Carnival plays at Mantua which the Duke had been unable to attend. This letter describes the whole room as the stage and describes in particular the arcades which furnished the perspective view of Mantegna's paintings of *The Triumph of Caesar*.

The description is very confusing because of the many sides the writer ascribes to the quadrangle. But a careful study of the description reveals the fact that the real stage scene was a grotto constructed for the occasion, and that these famous paintings of Mantegna which are generally recorded as the first scenes for·a theatre that have come down to us were merely paintings which adorned the walls of the theatre. That this is the true interpretation of their use becomes certain when we realize that, as Kristeller has pointed out, these paintings were partly finished in 1489 and were assumed to be completed in 1494[1].

---

[1] The letter, the pertinent portions of which I append in Mrs Ady's translation (*Isabella d'Este*, vol. I, pp. 183–5), was among the *Lettere artistiche inedite*, published by G. Campori in 1886. For discussions of it, cf. Kristeller, *op. cit.* pp. 272–83, and G. Bapst, *Essai sur l'histoire du théâtre* (1893), pp. 246, 247.

"The stage itself is quadrangular in form, but somewhat extended in length. Each side has eight arcades, with columns well proportioned

Again, Raffaello is sometimes said to have painted for Pope Leo a scene for a play, representing the Father Mariano as tortured by devils. This scene was the scene painted as a curtain for the performance of the *Suppositi* in 1518, as we shall see, and had nothing to do with the "perspective scene" of the play.

Likewise Vasari's account of the scenes made by

to the size and height of the arches. The base and the capitals of each pillar are richly painted with the finest colours and adorned with foliage, and the arches, with their reliefs of flowers, offer an admirable perspective, each being about four *braccia* wide and proportionately high, the whole representing an ancient and eternal temple of rare beauty. The back of the stage was hung with cloth of gold and foliage, as required for the recitations, and the sides were adorned by six paintings of the Triumphs of Caesar by the famous Mantegna. On the two other and smaller sides of the stage there were similar arcades, but only six in number. Two sides of the stage were given up to the actors and reciters; on the two others were steps occupied on the one hand by women, on the other by strangers, trumpeters, and musicians. At one angle were four very lofty columns with rounded bases, and between them a grotto designed with great art, but in the most natural manner. The roof overhead blazed with hundreds of lights like shining stars, with an artificial circle, showing the signs of the zodiac, and in the centre, the sun and moon moving in their accustomed orbits. Within the recess was a Wheel of Fortune inscribed with the words, *Regno, regnam, regnabo*, and in the midst, the golden goddess, seated on her throne, bearing a sceptre adorned with a dolphin. The lowest tier of the stage was hung with Triumphs of Petrarch, also painted by Mantegna, and large golden candelabra hung from the centre of the roof, each holding three double rows of torches and a shield with the arms of His Caesarean Majesty, the black eagle with the royal and imperial diadem. At the sides of the stage were two large banners with the arms of His Holiness the Pope and the Emperor, and smaller ensigns with those of the Most Christian King and illustrious Signory of Venice. Between the arches were banners with the arms of Your Excellency and of the German prince Duke Albert of Bavaria, and the devices of this Signor Marchese and the Signora Marchesana. Higher up on the walls were busts and statues of gold, silver, and other metals, which added greatly to the decorative effect of the whole. Last of all the roof was hung with sky-blue cloth to imitate the blue vault of heaven, studded over with the constellations of our hemisphere."

Federigo Zucchero for Palladio's theatre in 1561 or 1562 has often been misunderstood as referring to stage scenes instead of mural decorations for a theatre[1].

It is, of course, true that the same artists often painted scenes for a theatre and constructed also the stage scenery for dramatic performances, but in tracing the history of stage decoration, it is important that the two kinds of "scenes" be clearly differentiated in purpose as they are in kind.

The constructing of the perspective scene for the stage involved dividing the scene into its architectural units or "houses" and at the same time arranging these units so that they became constituent elements of a single scenic picture. As Vitruvius had suggested, and as perspective theory had shown, the arrangement of the houses was to be on the diverging lines of a triangle, the point of which was established "in a center in a definite place." As these houses receded, they must be foreshortened, and the proper amount of azure must be added to their colour according to the principles of aerial perspective.

As I have said, it is not clear when this method of staging was first adopted, but that it was accepted as a recent innovation in 1486 by Sulpitius is certain; that it represented an attempt to revive the classical method of staging dramatic productions is clear from the insistency with which its interpreters claimed their Vitruvian authority; and that it was characterized by the perspective treatment of a scene essentially architectural in construction and composed of architectural units is proved by the accounts of actual productions which have come down to us as well as by the descriptions of the theorists. That this method of constructing scenery was first adopted by the Roman Academy at a date approximately that at which they were responsible for the

[1] Cf. Vasari, *op. cit.* vol. VIII, pp. 233, 234.

introduction of the ancient drama on the modern stage is evident also from the testimony of Sulpitius.

That the acceptance of this method of staging the drama was elsewhere than in Rome a settled fact in the late fifteenth and early sixteenth centuries is proved by the scattered documents which record the history of the early stage. The first record of a performance of a classical drama at Ferrara, the *Menaechmi* of Plautus, which was performed January 25, 1486, on a stage erected in the court of the palace, describes the scene:

Et remis puppim et velo sine fluctibus actam Vidimus in portus nare, Epidamne, tuos, Vidimus effictam celsis cum moenibus urbem, Structaque per latas tecta superba vias. Ardua creverunt gradibus spectacula multis, Velaruntque omnes stragula picta foros. Graecia vix tales habuit vel Roma paratus Dum regerent longis finibus imperium[1].

Certainly it seems that there is here described some such scene as that used in the confessedly Vitruvian settings, and the phrase "per latas vias" apparently describes the arrangement of the houses in the usual fashion of a street in perspective.

A letter of January 29, 1502, from Isabella d'Este at Ferrara to her husband in Mantua described the festivities attending her brother's wedding. Describing the hall arranged for the comedies, Isabella wrote: "On the opposite side of the hall is a wooden stage about the height of a man, with battlements, and the scenery for the comedies, which are to be six in number[2]." Again there is at least a probability that the stage so arranged was a stage after the manner then affected by the antiquarians.

In March, 1508, the *Cassaria* of Ariosto was played

[1] Quoted from Guarino in A. d'Ancona, *Origini del Teatro* (1877), vol. II, p. 128, note 2. Cf. Cunliffe, *op. cit.* pp. xxxix–xli, and also *Intro.*, p. x, to ed. *Suppases* and *Jocasta* (1906).

[2] Ady, *Isabella d'Este*, vol. I, p. 199.

with the typical neo-Vitruvian scenery, which was described by Bernardino Prosperi to Isabella:

But what has been best in all those festivities and representations has been the scenery in which they have been played, which Master Peregrino, the Duke's painter [Pellegrino da San Daniele], has made. It has been a view in perspective of a town with houses, churches, belfries and gardens, such that one could never tire of looking at it, because of the different things that are there, all most cleverly designed and executed. I suppose that this will not be destroyed, but that they will preserve it to use on other occasions[1].

A setting so constructed as to serve as a more or less permanent background for the type of drama which it decorated is implied by this description and the writer's comment.

A more detailed description has been preserved of the two great performances of *La Calandria*, written by Cardinal Bibbiena and played first at the court of the Duke of Urbino and afterward before the pope. Mrs Ady translates a letter of 1513 from the famous Castiglione, the author of *The Courtier*, who supervised the production at the court of the Duke of Urbino, and who wrote the prologue that was delivered on this occasion. The letter to his friend Ludovico Canossa would seem to fix the date of production as 1513. In part Castiglione said:

Our comedies have gone off well, most of all the "Calandria," which was represented in a truly magnificent style.... The scene represented was an outer street of the town between the city wall and its last houses. The wall with its two towers was represented in the most natural way possible, rising from the

---

[1] E. G. Gardner, *The King of Court Poets: A Study of the Work, Life, and Times of Lodovico Ariosto* (1906), p. 323. Professor Cunliffe, *Intro.* to *Supposes*, p. xv, says that this performance gave "occasion for the first recorded use of modern scenery." Cf. also Bond, *op. cit.* pp. xlii, xliii.

floor of the stage to the top of the hall. One tower was occupied by the pipers, the other by the trumpeters, and between the two there was another finely constructed rampart. The hall itself where the audience sat, occupied the place of the moat, and was crossed as it were by two aqueducts[1].

So much seems clear; confusion comes to the reader later:

The scene was laid in a very fine city, with streets, palaces, churches, and towers, all in relief, and looking as if they were real, the effect being completed by admirable paintings in scientific perspective. Among other objects, there was an octagon temple in low relief, so well finished that, even if all the workmen in the duchy of Urbino had been employed, it seemed hardly possible to think that all this had been done in four months! This temple was completely covered with beautiful stucco reliefs, the windows were made to imitate alabaster, the architraves and cornices were of fine gold and ultramarine blue, with glass jewels here and there, looking exactly like real gems; there were roundels of marble containing figures, carved pillars, and much more that would take me too long to describe. This temple stood in the center of the stage. At one end there was a triumphal arch about two yards from the wall, marvelously executed. Between the architrave and the vault an admirable representation of the story of the Horatii had been painted to imitate marble. The two niches above the pillars supporting the arch were filled with little Victories bearing trophies in their hands made of stucco. On the top of the arch stood a most beautiful equestrian statue of a figure in armour, striking a vanquished man at his feet with his spear. To right and left of this rider were two little altars with vases of burning flame that lasted to the end of the comedy[2].

[1] It seems to me quite probable that the first part of the description relates to the curtain or painted scene which the spectator saw as he entered the hall.

[2] The letter is translated by Mrs Ady in her *Baldassare Castiglione* (1908), vol. I, pp. 336–9. Part of it is copied from this source in Mr Keith's article in *The Builder*, vol. cvii, pp. 152–4.

Castiglione's further description related to the intermezzi, which required for their presentation the bulls
of Jason, the sea-horses of Neptune, doves to draw the
car of Venus and peacocks to draw the car of Juno;
they showed Juno appearing in a cloud, nine gallants
ablaze with light bursting from a door that was set
fire to, and many other spectacular devices with which
we have become familiar in the masques at the court of
James I. The same attention to architectural detail, the
same emphasis on light effects, the same "machines"
and burning objects, the same frequent introduction of
men appearing as birds and beasts, that characterized
the masques, are here apparent.

Less detailed but more instructive is the account given
by Vasari of the work of Baldassare Peruzzi, who made
the scenery for the performance of *La Calandria* which
was given before the pope a little later. To Peruzzi,
Vasari gives the credit for having revived the art of the
scenic representation of the drama. He records:

When the Calandra, a play by Cardinal Bibbiena, was performed before the same Pope Leo, Baldassare made the scenic
setting, which was no less beautiful—much more so, indeed,
than that which he had made on another occasion....In such
works he deserved all the greater praise, because dramatic performances, and consequently the scenery for them, had been
out of fashion for a long time, festivals and sacred representations
taking their place. And either before or after (it matters little
which) the performance of the aforesaid Calandra, which was
one of the first plays in the vulgar tongue to be seen or performed,
in the time of Leo X, Baldassare made two such scenes, which
were marvellous, and opened the way to those who have since
made them in our own day. Nor is it possible to imagine how
he found room, in a space so limited, for so many streets, so
many palaces, and so many bizarre temples, loggie, and various
kinds of cornices, all so well executed that it seemed that they
were not counterfeited, but absolutely real, and that the piazza

was not a little thing, and merely painted, but real and very large. He designed, also, the chandeliers and the lights within which illuminated the scene, and all the other things that were necessary, with much judgment, although, as has been related, the drama had fallen almost completely out of fashion. This kind of spectacle, in my belief, when it has all its accessories, surpasses any other kind, however sumptuous and magnificent[1].

When, in 1514, at the death of Bramante, Raffaello was put in charge of the construction of St Peter's, he was also made by the pope general superintendent of fine arts, and accordingly he had charge of the fêtes of the papal court as well as of the excavations, buildings, and other works under that office. As I have already instanced, he was given Fra Giocondo as special adviser in architectural matters, and moreover, he caused a special translation of Vitruvius to be made for his guidance. The resulting interest in antiquity was evidenced chiefly in the scheme for the restoration of ancient Rome, but it is likewise noticeable in the work that Raffaello did in arranging dramatic productions. A particularly clear account of the arrangement for the production of the *Suppositi* of Ariosto in 1518 has been preserved in a letter from Pauluzzi to the Duke of Ferrara. We learn in this letter of the curtain upon which was painted "Father Mariano with a crowd of devils gamboling about him," and of the scene admirably arranged in perspective. We hear, too, of the pope's particular admiration for the sky which Raffaello had made. Campori instances other letters as to the productions at San Angelo, which show that the comedy scene was arranged, according to the precepts of Vitru-

[1] Vasari, *op. cit.* vol. v, p. 69. For an account of the scenery made by Peruzzi for a comedy acted as part of the festival celebration of the accession of Pope Leo X, cf. also p. 67. It is interesting to note Vasari's constant emphasis on Peruzzi's interest in perspective.

vius, as a street bordered by private dwellings, and Campori adds:

et comme non seulement le fond, mais les parties latérales et supérieures aussi, devaient être exposés à la vue du spectateur, Raphaël aura pu faire preuve de son habilité dans ce que mentionne Pauluzzi sous le nom de *forami di prospettiva*[1].

It seems quite certain, too, that Raffaello was responsible for the construction of the temporary theatre for the performance of the plays, and that he made it according to the precepts of Vitruvius.

Perhaps the best known record of the scenery provided for plays in the sixteenth century is that given by Vasari in his description of the work of the festive preparations for the nuptials of Prince Don Francesca of Tuscany (1565 or 1566). He describes "the vast and most lovely canvas painted with various animals hunted and taken in various ways, which upheld by a great cornice, and concealing the prospect scene" occupied one end of the great hall. At the fall of this scene, the prospect scene was revealed. Vasari describes spectacular features not included in Serlio's delectations when he describes the cloud which parted to let another cloud descend, and the ground opening to emit fire and smoke[2]. By this description we are made quite sure that the machines of the "heavens" and of the nether stage as well were used in the performance of this version of the Cupid and Psyche tale.

Showing as they do the incorporation of the plans of the theorists of the stage, these scattered descriptions are documents of supreme importance. But it must not be forgotten that the Renaissance interest in the theatre was broader than that in stage scenery. It is not my

---

[1] Cf. G. Campori, "Documents inédits sur Raphael," *Gazette des beaux arts* (1863), vol. XIV, pp. 442–56; Müntz, *Raphael*, pp. 404, 405, 421, 422; Bapst, *op. cit.* p. 247; D'Ancona, *op. cit.* vol. II, p. 89.

[2] Vasari, *op. cit.* vol. X, pp. 106 *sq.*

purpose to undertake here a survey of the Renaissance theatres, for every step in such a discussion must be taken on disputed territory. But it is important to note that theatres were built early in the Renaissance according to the instructions of Vitruvius, apparently much earlier than has generally been supposed. Professor Chambers says that

Alberti put a theatrum in the palace built in the Vatican for Nicholas V about 1452, but there is no record of its use for dramatic performances at that time, and the immediate successors of Nicholas did not love humanism[1].

Flechsig records a great theatre built at Rome in 1513 for the festival of September 13, 14[2]. There are to be found occasional references to the theatre of Ariosto[3]. Of the fact that by the opening of the sixteenth century practically every Italian court had its hall arranged temporarily or permanently as a theatre there is abundant evidence in dramatic records. The conception of the theatre was at first that of a rectangular theatre with an auditorium arranged about the semi-circle decreed by Vitruvius. With Serlio, at least, there was a conscious adaptation and modifying of Vitruvian precepts. Gradually, however, the confusion of the idea of the theatre with that of the amphitheatre seems to have grown, and it is to this confusion that we must look for the explanation of some of the vagaries of stage history.

In the latter part of the sixteenth century there was built, however, a theatre which was, to some extent at least, to standardize the ideas of theatrical construction. It was a theatre which fulfilled the long-cherished ideas of the antiquarians in its conformity to Vitruvian precepts. This was the famous Olympic Theatre of Vicenza, built by Andrea Palladio.

[1] E. K. Chambers, *The Mediaeval Stage* (1903), vol. II, p. 214.

[2] E. Flechsig, *Die Dekoration der Modernen Bühne in Italien* (to 1600), pp. 51 *sq.*   [3] Cf. especially Gardner, *op. cit.* p. 239.

PLATE III

THE STAGE OF THE OLYMPIC THEATRE
From Conte Montenari, *Del Teatro Olympico*, 1749

The Olympic Academy of Vicenza, founded in 1555 for the study of the ancients, centered its interest about the production of classical drama. Among its founders was Andrea Palladio, a geometrician, a student of antiquity, and an architect. Palladio's patron had been Giorgio Trissino, whom he refers to as "splendore de' tempi nostri[1]." In order to produce its plays the Olympic Academy had from time to time a stage built for the purpose. Serlio, as we have seen, records the building of a stage here, and Palladio himself built a temporary stage in the Basilica in 1562[2]. It was at length decided to build a permanent theatre, and Palladio was naturally chosen to have charge of its construction. He had already studied the remains of early Roman architecture, he was a thorough student of Vitruvius like his friend and fellow-worker Daniello Barbaro, with whom he constantly exchanged ideas and plans, and he and Barbaro had made careful estimates and drawings from the ancient theatre of Berga. On the basis of these studies he drew the plans for his theatre, modifying the Roman theatre of Vitruvius by substituting a semi-elliptical auditorium for the semi-circular auditorium of Vitruvius and thus giving a better view of the stage to more of the observers. The work on the theatre was begun May 23, 1580, and Palladio died August 19, 1580. The task of completing the theatre was then turned over to his son, and not until 1584 was the theatre finished.

Coryat in his *Crudities* described his visit to this theatre in 1611 and recorded: "He that showed me

[1] Our information concerning Palladio's life is largely drawn from the "Vita di Andrea Palladio" by Paolo Gualdo, written in 1648 but published by Conte Giovanni Montenari in his *Del Teatro Olympico* in 1735 (second edition of 1749 consulted).

[2] The occasion was probably the first performance of Trissino's *Sofonisba*, acted for the Olympic Academy in 1562. Cf. Vasari, *op. cit.* vol. VIII, pp. 233, 234.

this Theatre told me that the Orchestra and fourteen benches would containe about some three thousand persons. The Scene also is a very faire and beautifull place to behold." He also writes of performances that he had heard were held there, concluding the list:

But one of the latest great shewes that was made here was presented before the forenamed that famous Earle *Leonardas Walmarana*, in the year 1585. For at that time the Tragedy of Sophocles, which is intituled *Oedipus*, was most excellently acted in this theater. The history of the acting whereof is finely painted in the Court wal at the very entrance to the theater[1].

According to tradition elsewhere recorded the first play presented in this theatre was the *Oedipus*.

This theatre has become famous in history for many reasons, but its characteristic feature is found in the five scenic runways or "perspectives" which extend back of the five doors of entrance. These scenic additions were made, however, not by Palladio, but by Scamozzi, who in a dedicatory letter prefixed to the seventh book of his work on architecture records the fact that he added these scenes at the time of the visit of the Empress Maria of Austria in 1585, the scene being arranged for a tragedy[2]. The researches of Mr William Grant Keith have brought recently to light a description of this scene preserved in the *Palladio* of Inigo Jones and written in Jones's own hand. It is dated "Vicensa. Sundaie ye 23 of September 1623." It is an important document in the history of English stage decoration, and I quote it here as Mr Keith has transcribed it.

The Theater of Palladios ordering the front of the sceane of Bricke covered with stcco full of ornament and stattues as in

---

[1] Cf. vol. II, pp. 86, 87.

[2] The history and description of this theatre are most authoritatively recorded by Montenari, *op. cit.*, and by Ottavio Bertotti Scamozzi, *Il Forestiere instruito della Cose più rare di Architettura, e di alcune Pittura della Città di Vicenza* (1761).

the designe I have The Prospectives ar 5 the wiedest is a streete of houses Temples and suchlicke in front at ye end of ye scene an arck triumfall Painted. all the houses on ye sides ar of Releave the windoues look out and maad with bourdes inwardes to maak a thicknes the collumbs wear flatt but round tourd the edges ye stattues of marbel and bronze finto [imitation bronze —W. G. K.] I mean thos in shortning ar flatt but of hole Releave w^h sheaw strangly a neear but a farr of well. on the Passages of the sides all the lights wear Placed w^h as the said sheawed exelently the flouer was Playne Bourdes but Painted lyke Pavement ye Cornishes wear splaie Peeces of Deeal bourdes and Painted slightly The rufe was ye raffters and tiles covered with Canvase the cheaf artifice was that whear so ever you satt you sauw on of thes Prospects: In this sceane thear is no apparitions of nugole [no scenic cloud effects—W. G. K.] and suche licke but only the artifice of the sceane in Prospective Carrieth ytt...an otangell tempell an other in collomes against yt and Pallases on each side of them....

The figures of releave in shortning ar of Carta Pasta they are maad flatt as I saide to anenswear the narrownes of the shortning neeces in w^h the stande[1].

It is evident that the scenery so added to the Olympic Theatre in 1585 was of exactly the same sort as that described by Serlio in 1545 as having been familiar to him even in his early years. Indeed the scenery of this theatre seems to have been of the type established at the beginning of the dramatic revivals. Curiously, it seems to me, the decoration of the scene in perspective painting, described by Vitruvius, had become a painting in perspective of the separate architectural units of the scene, and these in turn were now introduced into the permanent scene wall as perspectives or scenic streetways. An examination of the plan of the Vitruvian theatre according to Barbaro will suggest that the placing

[1] Cf. "A Theatre Project," in the *Burlington Magazine*, vol. xxxi, pp. 65 *sq.*

of the *periaktoi* behind the doors of the scene wall probably suggested to Scamozzi the idea of introducing
the perspective scene in the same fashion.

Thus the century that had elapsed since the revival
of the classical drama in its Roman setting had seen

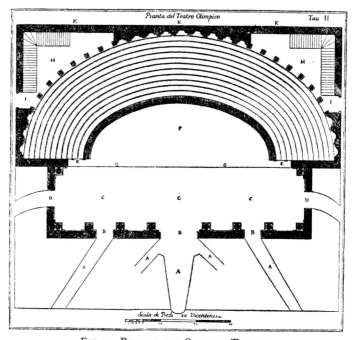

FIG. 7. PLAN OF THE OLYMPIC THEATRE
From Conte Montenari, *Del Teatro Olympico,* 1749

the development of a theory of scenic representation of
the drama, a knowledge of the theory and practice of
perspective which was more or less adequate to the
carrying out of this theory, and a fully equipped Roman
theatre with its classical stage adorned with the perspective scenery which had developed from the attempts
to follow classical authority.

CHAPTER IV

MACHINES

THE question of the use of "machines" is one which comes insistently to the student of the Renaissance drama. These machines are most familiar to us as they were used in connection with the sacred festivals of the church. Vasari describes the "Paradise" invented by Brunelleschi for the Festival of the Annunciation in Florence, with its representations of God, the angels, clouds, and heavenly lights, and he describes the great "engine" or "machine" which carried them. Vasari comments:

These engines, made thus, together with many others, were invented by Filippo [Brunelleschi], although others maintain that they had been invented long before. However this may be, it was well to speak of them, seeing that they have gone completely out of use.

Symonds discusses the question of the origin of these devices and conjectures that "Brunelleschi's study of ancient art may have induced him to adopt a classical device to the requirements of Christian pageantry[1]."

Whether or not Brunelleschi originated these "engines," Vasari's statement that they had gone completely out of use could not have been true for a very long period, for Isabella d'Este, writing in April of 1503 from Ferrara to her husband, described the representation of the Annunciation which she had witnessed on a stage at the house of the archbishop. After

[1] Cf. Vasari, *op. cit.* vol. II, pp. 229–32; Symonds, *Italian Literature,* vol. I, pp. 319–28; Burckhardt, *op. cit.* pp. 412–15; also Bapst, *op. cit.* p. 245, for a record of Leonardo da Vinci's invention of a *"théâtre machine"* entitled *il Paradiso* in 1489, and Burckhardt, *op. cit.* p. 412.

describing the appearance of the angel who first appeared, she wrote:

Then Mary appeared, under a portico supported by eight pillars and began to repeat some verses from the Prophets, and while she spoke, the sky opened, revealing a figure of God the Father, surrounded by a choir of angels. No support could be seen either for His feet or for those of the angels, and six other seraphs hovered in the air, suspended by chains. In the center of the group was the Archangel Gabriel, to whom God the Father addressed His word, and after receiving his orders, Gabriel descended with admirable artifice and stood, half-way in the air, at the same height as the organ. Then, all of a sudden, an infinite number of lights broke out at the foot of the angel choir, and hid them in a blaze of glory....At that moment the Angel Gabriel alighted on the ground, and the iron chain which he held was not seen, so that he seemed to float down on a cloud[1]....

Our most detailed account of the Florentine festivals, however, is found in Vasari's life of the Florentine engineer, Cecca, and of the mechanical devices perfected by him for accomplishing the spectacular effects required during these celebrations. We learn of the angels held by iron girdles and kept upright by weights of lead properly adjusted for balance, of cotton-wool clouds, of the ten circles of the ten heavens revolving wonderfully, of the effects produced by bronze lamps revolved mystifyingly[2].

The confusion of pagan and Christian elements in these spectacles is again most significant. Just as Caesariano recognized the thunder that accompanied the appearance of a god on the stage as being essentially like the accompaniment of the Passion by natural phenomena, so the descent of divine beings on clouds

[1] Ady, *Isabella d'Este* (1903), vol. I, pp. 251, 252.
[2] Cf. Vasari, *op. cit.* vol. III, pp. 193–200; also Symonds, *Italian Literature*, vol. I, pp. 325–7.

coming from heaven was accepted in the representation both of Christian festivals and of pagan dramas.

That machines were in use in the secular dramatic representations of the time also is evidenced by the instances already quoted in the descriptions of the intermezzi presented with *La Calandria* in 1513, and of the dramatic spectacles provided on the occasion of the marriage of Prince Don Francesca of Tuscany, as well as in the explanations of Serlio. That classical dramatic theory included or came to include provision for the representation of all the spectacular devices of the sacred representations as well as those usually associated with the secular drama is proved by the descriptive work of Sabbatini in the seventeenth century[1].

The possible source of the Renaissance knowledge of machines comes, then, to be a matter of significance. The modern classical scholar depends almost entirely for his knowledge of the machines of the ancient theatres upon the work of Vitruvius, the scholia of the early dramatists, and the work of Pollux, the Greek grammarian of the second century, whose *Onomasticon* contains a description of the machines of the Greek theatre. The fact that all of these sources of knowledge were likewise available to the scholars of the Renaissance has generally been forgotten. The popularity of Vitruvius we have already seen, and the Renaissance interest in the classical drama and in the comments of the scholiasts is too well known to need proof. The probable influence of Pollux on the Renaissance conception of dramatic representation has yet to be estimated.

A list of the early editions of the *Onomasticon*, however, is sufficient proof of an early and continued and widespread interest in it. The first edition was printed in Venice in 1502 by Aldus Manutius. There followed editions in Florence in 1520 (an edition edited by

[1] See Part III, chap. xi below.

Antonio Francesco Varchiese and dedicated to Linacre), in Basle in 1536 (Grynaeus), in Frankfurt in 1608 (Seberius), and in Amsterdam in 1706 (Hemsterhuys)[1].

Other unmistakable evidence of the influence of the *Onomasticon* is found in many quarters during the sixteenth and seventeenth centuries, however. I have already instanced Philander's reference to it, while the work of Barbaro seems also to indicate a familiarity with its descriptions[2]. Perhaps the most extensive use made of the *Onomasticon* comments on stage spectacle during this period, though, is to be found in Scaliger's *Poetices* (1561), where the chapter entitled "Theatrum" includes a section on the machines of the theatre which approximates a translation of the corresponding section of the *Onomasticon* in Book IV, chapter ix, sections 121–54. The *Nomenclator* of Adrien Junius or Du Jon, the great Holland scholar, likewise bears distinct indications of indebtedness to the *Onomasticon* in its form and arrangement as well as in its definitions, many of which are based on the authority of Pollux. This work was published at Augsburg in 1555, but its chief interest for students of the English drama is in the fact of its having been used as the basis of Higgins's English *Nomenclator* published in 1584[3]. In the seventeenth century the dependence of classical scholars upon Pollux is shown by explicit praise, such as Evelyn gives his work, and by constant citations of his words as authority, such as are found in the edition of Vitruvius by De Laet.

Pollux's discussion of the construction and arrangement of the Greek theatre is not relevant here, but it must be noted that he gives much more explicit information concerning the conventionally accepted significance

[1] Cf. Sandys, *op. cit.* vol. ii, p. 227, and *Index*.
[2] Cf. above, pp. 24, 25.
[3] I am indebted to Professor C. R. Baskervill for calling my attention to the theatrical terms defined in the English *Nomenclator*.

of the various stage doors as entrances and exits than Vitruvius gives. He explains in the same manner as Vitruvius the three types of stage decoration corresponding to the three types of drama, however. And he makes his unique contribution to the history of the stage in that he lists and describes the machines in use on the Greek stage[1].

The *periaktoi* are described differently by Pollux than by Vitruvius as "versatiles machinae," the functions of which are thus explained:

dextra quidem ea, quae extra urbem sunt repraesentans. sinistra vero ea, quae ex urbe ducit, maxime quae ex portu, & Deos inducit marinos, & alia omnia, quae graviora existentia, machina ferre nequit. Si vero machinae hae versatiles convertantur, dextra quidem locum mutat, utraeque vero locum subalternant. Ingressum porro, dextra quidem, ex agro, e portu, aut ex urbe ducit[2].

Other equipment of the stage is listed by Pollux:

Praeterea inter theatri partes quoque numeretur, pegma, & machina[3], exostra, specula, murus, turris, specula derectrix, duas contignationes habens domus, turris fulminea, tonitru, Deorum sedes, grus, pensilia, tapetia, semicirculus, strophium, semistrophium, & scalae Charonae, & anapiesmata[4].

Certain of these parts of theatrical apparatus are described more or less in detail, and these descriptions of Pollux seem to have been eagerly examined by the Renaissance students of the drama.

The *eccyclema* and *exostra*, which were generally regarded during the Renaissance as functioning similarly, are described by Pollux as differentiated by being used in tragedy and in comedy respectively. He says:

Sed pegma supra ligna quaedam alta scala est, cui thronus insidet. exhibet vero secreta, quae sub scena in domiciliis fiunt.

---

[1] The quotations below are taken from the Latin translation of 1706.

[2] Cf. Bk IV, § 126.

[3] Translating καὶ ἐκκύκλημα, καὶ μηχανή.   [4] § 127.

& hujus officii verbum est, in orbem circumvolvi. Machina autem, super quam pegma inducitur, εἰσκύκλημα nominatur. & hoc juxta singulas januas observandum est, & fere juxta singulas domos.

Later he adds, after having shown that the machine for use in presenting the gods in tragedy is in comedy called a crane: "Exostram porro idem, quod pegma, esse volunt[1]."

In regard to the machine by which the *deus ex machina* is introduced:

Machina vero, Deos exhibet, Heroës illos aërios, Bellerophontes scilicet, & Perseos. & dicitur juxta sinistrum introitum, super scenam esse altitudine. Quod vero in Tragoedia, machina, hoc in Comoedia, crade dicitur. Unde patet quod ficus imitatio est. Ficum etenim, Attici κράδην vocant[2].

Later he says also:

Ex Deorum autem sede, quae scenam excellit, apparent Dii, utpote Jupiter, & qui circa ipsum. Grus praeterea, machina quaedam est, ex alto demissa, ad corporis alicujus raptum idonea, qua Aurora usa est, corpus Memnonis rapiens. Pensilia vero nominabis funiculos, qui ex alto dependent, ut eos sustineant Heroës, Deosve, qui in aëre ferri videntur[3].

Of the making of thunder and lightning Pollux writes: "Machina autem fulminea, & tonitru. illa quidem, est alta versatilis machina. hoc vero in posteriore parte sub scena, urnae sunt lapillis plenae, qui impulsi, per aenea vasa delabuntur[4]." These machines were known as the *keraunoskopeion* and the *bronteion*. Haigh in his *Attic Theatre* comments on Pollux's definition of the *keraunoskopeion* as unintelligible, but he adds that "Heron, the mathematician, speaks of a device used in automaton theatres, by which a plank, with a flash of lightning painted on a dark background, was shot

---

[1] § 128.   [2] § 128.
[3] § 130.   [4] § 129.

out of a box into a receptacle below[1]," a device which was certainly utilized during the Renaissance. The freedom of interpretation given the thunder machine on classical authority is witnessed by the words of Barbaro already quoted in his note on Vitruvius as well as by Renaissance practice: "Tonitru in eorum [the gods] aduentu fiebant, utribus, & pellibus corijs inflatis, calculisq̃; repletis, uel ictibus percussis, quos nos tamburros nominamus."

Of Charon's steps by which ghosts ascended to the stage, and of the machines (which according to Haigh were in the Greek theatre probably trap-doors) by which the furies gained access to the stage, Pollux says:

Gradus porro Charonii, juxta sedilium descensus positi, Manes a se emittunt. Sed anapeismata, hoc quidem in scena est, veluti fluminis transgressionem repraesentans, aut aliud hujusmodi: illud vero circa scalas est, per quas ascendunt Furiae[2].

That the machines of Pollux include practically all the machines used in the Renaissance in both sacred representations and secular drama seems to be self-evident. That the *Onomasticon* was accessible throughout the Renaissance is shown by the list of printed editions; and borrowings from it as well as references to it prove its popularity as a source of information concerning ancient Greek life. It seems, therefore, inevitable that the influence of this work must have been very great in determining the use of machines in the early revivals of the classical drama and in the succeeding drama of the Renaissance.

[1] *Op. cit.* (1907), p. 218. [2] § 132.

CHAPTER V

THE THEORY OF THE DRAMA

WHILE the achievements of artistic theory and technique had led to such results in the work of the architect in the theatre, the interpretation of Aristotle's *Poetics* had been influencing the work of the creators and the critics of the drama alike. And it is necessary if we are to understand the evolution of the theory of the use of spectacle on the stage to see what had been the interpretations of Aristotelian doctrines.

Aristotle had, of course, differentiated tragedy and comedy[1]. He had included spectacle as one of the six parts of tragedy, and had concluded: "in fact, every play contains spectacular elements as well as Character, Plot, Fiction, Song, and Thought[2]." But he had given the credit for the addition of scene-painting to Sophocles rather than to Aeschylus as Vitruvius had done[3]. While saying that "spectacle has, indeed, an emotional attraction of its own[4]," and while claiming the supremacy of tragedy over epic because it has all the elements of epic with the addition of music and spectacle[5], he still had said that spectacle had the least to do with poetry, for "the production of spectacular effects depends more on the art of the stage machinist than on that of the poet[6]."

In the differentiation of types of the drama, in giving classical authority for the use of scene-painting, in in-

---

[1] Cf. S. H. Butcher, *Aristotle's Theory of Poetry and Fine Art* (1911), *Poetics*, ii, 4; and Spingarn, *op. cit.* pp. 66, 67.

[2] *Poetics*, vi, 7. [3] *Ibid.* iv, 13.

[4] *Ibid.* vi, 19. [5] *Ibid.* xxvi, 4.

[6] *Ibid.* vi, 19.

cluding spectacle as a part of the play, in assigning the work of stage decoration to the machinist, Aristotle and Vitruvius were on common ground, though Vitruvius did give Aeschylus rather than Sophocles the credit for originating scene-painting, and though it was to the architect who was also the engineer that he gave the business of planning the spectacle or decoration of the scene.

But there are certain elements that are introduced into the discussion by Aristotle alone. In the first place, the exciting of fear and pity by means of spectacle was discussed by Aristotle. Concerning this question he said:

Fear and pity may be aroused by spectacular means; but they may also result from the inner structure of the piece, which is the better way, and indicates a superior poet. For the plot ought to be so constructed that, even without the aid of the eye, he who hears the tale told will thrill with horror and melt to pity at what takes place....But to produce this effect by the mere spectacle is a less artistic method, and dependent on extraneous aids. Those who employ spectacular means to create a sense not of the terrible, but only of the monstrous, are strangers to the purpose of Tragedy; for we must not demand of Tragedy any and every kind of pleasure, but only that which is proper to it[1].

Yet in spite of this comment, the mere fact that Aristotle mentioned spectacle as a means of rousing pity and terror gave grounds for justifying the thunder and tolling bells of the drama as well as its ghosts and murders.

A second important addition to the discussion of the theory of spectacle was made by Aristotle's comment on the use of the *deus ex machina* in the plot of the drama:

It is therefore evident that the unravelling of the plot, no less than the complication, must arise out of the plot itself, it

[1] *Poetics*, xiv, 1, 2.

must not be brought about by the *Deus ex Machina*—as in the Medea, or in the Return of the Greeks in the Iliad. The *Deus ex Machina* should be employed only for events external to the drama,—for antecedent or subsequent events, which lie beyond the range of human knowledge, and which require to be reported or foretold; for to the gods we ascribe the power of seeing all things. Within the action there must be nothing irrational[1].

The prohibitions of this statement do not seem to have entered much into the discussions of the stage critics until the late seventeenth century, when all theory was a splitting of hairs, but in its suggestions of possible stage devices this passage seems to have been influential from the outset.

Incidentally Aristotle's mention as parts of tragedy of "Recognition," which was in the Renaissance translated as "Discovery" (a change from ignorance to knowledge); "Reversal of the Situation," which was earlier translated as "Revolution" ("a change by which the action veers round to its opposite"); and "Scene of Suffering" or "Disaster" ("a destruction or painful action, such as death on the stage, bodily agony, wounds and the like")[2] gave endless chances for revealing and concealing horrors on the stage with all manner of possible interpretations of the phrases as far as the theory of stage decoration goes.

But of course, the most important doctrine "fathered on Aristotle," as Friedland says, is the doctrine of unity

[1] *Poetics*, xv, 7. Cf. also Horace's prohibition in the *Ars Poetica* which was constantly referred to during the Renaissance:

> Nec deus intersit, nisi dignus vindice nodus
> Inciderit.

[2] *Poetics*, xi. Cf. also Horace:

> Non tamen intus
> Digna geri promes in scenam, multaque tolles
> Ex oculis quae mox narret facundia praesens.

of place. It is perhaps well to repeat once more exactly what Aristotle did say, which was that

Tragedy endeavours, as far as possible, to confine itself to a single revolution of the sun, or but slightly to exceed this limit; whereas the Epic action has no limits of time[1].

And again he said:

The Chorus too should be regarded as one of the actors; it should be an integral part of the whole, and share in the action, in the manner not of Euripides but of Sophocles[2].

The first genuine translation of Aristotle's *Poetics* was made into Latin by Georgius Valla between 1495 and 1498. Spingarn has told the story of the growing knowledge and popularity of the *Poetics* as well as of its changing interpretation. Friedland in his study of *The Dramatic Unities in England* has given in detail the growth of the idea of unity of place, and Charlton's recent study of Castelvetro has also given much information on the matter. But the history of Aristotle in the Renaissance needs no retelling here, save that it is necessary once more to stress certain outstanding facts. That the rules of dramatic construction as well as the rules of production or representation were accepted on classical authority is attested by the prefatory verses to the *Historia Betica* acted at Rome in 1492. Trissino's *Sofonisba*, usually reckoned the first regular modern tragedy, and though not produced until 1562, presumably written about 1515, is described by Spingarn as in reality little more than an attempt at putting Aristotelian theory into practice. With Robortello came the "artificial day," the twelve hours limit for the action of a play. With Scaliger (1561) came a full commitment of the dramatist to strict verisimilitude. He insisted upon the necessity of affecting the spectators as though they were actually witnessing the events enacted upon

---

[1] *Poetics*, v, 4.   [2] *Ibid.* xviii, 7.

the stage. In order to produce this effect, the time of the action could not be supposed to be more than six or eight hours. With Castelvetro's work (1570) the doctrine of the unity of place was determined, a necessary outgrowth of the strict application of the idea of unity of time, for verisimilitude could not admit great distances to be traversed in a short space of time. Later the argument for the essential unity of place presupposed by the constant presence of the chorus was also added.

It is thus apparent that during the sixteenth century the dramatist was finding himself bound by a more and more definite set of rules deduced from classical authority, while the architect was finding more and more diffuse explanation of an equally rigid system of rules for the scenic representation of the drama, his rules likewise drawn from classical authority. The record of stage decoration in England during the sixteenth and seventeenth centuries is a record of the convergence and the divergence of these two theories, while the record of the late seventeenth century is a record of compromise and conciliation in settling differences that grew up between them.

PART II

STAGE DECORATION IN ENGLAND
DURING THE SIXTEENTH CENTURY

CHAPTER VI

EARLY CLASSICAL INFLUENCES IN ENGLAND

THE beginnings of the scenic representation of the modern drama in England and of the revived classical drama antecedent to the modern native drama are veiled to us by the absence of adequate records of the early English drama in all its aspects. As a result, the scattered materials that remain have been diversely interpreted, especially in regard to the possible classical origin of the modern English drama. Such careful surveys of existing dramatic material as that of Sir A. W. Ward in his article on the English drama in the *Encyclopaedia Britannica* (eleventh edition) and that of Professor Wallace in his *Evolution of the English Drama* clearly illustrate this fact. Sir A. W. Ward finds significance in the early classical tendencies noted in the English drama, and concludes:

It was under the direct influence of the Renaissance, viewed primarily, in England as elsewhere, as a revival of classical studies, and in connexion with the growing taste in university and cognate circles of society, and at a court which prided itself on its love and patronage, that English tragedy and comedy took their actual beginnings.

Professor Wallace, emphasizing in his survey the importance of the native rather than the classical elements of the drama, disregards as isolated and comparatively inconsequential the instances of classical influence noted by Sir A. W. Ward, and on the basis of other scattered instances which he regards as more significant, he concludes:

For three quarters of a century the basis of Court entertainment had been spectacular appeal, that which was graspable with the greatest ease and the most sensuous delight. Dialogue had evolved partly as an essential accompanying feature—as the landscape painter gives the human touch by a living figure—and partly as a substitute for garish display and action. The thing lay rather in instinct than in imitation of the ancients[1].

Because, therefore, it is important to judge facts that are confessedly scattered and often inconsequential in themselves, in the light of the knowledge of what finally did prevail, it may as well be said at the outset of this review of the tendencies noted in the sixteenth century that perhaps the most important proof of the classical origin of spectacle on the modern English stage lies in the fact that the classical theory of stage decoration did prevail in the seventeenth century. The facts which I shall instance in this study of the sixteenth century can in no way be judged in their true significance save by a study of their relation to the full development of the classical theory in England under Inigo Jones and his seventeenth century contemporaries and successors.

That the sources of knowledge upon which the classical theory of dramatic representation was built up in Italy were early known at least to scholars in England seems as certain as merely circumstantial evidence can make it. Poggio, who discovered the Vitruvius manuscript at St Gall, spent the years 1420 to 1422 in England[2]. Vitruvius's *De Architectura* was among the works sent for out of Italy by Humphrey, Duke of Gloucester[3], whose gift to Oxford of his library of classical and Italian works is generally said to herald the English interest in humanism. Vives in his *Epistola*

[1] C. W. Wallace, *The Evolution of the English Drama up to Shakespeare* (1912), p. 120.

[2] Cf. Lewis Einstein, *The Italian Renaissance in England* (1902), p. 52.

[3] Cf. K. H. Vickers, *Humphrey, Duke of Gloucester* (1907), pp. 365, 369.

de Ratione Studii Puerilis addressed to Charles Mountjoy in 1514[1], as well as in his later *De Tradendis Disciplinis,* advocated a knowledge of Vitruvius as contributing to the vocabulary of the student of the classics a
knowledge of the practical and technical terms of ancient
life, and he also commented on the work of Pollux as
contributing Greek expressions and words, though con-
fessing him a better guide to the learned than the unlearned. In this later work Vives also instanced Vitruvius and Alberti as the authorities whom the architect
and builder should consult; yet he confessed Vitruvius
difficult to understand, even with the help of Jocundus's
illustrations[2]. Daniello Barbaro, the translator and anno-
tator of the *De Architectura* and exponent of the art and
science of perspective as well, was appointed ambassador
from the Venetian court to the court of England in
1548 and spent some eighteen months in England[3].

The fact that the 1520 edition of Pollux's *Onomasticon*
was dedicated to Linacre has already been noted, and
constant references to Pollux in the English *Nomenclator* (1584) show his recognized authority. It is unnecessary even to repeat the long-accepted proof of the
authority which attached to the pronouncements of
Aristotle and Horace and Pliny in sixteenth-century
England[4]. Certainly it seems that the English scholars
of the Renaissance had ample knowledge of the sources

[1] Cf. Foster Watson, *Vives and the Renaissance Education of Women*
(1912), Appendix, p. 246.

[2] Cf. Foster Watson, *Vives: On Education.* A translation of *De Tradendis Disciplinis* of Juan Luis Vives (1913).

[3] Reginald Blomfield, *A History of Renaissance Architecture in
England,* 1500–1800 (1897), vol. i, p. 25. For proof that Vitruvius
was known to Dr John Dee, John Shute, and Ben Jonson, see below.

[4] See the works of Spingarn, Saintsbury, Friedland, and Sandys
already instanced, where the influence of the classical revival is treated
at length. See also H. C. Taylor, *Thought and Expression in the Sixteenth Century* (1920).

from which the theory of dramatic representation took its beginnings.

Nor could it have been otherwise in view of the international character of the new learning. It is impossible to estimate the influence of such emissaries of humanism as Erasmus and Vives or of the early English humanists such as Robert Fleming, William Gray, Linacre, More, Grocyn, Colet and Fisher, many of them long resident at Italian courts[1]; but it is possible to assert that the knowledge of the ancients, at first gathered for the most part by Italian scholars, early became knowledge common to the scholars of the Renaissance in all countries. To English scholars, therefore, a knowledge of Italian neo-classical theories and methods of dramatic representation was as ineluctable as a knowledge of the classical sources of the Italian theory and practice.

Indeed, it seems impossible that the desirability of such ornamental addition to court and academic circles as was afforded in the presentation of plays in the classical manner should not have been brought to the consciousness of the early English churchmen and courtiers and scholars alike who went to Italy on business of church or state or in pursuit of knowledge of the ancients[2]. It will be remembered that it was particularly to the courts of Ferrara and Urbino that early

[1] Cf. especially the article on "Englishmen and the Classical Renaissance," by T. M. Lindsay, in vol. III of the *Cambridge History of English Literature*; and Richard Fiddes, *Life of Cardinal Wolsey* (1724), pp. 214–18.

[2] The interesting speculations concerning the stage erected by John Rastell about 1526 discussed by Professor C. R. Baskervill in an article on "John Rastell's Dramatic Activities," in *Modern Philology* (vol. XIII, pp. 557 *sq.*) are not to be ignored in this connection. The papers on which Professor Baskervill bases his discussion are published in full in A. W. Pollard, *Fifteenth Century Prose and Verse* (1903). The record of Sir Thomas More's childish interest in the drama and of his early participation in the performances at the house of Cardinal Morton should be remembered too. Cf. Roper's *Life of More*.

scholars and courtiers went[1], and in those courts dramatic representations were known in their most luxurious neo-Vitruvian dress, as has already been illustrated in this discussion. Englishmen at the courts where Castiglione and Genga, Bibbiena and Peruzzi, Ariosto and Raffaello were responsible for dramatic representations must have been influenced by this "fad of the Renaissance."

Blomfield, Einstein, and Reyher have all recounted the history of the importation of Italian artists and craftsmen, begun under Henry VII and fostered under Henry VIII, especially after Wolsey had undertaken the rebuilding of Hampton Court in 1515[2]. Among the greatest of Italian artists at the court of Henry VIII were the architects Pietro Torrigiano (Peter Torresany), Benedetto da Rovezzano, "John" de Majona, and Girolamo de Treviso, the last of whom entered the service of the King as engineer and architect rather than painter, though he seems to have been renowned for his excellence in colour, and Vasari records that at Bologna Peruzzi made the design of a Nativity for Count Giovanni Battista Bentivogli, which the count then gave to Treviso to colour. Among the Italian painters at the English court were Antonio Toto del Nunziato (Anthony Toto), sergeant-painter to the King, Bar-

---

[1] Perhaps the most interesting of these exchanges of civilities between courts is that recorded by Holinshed (*Chronicles of England, Scotland, and Ireland* (1808), vol. III, p. 538) for 1507. In that year Henry VII caused "Guidebald duke of Urbine" to be elected Knight of the Garter as his father had been before him. "Sir Gilbert Talbot, and the other two ambassadors being appointed to kéepe on their iournie vnto pope Iulie the second, elected after the death of said Pius the third, bare the habit and collar also vnto the said duke Guidebald; which after he had receiued the same, sent sir Balshasar Castalio...vnto king Henrie, which was for him installed, according to the ordinances of the order."

[2] Cf. Blomfield, *op. cit.* vol. I, pp. 3–5; Einstein, *op. cit.* pp. 192–207; Reyher, *op. cit.* pp. 73–5.

tholomew Penni, said to have worked under Raffaello until Raffaello's death, Niccolo Bellini of Modena, Antonio Cavallari, and Elys or Alice Carmellion. Other foreign artists were in service at court also, the only supremely great artist among them being, however, Hans Holbein. The names of many of these artists have been anglicized beyond recognition[1].

But workmen as well as more skilled artists were imported throughout the sixteenth century, to the great discontent of the native workmen, as Hall's chronicle sufficiently shows, for the uprisings of native workmen are seen to have been as violent as they were continuous from 1516 onwards. The importation of foreign wares, among them "painted cloths," was likewise the source of constant friction, and the eloquent plea in Parliament for the protection of the baby industry of painting as late as 1601 has a curiously modern ring[2]. Also it is interesting to note that the description of the decorations which marked Elizabeth's progress through London the day before her coronation remarks: "Thus the Queenes hyghnesse passed through the citie, whiche, without any forreyne persone, of itselfe beawtifyed itselfe[3]."

That the artistic influences of the first half of the century were predominantly Italian is generally recog-

[1] In addition to the references already cited, see "Notices of the Contemporaries and Successors of Holbein," by J. G. Nichols, and "Additional Observations," by George Scharf, in *Archaeologia*, vol. XXXIX, pp. 19–46, 47–56. See also Vasari, *op. cit.* vol. v, pp. 167–71, for account of Treviso; Bryan's *Dictionary of Artists* on the life of Penni; and the *Dictionary of National Biography* for the life of Anthony Toto.

[2] The interesting records which mark the progress of the discussion in both houses are to be found in Heywood Townshend's *Historical Collections* (1680), pp. 147, 270, 313–15.

[3] J. Nichols, *The Progresses, and Public Processions, of Queen Elizabeth* (1788–1805), vol. I, "The Passage of...Quene Elyzabeth... through the Citie of London to Westminster...," p. 25.

nized. Partly because of the growing Protestantism in England and partly because of other political and economic reasons, the influence of Germany increased rather unfortunately for things artistic. And while the influence of Italy did not cease, and while the architects of Elizabeth's reign went to Italy to study, much of the Italian theory of architecture came to England filtered through German interpretation. The edition of Vitruvius which was perhaps best known in Elizabethan England was that of Rivius[1].

However, during Elizabeth's reign there was published, in 1563, the first English work on architecture, John Shute's *First and Chief Grounds of Architecture*[2]. Shute was one of the first English architects to study in Italy, having been sent over about 1550 by the Duke of Northumberland. In explanation of his work Shute says:

I haue for the first parte taken for my author chieflye to be followed the noble and excellent writer Vitruuius one of the most parfaictest of all the Antiques, and for that, neither any one man in what art so euer it be is absolute, and that other singuler men of the Antiques and he in many poinctes do disagre and differ (which Sebastianus Serlius, a meruelous conning artificer in our time) in many places of his workes learnedly doth declare. I haue added vnto him vpon what soeuer in any thing semed nedfull the opinion and meaning of the sayd experte writer Sebastianus, here and there also wher I thought meete I haue ioyned the minde and iudgement of one Gulielmus Philander a notable man whiche about the yere of our lorde 1546. wrote vnto the frenche king Anotacions vpon Vitruuius, concerning this matter or such like.

[1] Blomfield, *op. cit.* vol. 1, pp. 25–36.

[2] Shute's work was republished by *Country Life* in 1912 in a limited edition of 1000 copies. Cf. Blomfield, *op. cit.* vol. 1, pp. 86, 87, for comment on the influence of this work. It should be noted too that in the preface to his work Shute says that he had shown his drawings to Edward VI.

Thus while Shute confined himself in this work to a discussion of the five orders, he showed familiarity with the best of contemporary writing on architecture. It seems probable that this work was intended as a part of a larger work which was never written or which has been lost to us. The book was reissued in 1579 and in 1584, but it was not until the translation of Serlio's work in 1611 that there was a complete architectural treatise in English.

Meanwhile the first English translation of Euclid's *Elements* was made by Sir Henry Billingsley, lord mayor of London, and was published in 1570, with a long introduction by Dr John Dee. This introduction is a very important contribution to the history of mathematical studies in England, and among the mathematical arts are discussed perspective, "zographie," and architecture. Perspective, Dee defines as "an Art Mathematicall, which demonstrateth the maner, and properties, of all Radiations Direct, Broken, and Reflected." And he adds, "This Description, or Notation, is brief, but it reacheth so farre, as the world is wyde." Of "zographie," Dee says that it is

an Arte Mathematicall, which teacheth and demonstrateth, how, the Intersection of all visuall Pyramids made by any playne assigned, (the Centre, distance, and lightes, beyng determined) may be by lynes, and due propre colours, represented.

The painter is but the mechanician of the "zographer," who needs to know geometry, arithmetic, perspective, anthropology, etc. Dee adds that of sculpture and "picture" great books have been written, and he instances those of Giorgio Vasari, Pittore Aretino, and Pomponius Gauricus. But it is in defence of the profession of architect that Dee grows most eloquent, quoting at length from Vitruvius in regard to the education of the architect. The architect is, he says, "neither

Smith, nor Builder; nor, separately, any Artificer: but the Hed, the Prouost, the Director, and Iudge of all Artificiall workes, and all Artificers." The two "most perfect Architects" are Vitruvius and Alberti, and from them he quotes, being led to exclaim in regard to Vitruvius,

Thus much, and the same wordes (in sense) in one onely Chapter of this Incôparable *Architect Vitruvius*, shall you finde. And if you should, but take his boke in your hand, and slightly loke through it, you would say straight way: This is Geometrie, Arithmetike, Astronomie, Musike, Anthropographie, Hydragogie, Horometrie, &c. and (to côclude) the Storehouse of all workmanship.

In 1598 Richard Haydocke published a translation of the work of Lomazzo (or Lomatius) as *A Tracte containing the Artes of curious Paintinge, Carvinge, & Buildinge*[1], but part of this work, including the book on perspective, though duly represented in the index, seems never to have been printed.

That England depended upon foreign sources for architectural theory and for architectural skill is shown by the bringing of foreign artists and workmen to England, and later, during the reign of Elizabeth, by the first English architects' going to Italy to study, as did John Shute and Inigo Jones. Furthermore the early works on architecture published in England, tardy as they were, were merely translations or adaptations of the works of Italian artists.

With a knowledge of the classical sources upon which the Italian theory of dramatic spectacle was based, with

---

[1] The book is entitled "*A Tracte containing the Artes of curious Paintinge, Carvinge, & Buildinge* written first in Italian by Jo: Paul Lomatius, painter of Milan. And Englished by R. H. student in Physik." The signature is that of Richard Haydocke. References to the authority of Vitruvius, Michael Angelo, Aristotle, and Pliny are frequent in the work.

c s

6

an acquaintance with Italian performances of the drama in a neo-classical setting, with Italian artists and craftsmen present in England in sufficient numbers to make the execution of such settings possible, with a conscious dependence on Italy for artistic precept and example, the English court and the English academic circles in the sixteenth century might well have been led to adopt the method of staging their dramas which was then prevalent in Italy. For the answer to the question as to whether this was the method adopted the records of the classical drama and of the early native modern drama in England must be examined as they are found in connection with the grammar schools, the universities and inns of court, and the court itself.

CHAPTER VII

DRAMATIC REPRESENTATIONS IN THE GRAMMAR SCHOOLS, UNIVERSITIES AND INNS OF COURT

WE have abundant proof of the fact that in the early grammar schools of England the acting of classical dramas was traditionally regarded as the best method by which to give students facility of speech and familiarity with common Latin idiom. And that the tradition persisted is shown by Jonson's *Staple of News* (1625), in which he wrote:

Is't not a fine sight, to see all our children made interluders? Do we pay our money for this? We send them to learn their grammar and their Terence, and they learn their play-books[1].

When Dean Colet re-established the old foundation of St Paul's Grammar School in 1512, William Lily was appointed head-master. At his death in 1522, he was succeeded by his son-in-law, a former usher in the school, John Ritwise (or Rightwise). During the incumbency of Ritwise the boys of the school acted before the cardinal and before the King. Thus while no record exists, so far as I know, of plays given by the boys of Paul's during the rule of Lily, it is well to recall that Lily came to the school after a sojourn in Rome, where he had gone to perfect himself in Latin under Pomponius Laetus and Sulpitius. It is difficult to conceive

[1] Act III, Scene II. On the whole subject see particularly A. F. Leach, *The Schools of Mediaeval England* (1915). See also W. H. Woodward, "English Universities, Schools, and Scholarship in the Sixteenth Century," in the *Cambridge History of English Literature*, vol. III, and Foster Watson, *The English Grammar Schools to 1660* (1908).

of one who had received his Latin training under the first editor of Vitruvius and under the first scholar to arrange Roman plays acted in the Roman fashion in a setting designed according to the precepts of Vitruvius, as returning to England and failing to make use both of the Latin play as a method of teaching Latin and of the Vitruvian principles of scenic representation of the drama[1]. Especially does it seem that Lily brought back the ideals of the Roman Academy when we find his successor very early in his reign responsible for dramatic presentations at court, and we have record of Paul's boys under Ritwise acting in 1527 an anti-Lutheran play before the King and the French ambassadors[2]. In 1528 the boys acted the *Phormio* of Terence on the occasion of a banquet given by Cardinal Wolsey in honour of the King and the foreign ambassadors and in celebration of the release from captivity of Pope Clement VII[3]. Paul's boys also acted the play

[1] For the facts herein contained see especially Anthony à Wood, *Athenae Oxoniensis*, vol. 1, col. 35, "William Lily"; article on Lily in *Dictionary of National Biography*; Thomas Warton, *History of English Poetry* (1871), vol. IV, p. 1.

[2] Thorndike, *op. cit.* p. 253, says that the boys of St Paul's grammar school appeared at court in 1517, but I have not been able to ascertain his authority for this statement. For the record of the 1527 performance, cf. Hall's *Chronicle* (1809), p. 735, where we are told that the "great chamber of disguisings" was for this evening fitted up with most cunning workmanship, a great fountain occupying the centre of the picture, while at one side was a hawthorn tree of silk and at the other side a similar mulberry tree. Eight fair ladies sat in gorgeous apparel on the benches about the fountain. After the play four companies of maskers danced, and the setting seems to have been arranged for them. Whether the play "in the Latin tongue in maner of tragedy" was played with this setting and these eight fair ladies as background is not made clear by the chronicler. Chambers, Wallace, Herford, Froude, Lupton, and others have recorded this event.

[3] Cf. *Calendar State Papers (Venetian)*, 1527–1532, no. 225, letter of Spinelli dated Jan. 8, 1528, which letter is cited by Wallace, *Evolution of the English Drama*, p. 89. The letter itself is interesting in the description of the mottoes used as decoration on this occasion.

of *Dido* before Wolsey, the play being fashioned by their master from Vergil[1].

The boys of Eton were early instructed in play-acting also, as is shown by a record of expense in connection with the performance of two plays in 1525[2]. In 1538 they acted before Cromwell[3], and their habit of acting is established by the evidence of the *Consuetudinary*, written in 1561, and recording the traditions of plays and their production[4]. The mastership of Nicholas Udall (1534–41) was the mastership of an avowed classicist, to whom Queen Mary later gave full authority for requisitions from the Master of the Revels for whatever he considered necessary for the fit setting out of plays and masques at court[5], a fact which proves his interest and skill in the realm of dramatic spectacle.

We have no certain early records of Westminster productions, but it now seems probable that Udall wrote for the boys of Westminster his *Ralph Roister Doister* during his mastership there[6].

Bishop Bale has recorded a list of plays which were among those acted by the boys of the grammar school at Hitchin after 1538, when Ralph Radcliffe set up a stage in a large hall purposely for the acting of plays in his school[7].

Of the performances of the boys of the grammar schools at the court of Elizabeth record was made in the Office of the Revels accounts along with those of other companies, and it is difficult to isolate their expenses from the mass in order to make any possible

[1] Cf. Wood, *op. cit.* vol. I, col. 35.

[2] Cf. Wallace, *Evolution of the English Drama*, p. 88, note 3, and E. K. Chambers, *The Mediaeval Stage* (1903), vol. II, pp. 195, 196.

[3] Cf. Chambers, *op. cit.* vol. II, pp. 195, 196.

[4] *Ibid.* Cf. also Warton, *op. cit.* vol. III, p. 308.

[5] Cf. *The Losely Manuscripts*, ed. A. J. Kempe (1835), pp. 62, 63.

[6] Cf. Chambers, *op. cit.* vol. II, pp. 195, 196.

[7] *Ibid.* Also cf. Wallace, *op. cit.* p. 88, and Thorndike, *op. cit.* p. 253.

generalization as to the method of their scenic production.

As to these early productions of the grammar schools, it is possible only to say, in view of the meagreness of the records, that from early in the sixteenth century we find the boys acting classical plays or plays modelled on classical lines not only in their schools but also before the court and the courtly circle, and acting them under the direction of masters known to be able to direct the representation of the plays in the manner then reckoned as the classical manner.

That the universities, like the grammar schools, early accepted the acting of classical plays as a method of educational training is proved beyond dispute by the statutes of several colleges quoted by Professor Boas in his *University Drama under the Tudors*[1]. But perhaps more significant even than these statutes is the record of the famous performance of *Plutus* at St John's College, Cambridge, in 1536, for this performance was arranged by the advocates of the reformed pronunciation of Greek, apparently as a challenge to the supporters of the old "Reuchlinian" pronunciation, who won temporarily the academic battle that ensued, only to be defeated later by the Erasmians[2].

The statutes regulating plays in the colleges date from 1545 for St John's; 1546, Queens'; 1560, Trinity, Cambridge; and from 1554, Christ Church, Oxford. These statutes, it must be remembered, however, regulate and do not establish customs[3]. It is certain that plays were very early enacted in the colleges. The Magdalen account books (Oxford) show some sort of dramatic performances as early as 1486, and while the terms *comoedia* and *tragoedia* are not used therein until

[1] Cf. pp. 16, 17.
[2] Cf. Sandys, *op. cit.* vol. II, p. 232, and Boas, *op. cit.* pp. 16, 17.
[3] Boas, *op. cit.* pp. 16, 17.

1535, the terms must have been used and the dramatic forms they denoted must have been recognized at least as early as 1511–12 in Oxford, when one Edmund Watson was granted a degree on condition that he compose "*C carmina in laudem universitatis et unam comoediam infra annum post gradum susceptum*[1]."

How much decoration and stage spectacle was regularly provided for these college performances we do not know. That the afterwards famous Dr John Dee came dangerously near disrepute because of the "machine" which he arranged for the performance of the *Pax* of Aristophanes at Trinity College in 1546 we know from his own words, however. Having been appointed under-reader in Greek, he arranged the presentation of the play, as he says,

with the performance of the Scarabaeus, his flying up to Jupiter's palace, with a man and his basket of victuals on her back: whereat was great wondering, and many vain reports spread abroad of the means how it was effected[2].

The fact that Scaliger, writing of the κράδη used in comedy after the fashion of the machine by which in tragedy the *deus ex machina* came upon the scene, added to the description of Pollux the remark, "qualis Cantharus siue Scarabaeus Aristophanis[3]," makes it clear that this experiment by Dee was in the nature of an attempt to follow classical tradition.

That the university plays were not acted in a bare hall is indicated also by an extract from one of Roger Ascham's *Epistles*, written about 1550 while he was travelling in Flanders, asserting

that the city of Antwerp as much exceeds all other cities, as the refectory of St John's Hall, Cambridge, exceeds itself when

[1] Cf. Boas, *op. cit.* pp. 11, 12.
[2] Cf. article on John Dee in *Dictionary of National Biography*.
[3] Cf. Scaliger, *Poetices* (1561), p. 36.

furnished, at Christmas, with its theatrical apparatus for acting plays[1].

The performance of the *Hymenaeus* at St John's in 1578–9 cost about £35[2], and the Rainolds-Gager letters of 1591 and 1592 dispute the wisdom as well as the professionalism of an expenditure of £30 on a play and refer to borrowing robes from the Revels[3]. And, in spite of Gager's contention that the university performances were set forth "thriftely warely, allmost beggerly," the evidence leads directly to Professor Boas's conclusion: "There is little here to give countenance to the traditional view of the primitive simplicity of Elizabethan stage-arrangements[4]." Nor is there any evidence to show that the university stage known to John Dee and Roger Ascham was habitually any more meagerly adorned than that of the reign of Elizabeth.

As to the nature of the stage arrangements, we get our first glimpse from the record of 1551–2 at Christ's, where 12*d*. was paid to the carpenter "for removing ye tables in ye haull & setting y^em vp again wth ye houses and other things[5]."

But it was in connection with the royal visits that the university stage achieved its great renown. And the contemporary records of these occasions are more

---

[1] Quoted in "Latin Plays acted before the University of Cambridge," printed in the *Retrospective Review*, vol. XII, pp. 1–42.

[2] Cf. G. C. Moore-Smith, introduction to edition of *Hymenaeus* (1908).

[3] Cf. John Rainolds, *The Overthrow of Stage-plays* (second ed. 1629), and letter from William Gager, quoted by Karl Young, "William Gager's Defense of the Academic Stage," in *Publications of the Wisconsin Academy of Sciences*, vol. XVIII.

[4] Boas, *op. cit.* p. 349.

[5] Cf. Boas, *op. cit.* p. 23. Of the various university performances Professor Boas's work gives most of the known evidence, and I have, therefore, not attempted to review evidence save such as has a direct bearing on the subject under consideration.

or less adequate to the picturing of the performances. When Queen Elizabeth visited Cambridge in August, 1564, she spent her evenings in witnessing "comedies and tragedies, set forth partly by the whole university, and partly by the students of the King's College." It is recorded that

There was, before her Majesty's coming, made in the King's College Hall, a great stage. But, because it was judged by divers to be too little, and too close for her Highness and her company, also far from her lodging, it was taken down.

Evidently some regard was had to the perspective view of the stage, if this account of the criticisms levelled against it be accurate. In consequence of these objections, it is recorded, after evening prayer on Sunday evening, the Queen attended the play, Plautus's *Aulularia*,

For the hearing and playing whereof, was made, by her Highnes surveyor and at her own cost, in the body of the (King's College) Church, a great stage containing the breadth of the church from one side to the other, that the chappels might serve for houses.

On Monday the play of *Dido* "was exhibited and played by and at the charges of the company of the King's College." Udall's *Ezechias* was the third and last play presented, the Queen being too weary to attend the proposed performance of *Ajax Flagellifer* which had been prepared for presentation[1]. The record in this case is not convincing, though the use of the chapels as stage houses certainly suggests the habitual use of houses constructed on the stage.

The accounts of the Queen's visit to Oxford in 1566, however, provide us with more important information.

[1] Nichols, *op. cit.* vol. i, "The Triumphs of the Muses: Or, the Grand Reception and Entertainment of Queen Elizabeth at Cambridge...1564," p. 13.

The fullest record of the arrangement of the hall and the stage at Christ Church, where were presented *Marcus Geminus*, *Palamon and Arcyte*, and *Progne*, is that given by John Bereblock. For the first performance Bereblock says:

> Erat aula laqueari aurato, et picto arcuatoque introrsus tecto, granditate ac superbia sua veteris Romani palatii amplitudinem, et magnificentia imaginem antiquitatis diceres imitari. Parte illius superiori, qua occidentem respicit, theatrum excitatur magnum et erectum, gradibusque multis excelsum. Juxta omnes parietes podia et pegmata extructa sunt, subsellia eisdem superiora fuerunt multorum fastigiorum, unde viri illustres ac matronae suspicerentur, et populus circum circa ludos prospicere potuit. Lucernae, lichni, candelaeque ardentes clarissam ibi lucem fecerunt....Ex utroque scenae latere comoedis ac personatis magnifica palatia aedesque apparatissimae extruuntur. Sublime fixa sella fuit, pulvinaribus ac tapetiis ornata aureoque umbraculo operta.

The most important part of this description is, of course, that contained in the passage pertaining to the erecting at both sides of the stage *magnifica palatia aedesque apparatissimae*, for such differentiation of structures and such indications of magnificent and appropriate construction would be pointless unless the scene revealed the glories of architectural achievement of the neo-Vitruvian stage. However, only less important than the description of the construction and arrangement of the houses is that contained in the first sentence I have quoted:

> *Erat aula laqueari aurato, et picto arcuatoque introrsus tecto, granditate ac superbia sua veteris Romani palatii amplitudinem, et magnificentia imaginem antiquitatis diceres imitari,*

for this description seems clearly to indicate a conscious imitation of antiquity. It is also to be remarked that the whole arrangement of the hall must have been similar to that indicated by Serlio as the Vitruvian arrangement adapted to the rectangular hall.

The play of *Palamon and Arcyte* acted in two parts on successive nights received much attention from the historians of the royal visit, but they gave more time to the casualties resulting from an accident at the beginning of the performance and to the excitement caused by the hearing of the cry of the hounds from the court at the proper moment than to the scene itself. Enthusiasm is expressed, however, over the magnificence and beauty of the scene, and we are told that the lady Amelia gathered flowers "in her garden there represented."

Progne, we are likewise told, was enacted in a scene of wondrous beauty, but the most interesting and the most detailed part of the description is that relating to the trap-door device and the realistic flames used, to the exceeding great admiration of the spectators:

Primo ibi exauditus est strepitus quidam subterraneus, reconditus & formidabilis. Hinc sese infernis e partibus erigit Diomedes. Illud vero tum fuit horribile, spumas agere in ore, caput, pedes, braccia, flagrantia habere, non fortuito, sed insito et innato incendio, ipsum vero misere nimis perterreri ac agitari furiarum taediis ardentibus[1]....

It is evident that the subterranean thunder and Charon's ladder described by Pollux were thus in use on the university stage.

In 1583, on the occasion of the Palatine of Siradia's visit to Oxford, elaborate preparations were made for the plays to be presented before him, *Rivales* and *Dido*.

[1] Cf. Nichols, *op. cit.* vol. I, "The Queen's Progress, 1566," pp. 41–55, and also vol. III, p. 109. A translation of the account by Bereblock is included in W. Y. Durand's "Palamon and Arcyte, Progne, Marcus Geminus and the Theatre in which They Were Acted, as Described by John Bereblock (1566)," in *Publications of the Modern Language Association*, vol. XX, pp. 502–28.

We have no adequate record of the decorations provided on this occasion for the plays, but the account of the performance of *Dido* suggests again the use of thunder and lightning as well as the *deus ex machina* and other devices regularly a part of Italian court performances. The Queen's banquet was graced with the destruction of Troy set forth in a "marchpaine patterne." There were also

a goodlie sight of hunters with full crie of a kennel of houndes, Mercurie and Iris descending and ascending from and to an high place, the tempest wherein it hailed small comfects, rained rose water, and snew an artificial kind of snew, all strange, marvellous, and abundant[1].

The Queen's visit to Oxford in 1592 was the occasion for more plays, but the chroniclers record that the plays were "both of them but meanely performed (as we thought), and yet most graciouslye, and with great patience, heard by hir Majestie[2]."

It is improbable that rose-water rain was provided by the university for undergraduate performances save on the occasion of royal visits, but it is likewise improbable that the performance of plays on these glorified occasions should have differed in kind from their usual performance. It is much more likely that these presentations differed only in the degree of the luxury and costliness of their setting.

That the "Students in the Universities of the Laws[3]," like the students of Oxford and Cambridge, were early interested in the drama is generally believed, though

[1] Nichols, *op. cit.* vol. ii, "Palatine of Siradia's Visit, 1583," pp. 204–6.

[2] Nichols, *op. cit.* vol. ii, "The Queen's Progress, 1592," p. 23.

[3] For an interesting account of this term and of the relation of the gentlemen of the inns of court to the court, see M. Thynne, "Of the Antiquity of the Houses of Law," published in *Curious Discourses* by Thomas Hearne (1720).

the first recorded performance of the members of the inns of court took place in 1526[1]. At Christmas of 1526, Hall records, there was a "goodly disguising plaied at Greis inne," the invention of one "Master Roo," and he adds, "This plaie was so set furth with riche and costly apparel, with straunge diuises of Maskes & Morrishes that it was highly praised of all menne, sauyng of the Cardinall[2]...." It is probable that the offence taken by Cardinal Wolsey, who imagined a personal attack in the theme of the play, was the reason for its being specially noted by Hall. At any rate, the prohibition by an order of the bench in 1550 of all "comedies called interludes" save at the Christmas season proves the existence of the custom of acting plays in the inns of court[3]. And it is significant that the four earliest English classical tragedies[4] which have been preserved were all played by the gentlemen of the inns of court. The stage directions for three of these tragedies give us perhaps our clearest picture of the Elizabethan stage arranged for elaborate performances.

The earliest of the extant English classical tragedies, *Gorboduc: or Ferrex and Porrex*, does not in its stage directions give any clear notion of the stage setting,

[1] Cf. Chambers, *Mediaeval Drama*, vol. II, p. 194.

[2] Hall, *op. cit.* p. 719, account of the "xviii yere of King Henry the Viii."

[3] Cf. Chambers, *Mediaeval Drama*, vol. II, p. 194; Warton, *op. cit.* vol. III, pp. 316, 317.

[4] Unfortunately, early comedies that have persisted do not contain stage directions that throw much light on the matter of their original stage setting. Cf. Professor Bond's introduction to his *Early Plays from the Italian* for a discussion of the possible relation between Italian and English methods of presenting plays like the *Supposes*, which was performed at Gray's Inn in 1566. To me it seems impossible that the English projectors of this play which had received such luxurious presentation in Italy (cf. above, p. 52) should not have followed the Italian model in its presentation also.

but Professor Cunliffe's comment on its stage arrangement cannot be ignored.

> In the fourth dumb-shew [he says] the three furies come "from under the stage as though out of hell"; and this, as well as the phrase in Machyn's diary with reference to the second performance, "there was a grett skaffold in the hall," seems to indicate that the stage of _Gorboduc_ was, substantially, that of the miracle plays[1].

Sir A. W. Ward's statement concerning _Apius and Virginia_ that the stage direction, "Here let Virginius goe about the scaffold" indicates "that the stage was still that of the mystery-dramas and moralities[2]" is a conclusion reasoned from the same premises. If such conclusions are justified, then wherever we have noted the presence of a temporary stage, or indeed a stage of any sort, and wherever we have indications of the use of a trap-door or Charon's ladder, we are justified in assuming a miracle-play stage. No one so well as Professor Cunliffe has traced the relationship between the requirements of the classical stage and the trap-doors and their emitted ghosts and infernal beings of the Elizabethan stage[3]. And of the accepted classicism of Charon's ladder and the _anapeismata_ I have spoken earlier in this study. But the misunderstanding of the use of the word _scaffold_ is general. It is quite clear that the word is used definitely in two senses, both of which are fortunately recorded in Higgins's _Nomenclator_ of 1584[4], where the English equivalent of _proscenium_ is given as "the stage or scaffold it selfe, upon which they

---

[1] Cf. J. W. Cunliffe, "Early English Tragedy," in the _Cambridge History of English Literature_, vol. v, p. 78.

[2] A. W. Ward, _A History of English Dramatic Literature to the Death of Queen Anne_ (1899), vol. i, pp. 206, 207.

[3] Cf. J. W. Cunliffe, _The Influence of Seneca on Elizabethan Tragedy_ (1893 and 1907).

[4] Cf. above, p. 62.

played," and the English definition of *fori* is given as "the galleries or standings for the beholders of plaies: the scaffolds." Florio likewise illustrates the interchangeable nature of the words *stage* and *scaffold* (in the first sense of the word) in his definitions of *palco*, "a stage, or scaffold," *proscenio*, "a stage—but properly the place before a scaffold...," *scena*, "a stage or scaffold in a theater or play-house[1]." There are many similar instances, but these should suffice to show that arguments like that of Professor Cunliffe in regard to this famous performance of the inns of court are based on an unwarrantable limitation of the meaning of the word *scaffold*.

But in three others of these earliest English classical tragedies[2], there is more than negative evidence to be considered. "*Iocasta*: a Tragedie written in Greeke by *Euripides*, translated and digested into Actes by George Gascoygne, and Francis Kinwelmershe of Grayes Inne, and there by them presented, 1566," states that it is "presented as it were in *Thebes*." The stage directions are clear. "Iocasta the Queene issued out of her house," and then "Iocasta the Queene issueth out of her Pallace," an interesting change from the technical stage term "house" to the dramatic term "Pallace." "Iocasta goeth off the stage into hir pallace, hir foure handmaids follow hir, the foure chorus also follow hir to the gates of hir pallace," and later Servus

goeth off the stage by the gates called *Electrae* [leading to the city], Antygone attended with iij. gentlewomen and hir gouern-

---

[1] Florio's *Queen Anna's New World of Words* (1611). Malone quotes from an edition of 1598.

[2] Unless specifically stated otherwise references are to the texts printed by Professor Cunliffe in his *Early English Classical Tragedies*, the text of *Iocasta* being printed from the edition of 1575, that of *Misfortunes of Arthur* from the edition of 1587, and that of *Gismund of Salerne* (or *Tancred and Gismund*) from the undated edition of probably 1568.

our commeth out of the Queene hir mothers Pallace [and] Antigone with hir maids returneth into hir mothers pallace, hir gouernour goeth out by the gates *Homoloydes* [leading to the camp of Pollinyces].

The palace with its gates, the gates Electrae, and the gates Homoloydes are used throughout the play for entrances and exits, the characters carefully directed as to the appropriate entrance or exit in every case. The stage connoted by this description is an effective one, whether huge gates constituted the only decorations at sides and back, or whether they were made but part of an appropriate stage design. The directions indicate also a trap-door in the stage, for in the third dumb show a great gulf opens.

"*The misfortunes of Arthur*...reduced into Tragicall notes by *Thomas Hvghes* one of the societie of Grayes-Inne" was presented "to her Maiestie by the Gentle-men of Grayes-Inne at her Highnesse Court in Green-wich, the twenty-eighth day of Februarie in the thirtieth yeare of her Maiesties most happy Raigne," it being noted that "Maister Flower," "Maister Penroodocke," and "Maister Lancaster" directed the proceedings at court. It is from the directions for the dumb shows prefixed to the acts that we get our idea of stage ar-rangements in this play. The first dumb show revealed three furies rising from under the stage, and

Whiles they went masking about the stage, there came from another place three *Nuns* which walked by them selues. Then after a full sight giuen to the beholders, they all parted, the furies to *Mordred's* house, the *Nuns* to the Cloister.

In the second dumb show, "Whiles the Musicke sounded there came out of *Mordred's* house a man stately attyred....Then out of the house appointed for *Arthur* there came three *Nymphes*." For the fourth dumb show, "Dvring the Musicke...there came a Lady

Courtly attyred with a counterfaite Childe in her armes...," and the dumb show closed with the "counterfaite Childe" flung against the walls. Again it is clear that the "houses" were differentiated, and it seems quite possible that the specific houses named were only constituent elements of a more inclusive scene.

The Tragedy of Tancred and Gismund, presented by the gentlemen of the Inner Temple before the Queen, has come down to us in two forms. The 1592 edition, reprinted in the *Tudor Facsimile Series* and also in the *Malone Society Reprints*, is declared by the author to be "newly revised and polished according to the decorum of these daies," and hence it is particularly well worth while to notice what were the revisions incorporated in the interests of decorum in this edition of 1592, since the earlier edition—probably of 1568—is available in *Quellen und Forschungen*[1] and in Professor Cunliffe's *Early English Classical Tragedies*. In both the earlier and the later editions Cupid descends from heaven; in the second edition he comes down in a cradle of flowers. In both editions Megara and the furies rise out of hell. In both editions Tancred's palace and Gismunda's chamber are constantly used as entrances and exits, and Guiscard is led to the probably less visible prison. But the two versions differ significantly in the fifth act. The dumb show before the second and fourth acts in the second edition shows clearly that Gismunda's chamber had curtains before it which could be drawn back, as they must have been during part of the fifth act according to the earlier version, and yet the final scenes of the last act are in the second version brought outside the chamber. According to the early version Renuchio delivers the cup containing the warm heart of her lover

[1] Cf. vol. LXXX, pp. 536–95. See the preface of W. W. Greg to the edition printed in the *Malone Society Reprints* (1914) for the history of the two editions and an account of the dates of the extant copies.

to Gismunda in her chamber. She fills the cup with poison, drinks the poison, and dies in her chamber after her father, summoned, has arrived. We are told that Tancred then kills himself. In the later version Gismunda comes out of her chamber. Renuchio gives her the cup. She undresses her hair, takes a vial of poison from her pocket, drinks the poison, lies down and covers her face with her hair, the chorus meanwhile departing into the palace, presumably that she may be given the probable setting of solitude for her self-murder. Her father then comes out of his palace, and at the last plucks out his eyes and then kills himself. Why the horrible scene at the close of the play should have been added is not easily perceived, and whether the death of Gismunda was transferred to an outdoor scene because of classical precedent or because of more than classical reverence for unity of place (which is scarcely probable) or because of the difficulty in letting the audience see and hear indoor scenes, it is impossible to state. But the author's avowed purpose of achieving decorum should be taken into account[1].

[1] Professor Cunliffe notes this change as a particular instance of succumbing to Senecan influence. But if such is the case, the word *decorum* must be here used in a sense different from that in which it is used elsewhere during the period.

CHAPTER VIII

DRAMATIC REPRESENTATIONS AT COURT

AFTER all, the academical drama might, as Professor Wallace asserts that it did, have gone on its way "undisturbed and undisturbing." And even though the neo-classical method of dramatic representation had been adopted in grammar schools, universities, and inns of court, it is still possible, though I think scarcely probable, that the court drama might have been staged in some different fashion, the result of native inventiveness. How it was staged is merely a question of fact. There are, however, fundamentally three questions involved: the probability of decoration for the court drama, the date when decoration was adopted, and the kind of decoration adopted. As to the first of these considerations, any student familiar with the work of Withington and of Reyher on English pageants and masques[1], or anyone familiar with the chronicles of Holinshed and of Hall, cannot doubt the love of spectacle which characterized alike the courts of Henry VII and his successors and the people whom they ruled. The pageants and the masques of the century were extravagantly luxurious, exhibiting a surprisingly highly developed technique. Merely by way of illustration I quote here two fragments from the description given by Hall of the King's triumphal entry into London with the Emperor Charles in 1521:

...they came to the Stockes where there was a quadrant stage where on was an Herber full of Roses, Lyllies & all other

---

[1] Cf. Robert Withington, *English Pageantry* (1918), and Reyher, *op. cit.* Malone, *op. cit.* vol. III, p. 103, commented on the significance of such a "natural introduction to scenery on the stage."

flowers curiously wrought, and byrds, beastes, and all other thynges of pleasure. And aboute the Herber was made the water full of Fyshe, and about it was the Elementes, the Planettes and Starres in their places and euery thing moued, and in a Type in the Toppe was made the Trinitie with the Angels singing, and the Trinitie blessed the Kyng & the Emperor, and vnder his feete was written, *behold the louer of peace and concorde.*

[Later] they came to the litle Conduite in Chepe where was buylded a place like heauen curiously painted with cloudes, erbes, starres & the Ierarchies of angels, in the top of this pagiant was a great type & out of this type sodainly issued out of a cloude a fayre Lady richely appareled, & then al the minstrels whiche wer in the pagiant plaied & the angels sang, & sodainly againe she was assumpted into the cloud whiche was very curiously done[1].

The perfection of realistic detail and the use of a machine which let a "fayre Lady" suddenly issue out of a cloud and let her be as suddenly "assumpted into the cloud" are to be specially heeded in this description, while it must also be remarked that the machine is clearly set in a Christian rather than a pagan heaven.

The highly developed detail that characterized the palace and the castle, the rock and the mountain, the forest and the ship of pageant and masque scenery indicates that the English were prepared to present their plays with a scenic background if they so desired. And the presence of foreign artists and workmen who must have had practice in making settings of the sort familiar in all the Italian courts makes assurance doubly sure on this point. Henry VII and Henry VIII certainly do not seem to have been kings who would have chosen their drama unadorned, and they had no need to have it so.

As to the date when decoration or spectacle was first

[1] Hall, *op. cit.* pp. 639, 640.

added to the presentation of the drama, the evidence all points to the conclusion that the drama and its sensuous representation have always been inseparable when the drama has been considered as entertainment, and in England as elsewhere the early records of dramatic representations make it apparent that preparations were regularly made for appropriate decoration of the drama. The documents cited by Professor Wallace prove that there were dramatic performances at the court of Henry VIII from the first year of his reign onward[1]. That the hall in which a play was presented was decorated and arranged as a theatre is indicated by Holinshed's description of the events of February 13, 1510:

After supper, his grace with the quéene, lords & ladies came into the White hall within the said palace, which was hanged richlie, the hall was scaffolded and railed on all parts. There was an enterlude of the gentlemen of his chappell before his grace, and diverse fresh songs[2].

Among the Revels accounts for 1516 there is the following interesting record:

The King being at Eltham, Christmas 7 Hen. viii., instructions were issued to Richard Gibson, by Mr Wm Cornish and the master of the revels, to prepare a castle of timber in the King's hall, garnished after such devices as shall ensue. Cornish and the children of the Chapel also performed "the story of Troylous and Pandor" rychly imparylled, allso Kallkas and Kryssyd imparylled lyke a wedow of onour, in blake sarsnet and other abelements for seche mater; Dyomed and the Greks imparylled lyke men of warre, akordyng to the intent or porpoos. After weche komedy playd and doon, an harroud tryd and mad an oy that 3 strange knyghts wer com to do batell with [those] of the sayd kastell.

---

[1] Cf. Wallace, *Evolution of the English Drama*, pp. 71 *sq.*
[2] Holinshed, *op. cit.* vol. III, p. 560.

The expense noted for the painting of the castle was 18s. 4½d., and it is further indicated that

> 7 mynstrells imparylled in long garments and bonets to the saam of saten of Bregys, whyght and greeyn, on the walls and towyrs of the sayd kastell played a melodyus song[1].

The castle with its walls and towers so substantial that they afforded refuge to the minstrels playing for the performance was a stage scene that might well have adorned an Italian performance of the period, but the record here does not make it certain whether or not it was built for the tournament rather than the play.

A more convincing record is that given by Holinshed for the year 1520. He tells us that the King

> on the seuenth daie of Maie prepared a disguising, and caused his great chamber at Gréenwich to be staged, and great lights to be set on pillors that were gilt, with basons gilt, and the roofe was couered with blue sattin set full of presses of fine gold and flowers: and under was written Iammes, the meaning whereof was, that the flower of youth could not be oppressed,

and

> Into this chamber came the King, and the queene, with the hostages, and there was a goodlie comedie of Plautus plaied[2]....

That these early stages were decorated in some fashion is thus apparent, but in 1527 a more significant account was given in a letter written by the Venetian ambassador, Gasparo Spinelli, to his brother Ludovico describing the magnificent feast given by Cardinal Wolsey at which all the foreign ambassadors as well as the English king and the greatest noblemen were present:

> Supper being ended, they proceeded to the first hall...where a very well designed stage had been prepared, on which the

---

[1] *Letters and Papers of Henry VIII* (1862), vol. II, pt II, p. 1505.
[2] Holinshed, *op. cit.* vol. III, p. 635.

Cardinal's gentlemen recited Plautus's Latin comedy entitled the Menaechmi[1].

It seems unlikely that one familiar with the methods of courtly representations of the drama in Italy should fail to mention any difference in the manner of staging a play at the English court, and his comment on "a very well designed stage" seems therefore particularly interesting.

We are so rich in descriptions of masque scenery throughout the sixteenth century that it seems that we should be able to get some light on the progress of the technique of scenic representation of the drama from this source. Yet as a matter of fact, there is little that is pertinent in these descriptions. The early masques had scenery of a pageant nature constructed on movable cars. In 1516, as Reyher indicates, we have record of a fixed building for a masque. In 1527 the combination of fixed and movable scenery was used in a masque, but until the time of Inigo Jones the masque setting was not definitely fixed and immovable[2]. Consequently we can, in any case, learn comparatively little from the accounts of masque settings in regard to the painting of scenes in perspective suitable for dramatic presentations.

Therefore, aside from contemporary stage directions including references to the stage scene, which in the case of a limited number of Elizabethan plays have come down to us, we have to rely chiefly on information contained in the records of the Office of the Revels and particularly in the records of the accounts of that office. However, in the Revels accounts now accessible there is no unmistakable record of expenses for scenes for plays before 1564, the earlier documents containing the accounts of the office being those which pertain chiefly to the provision of costumes and properties. The possible

---

[1] *Calendar State Papers (Venetian)*, 1527–1533, no. 4.

[2] Cf. Reyher, *op. cit.* p. 354.

reason for this omission is considered below. Certainly there was cause enough why "Iohn Houlte yeoman of the Revelles vsed to saye Concerninge allowaunce of charges in the office of the Revelles it hath bene but a Taylers Bill."

Students familiar with the history of the office as recounted by both Chambers and Feuillerat will recall that an account of the history and duties of the office contained in a document preserved among the papers of the office and believed to date from 1573 and to relate to a proposed reorganization of the office, explains this remark of John Holt on the basis of the appointment from time to time of one who arranged special "devices," the tailor having charge of the work preliminary to these events. According to this same document the Revels was later united with the Tents and Toils into an office in the King's household. In March 1544–5, Sir Thomas Cawarden, having too much pride to enjoy the title of sergeant, which the previous incumbent, Travers, had held, was appointed Master of the Revels. Later the Revels, the Tents, and the Toils were made separate offices[1].

Certain recommendations in this important document are clearly indicative of the tasks of the office as they were allocated to the office at this period. The writer specifically says:

The cheife busynes of the office resteth specially in three poyntes. In makinge of garmentes In makinge of hedpeces and in payntinge.

He says also:

The connynge of the office resteth in skill of devise, in understandinge of historyes, in iudgement of comedies, tragedyes and

---

[1] Cf. E. K. Chambers, *Notes on the History of the Revels Office under the Tudors* (1906), and A. Feuillerat, *Documents Relating to the Office of the Revels in the Time of Elizabeth* (1908). Cf. Feuillerat, p. 5, and note concerning John Holt, p. 426.

shewes, in sight of perspective and architecture, some smacke of geometrye and other thinges wherefore the best helpe is for the officers to make good choyce of cunynge artificers severally according to their best qualitie, and for one man to allowe of an other mans invencion as it is worthie.

This memorandum also gives advice in regard to the "plat" to be made when the office is called upon to serve "the Prince," "which Platte deuised to be drawen and sett fourthe in payntinge by some connynge Artificer in that Arte and to be considered of by all the officers[1]."

That the tasks of the Office of the Revels were exactly the tasks necessarily performed by the creators of the neo-Vitruvian scenic background for the representations of the drama is at once obvious. The business of the office consisted in costuming and painting, and for the execution of this business there were required in its officers "skill of devise," a knowledge of dramatic types or *genres*, "sight of perspective and architecture, some smacke of geometrye and other thinges." Feuillerat has already called attention to the importance of the requirement of a knowledge of perspective, but it seems to me equally significant, if not more so, that knowledge of architecture and geometry is demanded. It will also be noted that the whole scenic design for play or masque was to be set forth in a pattern, as Serlio had advised.

As Feuillerat and Boas have both remarked, a study of the records of payments made in connection with dramatic productions at the court and in the universities on the occasions of royal visits shows that, to use the words of Feuillerat,

it was part of the task of the Works to help the Revels in the preparation of the Court festivities. The Declared Account for 1567–70 mentions the "newe making and setting vp of Scaffoldes,

---

[1] Feuillerat, *op. cit.* pp. 11, 12.

particions and dores and other necessaries for the Maundayes, Playes, Tragedyes, Maskes, Revelles, and Tryvmphes at diuers and sondry tymes."

Records of payments made to Lewis Stocket, Surveyor of her Majesty's Works, exist for the periods 1563–6, 1567–70, 1572, 1575–6[1]. Boas notes that Stocket was called on to aid Cambridge and apparently Oxford also in the presentation of plays before Queen Elizabeth on her 1564 and 1566 visits to those universities[2]. Since Inigo Jones as Surveyor of the Works under James was evidently officially responsible for a share in the decoration of masques and plays at court, I am very much inclined to think that a further knowledge of the history of the Office of the Works before the time of Elizabeth will reveal information pertinent to the early staging of the court drama in England, and that the absence in the Revels accounts of items of expense for scenes previous to 1563–4 is by no means to be taken as proof of the non-existence of such scenes.

The expenses in connection with the erecting of the scaffold on which the plays were acted are recorded in a single document printed by Feuillerat with the Revels records for 1567–8 but noted by him as probably belonging to the Works rather than the Revels[3]. These expenses, however, indicate the elaborate structure that must have been created for the staging of plays, though in this particular instance an old frame was used as the basis of the structure.

The accounts for properties and costumes recorded in the earlier documents are supplemented in 1564 and thereafter by those dealing with the provision of scenes. The first clear record of such provision is for a performance of "Edwardes tragedy," and other entertain-

---

[1] Feuillerat, *op. cit.* p. 452.

[2] Boas, *op. cit.* pp. 91, 100.

[3] Feuillerat, *op. cit.* pp. 120–4, and notes on pp. 449, 450.

ments of the Christmas season, where charges are entered for

> wages or dieats of the officers and Tayllours payntars workinge diuers Cities and Townes carvars Silkewemen for fringe & tassells mercers ffor Sarsnett & other stuf and Lynen drapars for canvas to couer diuers townes and howsses and other devisses and Clowds ffor a maske and a showe and a play by the childerne of the chaple ffor Rugge bumbayst an cottone ffor hosse and other provicions and necessairies.

A little less than two months later we find:

> The xviij[th] of fabruerie wages or dieats of the officers and Tayllors paynttars workinge vppon diuers Cities and Townes and the Emperours pallace & other devisses carvars mercers for Sarsnett and other Stuf & lynen drappars ffor canvas to couer the Townes with all and other provicions for A play maid by Sir percivall hartts Sones with a maske of huntars and diuers devisses and a Rocke, or hill ffor the ix musses to Singe vppone with a vayne of Sarsnett Dravven vpp and downe before them &c.[1]

It will be noted that the phrases used in these entries are "canvas to couer diuers townes and howsses," and "canvas to couer the Townes with all," indicating that the towns were not painted on a curtain or flat but were constructed in some such fashion as the Italian scenes, a series of houses or buildings at the sides of the stage. That certain "houses" were given prominence and treated individually, perhaps placed at the back of the stage, is quite possible. The provision for clouds is also to be noted.

It is undesirable here to make record of all the entries, which for the next ten years include constantly the same items of expense more or less curiously analysed. We know from these entries that the houses were constructed on frames made from "sparres," that they

---

[1] Feuillerat, *op. cit.* p. 116.

were covered with canvas—canvas probably treated with "syse"—and that they were painted with colours including gold and silver.

But the entries for the period between December 20, 1578, and the following January 15, seem to me significantly changed. The list of plays reads as follows:

An Inventyon or playe of the three Systers of Mantua shewen at Richmond on St Stephens daie at night enacted by thearle of warwick his servauntes) furnished in this office with sondrey thinges as was requisite for the same.

The historie of ....shewen at Richmond on St Iohns daie at night enacted by the children of the Quenes maiesties chappell furnished in this office with verie manie thinges aptly fitted for the same.

An history of the creweltie of A Stepmother shewen at Richmond on Innocentes daie at night enacted by the Lord Chamberlaynes servauntes furnished in this office with sondrey thinges.

A Morrall of the marryage of Mynde and Measure shewen at Richmond on the sondaie next after Newe yeares daie enacted by the children of Pawles furnished somethinges in this office.

A pastorell or historie of A Greeke maide shewen at Richmond on the sondaie next after Newe yeares daie enacted by the Earle of Leicester his servauntes furnished with some thinges in this office.

The historie of the Rape of the second Helene shewen at Richmond on Twelf daie at night well furnished in this office with manie thinges for them[1].

Similar entries are found in the records for the period between February 1 and March 6, 1578–9[2]. The records for the period November 1, 1579, to February 20, 1579–80, use a terminology slightly differentiated, each play being commented on as "wholly furnished in this office" or as "furnished in this office with[3]...." The significance of these various phrasings is not obvious.

[1] Feuillerat, *op. cit.* p. 286.
[2] *Ibid.* p. 303.   [3] *Ibid.* p. 320.

Furthermore the question naturally arises as to how the furnishings for the plays were provided in cases where the Office of the Revels seems to have provided only part of those necessary to their adequate setting forth.

The entries for the year from November 1, 1580, to October 31, 1581, are for the most part phrased "whereon was employed new[1]"; and similar phrasing is found in the entries of the following years. Such entries are, to my mind, clearly indicative of the fact that entries were made only for newly provided furnishings, and that it is consequently impossible to assume that play and players were fully equipped with "one howse one battlement and thirtene paire of gloves." In fact, it seems impossible to estimate on the basis of the Revels accounts the number of houses used or the stage equipment provided for any single performance.

In the November 1, 1579, to February 20, 1579–80, accounts the phrase is used "sondrye payntinges howses vestures garments[2]...." The succeeding records are

[1] Feuillerat, *op. cit.* p. 336. Mr Lawrence, *op. cit.* First Series, p. 237, says in his discussion of "New Facts about the Blackfriars: Monsieur Feuillerat's Discoveries" that the normal number of *mansions* used at the English court performances was three. There seems to me to be no proof of such a thesis in these records. Mr Lawrence in a note on p. 238 says also in regard to the word *mansion*: "The French term is used by me throughout in a broad technical sense to signify a component part of the multiple setting. It would comprise a cave, or a wood (as symbolized by a couple of trees)." The use of the word *mansion* by Mr Lawrence and other writers seems to me unnecessary when the English translation *house* was in constant use during the time of Elizabeth and in the first half of the seventeenth century. The records of the Revels seem, however, to indicate that the *house* was differentiated from the mount or cave or forest. The mount seems to have been listed as the work of the property-maker, and the trees bought for the stage forests are certainly not to be confused with the *houses* constructed by the carpenters. Yet it must be granted that Serlio's description would permit the broader interpretation of the word.

[2] Feuillerat, *op. cit.* p. 320.

distinguished by many entries of "a city," "a battle-ment," "a town," as well as of "a house," or "a country house." For 1584 and 1585 there are references to "one greate curteyne," "one great cloth of canvas," and "a greate cloth[1]."

The later records indicate that much of the work was done on contract by painters and carpenters as piece work rather than time work; hence even the painting of "ccx. yardes of Canvas at xij[d]. the yard" is not particularly significant[2], but the consecutive entries of payments made to William Lyzard in 1580–1580/1, "Paynting by great of .vj. small citties & three battle-mentes" and "Paynting by great of twoe great clothes at iij[li]. x[s]. the peece" probably are significant[3].

Many vexed questions are raised by these entries. In the light of the preceding evidence, however, it seems to me that we must conclude that during the reign of Elizabeth the court stage was decorated by the usual houses erected on the stage, that these houses were elaborately painted and adorned, that they were sometimes assigned to the *dramatis personae* as stage possessions by which to make appropriate entrances and exits, that the stage effect was sometimes achieved, at least after 1579, by "painted cloths." It is necessary to remember that the "painted cloths" may in some cases have been the painted canvas covers for the frames of the houses, though wherever sufficient skill in per-spective painting had been attained, it was quite legiti-mate to furnish the back of the stage with flat houses. As to the painting of "cities" and "villages" and "towns," it is to be remembered that the comedy and tragedy scenes such as Serlio pictured were described as "a city" or "a town," that the "city" need not be considered as other than an appropriate group of houses

---

[1] Feuillerat, *op. cit.* p. 365.
[2] *Ibid.* p. 356.　　　　　　　[3] *Ibid.* p. 338.

arranged to meet the demands of perspective. The phrase "country house," which recurs in these Revels entries, is the phrase regularly employed by the English translator of Serlio to indicate the kind of house employed in the satyric scene.

Professor Reynolds has already shown that it is probable that real trees were used on the stage to indicate a forest[1], but I wish here to emphasize the significance of such traditional usage in the light of classical theory. The entries of expenditures for holly and ivy are constant, and the entries for "A tree of Holly for the Duttons playe...other holly for the forest," as well as for "provizion & cariage of trees & other things to the Coorte for A wildernesse in A playe" but indicate the nature of the pastoral setting[2]. However, the constant record of payments for silk flowers and trees would indicate the fact that Serlio's interpretation of Vitruvius's directions in this regard had not been ignored.

A record of 1571–2 of xxij[s]. paid to "Iohn Izarde for mony to him due for his device in counterfeting Thunder & Lightning in the playe of Narcisses" is more interesting because it is unique than because it proves the use of such a device[3].

Elaborate properties were provided, the concluding payment to the estate of the property-maker John Carow in 1574–5 after his death giving perhaps the most representative list, comprising

propertyes videlicet Monsters, Mountaynes, fforestes, Beastes, Serpentes, Weapons for warr as gvnnes, dagges, bowes, Arowes, Biils, holberdes, borespeares, fawchions daggers, Targettes, poll-axes, clubbes headdes & headpeeces Armor counterfet Mosse, holly, Ivye, Bayes, flowers quarters, glew, past.paper. and suche

---

[1] Cf. G. F. Reynolds, "Trees on the Stage of Shakespeare," in *Modern Philology*, vol. v, pp. 153–68.

[2] Feuillerat, *op. cit.* pp. 175, 180.

[3] *Ibid.* p. 142.

lyke with Nayles hoopes horstails dishes for devells eyes heaven, hell, & the devell & all the devell I should saie but not all[1].

The properties provided include a rock and aqua-vitae to make the rock burn, as well as "Rosewater to Alay the smell therof[2]," the rosewater being an addition to Serlio's method. It seems that the list of properties is all-inclusive, but it should be noted that no furniture conceivably indicative of interior scenes is recorded, with the possible exception of "two formes for the Senatours in the historie of Titus and Gisippus[3]."

The decoration of the heavens is conclusively proved in the Revels accounts from 1564 onwards, and the entries for 1574–5 of payments made to John Ross (or Rose) for "Long boordes for the Stere of a clowde... Pulleyes for the Clowdes and curteynes...Dubble gyrtes to hange the soon in the Clowde[4]," as well as the even more interesting items in the 1578–9 accounts for

A hoope and blewe Lynnen cloth to mend the clowde that was Borrowed and cut to serve the rock in the plaie of the burnyng knight and for the hire therof and setting vpp the same where it was borrowed[5],

show quite convincingly the provisions for movable clouds in the heavens and also for a sun, which perhaps went down at the close of the play as Serlio had written.

That the same care for detail which characterized the performances at the court of the Duke of Urbino must have been approximated at the English court is indicated by the charges for the "counterfeit" animals used in both masques and plays. For instance, the entry in the 1573–4 accounts of "Holly and Ivye for the play of predor" is followed by "ffyshes Cownterfete for the

[1] Feuillerat, *op. cit.* p. 241. [2] *Ibid.* p. 308.
[3] *Ibid.* p. 276. [4] *Ibid.* p. 240.
[5] *Ibid.* p. 308. This item is of special significance, of course, in connection with the consideration of the place whence it was borrowed.

same viz. whiting, playce, Mackarell, &c.¹" The making of monsters seems to have been also a constant occupation of the property-makers. And entries for charges relating to the making of cats and monkeys and horses and lions are too familiar to all students of the Revels to need comment, but the entry of 1571–2

for x dosen of Kyddes skynnes together with the woorkmanship ...doone vpon the Hobby horses that served the children of Westminster in the triumphe (where parris wan the Christall sheelde for vienna. at the Turneye and Barryers)²

is indicative of the care lavished upon such performances.

More important but apparently thus far unnoted are the constant items in the Revels accounts of charges for pasteboards of various sizes. The amount of pasteboard used in the office seems to be entirely inexplicable unless we assume that it was used in the manner described by Serlio to construct chimneys, pillars, cornices, and other "juttings out," and to fashion the pasteboard figures by which the scene was varied and the audience kept from weariness while the "personages" were off the stage. It is impossible to prove the actual use of pasteboard in effecting relief from the wearisome regularity of outline that must otherwise have characterized the "houses." But that figures such as those described by Serlio, which were made to pass across the stage between acts or were made to stand fixed on their wooden props during the play, were actually used in the plays presented before Elizabeth is indicated by items of expense for "Bodyes of men in timber," and for "hermytage & hermytt, Savages, Enchaunter³."

That the lights and their arrangement received much attention is certain, but because the plays at court were

---

¹ Feuillerat, *op. cit.* p. 203.　　²　*Ibid.* p. 141.

³ *Ibid.* pp. 140, 345. Cf. also p. 175 for payment made for an "Image of canvas stuft."

given at night, and much of their effectiveness was dependent on the skill with which the lights in the hall were arranged, it is not possible to differentiate the supplies provided for the lights in the hall and those that may have adorned the scene itself. Whether the frequently recurring items of expense for "colors for lights" and "pots for colors" ever had to do with the bottled waters and wines such as those through which the lights shone in the scenes on the court stages of Italy there is no way of knowing.

Certainly the provisions for plays and masques in the time of Elizabeth show that there were provided the materials requisite to the devices for scenes and spectacles described by Serlio. If one were to construct in imagination the expense accounts for the performances at the court of Urbino, he would inevitably construct accounts with items practically identical with those of the Office of the Revels under Elizabeth: frames for players' houses, canvas to cover the houses, paints to paint them, wages for workers, trees and boughs, flowers and branches of silk, stuffed animals, moulded fruits, lights, colours for lights, pasteboard, aqua-vitae—an infinite variety[1].

There are, moreover, two incidental suggestions of relationship with the Italian neo-classical methods of

[1] Mr Lawrence, *op. cit.* First Series, pp. 42–71, in his study of "Title and Locality Boards on the Pre-Restoration Stage" says that in the indoor court theatre the *mansions* were arranged "along the two sides of an equilateral triangle, the apex of which marked the position of the third or fourth *mansion*....This arrangement was a distinct advance as it admitted of the whole being constructed and painted in perspective, a device whereby a sort of pictorial homogeneity was given to the heterogeneous constituents." It seems to me that the evidence tends to show that the homogeneity of the picture was established—at least to contemporary writers—by the essential unity of its conception. The unity given by perspective was merely the unity of the correlated parts of a whole.

staging which come from a perusal of the Revels accounts. The first is the presence of Italian players at the court of Elizabeth indicated in these accounts for 1573–4[1]. Professor Wallace has recorded additional evidence of their presence, so that we also have knowledge of their being paid in July of 1574 for two plays and on February 27, 1576/7 for one play[2].

The second suggestion is purely a conjecture based on two entries during the season of 1576–7 for payments made to one Robert Peake for his services as a painter[3]. Feuillerat raises the question in a note as to whether this is the Robert Peake who is known to have been sergeant-painter to King James. Now the first translation of Serlio, made in 1611, was made under the supervision of Robert Peake, and the conjecture is at least stimulating that one of the court painters under Elizabeth may have known the work of Serlio and proposed its translation, making an interesting link between the sixteenth and the seventeenth centuries.

[1] Feuillerat, *op. cit.* pp. 225, 227, 228.
[2] Wallace, *Evolution of the English Drama*, pp. 205, 218.
[3] Feuillerat, *op. cit.* pp. 257, 460. See below, p. 159.

CHAPTER IX

SCENERY IN THE PUBLIC THEATRES

THE consideration of the public stage is, it is evident, a matter of secondary importance in the history of Renaissance stage scenery, for stage decoration had its rise in the imitation of the classical stage through the careful research of scholars devoted to the revival of the art and learning of the ancients, and their theories found early embodiment in luxurious dramatic representations before courtly circles prepared by the greatest artists of the time. Of necessity this neo-classical stage decoration was a product of scholarship and was consecrated from its inception to the pleasure of the courtly and the academic circles of the period. A commercial theatre, during the sixteenth as well as during the twentieth century, must depend for its success upon the popularity of its representations. When the demand for scenic representation of the drama became apparent, there was a willingness on the part of managers to meet the demand. Therefore it is *a priori* probable that a spectacular drama at court would ultimately result in a spectacular drama in the public theatre, and the evidence that such was indeed the case has been reviewed by both Feuillerat and Graves[1]. Yet in the very nature of things it is improbable that the public theatre should in its early years rival in its presentations the costliness of the court drama.

The wave of enthusiasm for theatre building that swept over western Europe in the late sixteenth and the seventeenth centuries as a consequence of the interest disseminated by the study of Vitruvius has been else-

[1] Feuillerat, *Le Bureau des Menus-Plaisirs*, and Graves, *op. cit.*

where discussed[1]. Evidence that England shared in this enthusiasm is not wanting, for Professor Adams's study of *Shakespearean Playhouses* assembles the facts which prove this enthusiasm without possibility of challenge. That the same neo-Vitruvian theories that determined the structure of the playhouses on the Continent were also at work in England to determine the kind of early theatres built has not, however, generally been considered. It is necessary, therefore, to recall the fact that the earliest Continental theatres were those arranged for the most part in the palaces of Italian princes, that the first pictured interpretations of the Vitruvian theatre were those of Jocundus and were made in terms of a rectangular theatre, that the theatre of Serlio was essentially a theatre for a palace and was constructed as a conscious adaptation of the Vitruvian theatre to a rectangular hall.

The early public representations of the drama in the neo-classical fashion took place on stages specially constructed for that purpose, as is shown by the account of Sulpitius of the first painted scene and by the records of the temporary stages constructed for the Olympic Academy and elsewhere which have been already instanced[2]. That these temporary theatres were followed by public theatres constructed as amphitheatres after the Vitruvian model as it was interpreted in terms of the circular amphitheatre from Caesariano onward has also been noted, as has the significance of the union of the scenic stage with the amphitheatrical stage in the Olympic Theatre of Palladio and Scamozzi.

It is not part of my plan to follow in detail the progress of the English stage along these same lines of development, but I wish to call attention to the fact that the earliest theatres of England were undoubtedly halls in the palaces and great houses. The uncontested

[1] Cf. pp. 53–56.   [2] Cf. pp. 13, 14, 42.

evidence of companies of players attached to the court and to the establishments of the nobles in the latter part of the fifteenth century as well as in the sixteenth century[1] argues that a playing-place must have been provided in the great houses of England as well as at the Italian courts. The halls used for these more or less temporary theatres, the banqueting halls which were often the scene of court representations, the halls of the school, university, and inns of court representations were typically rectangular, and it is reasonable to suppose that they came to be arranged according to the demands of the neo-Vitruvian stage. That there is also probable a direct relationship between these private theatres and the so-called "private" commercial theatres in that they were rectangular in shape, in that they were provided with stages on which scenery could be used, and in that they had scaffolds or galleries built up for the audience according to the adaptations of the Vitruvian design will, I think, appear in the consideration of the stage of the seventeenth century[2].

The early confusion of the terms *theatre* and *amphitheatre* previously mentioned, together with the later Renaissance interpretations of the Vitruvian theatre in terms of an amphitheatre, which determined the theatre building in the latter half of the sixteenth century on the Continent, seems equally to have determined the design of the early public theatres in England. At least, such a conclusion seems to be justified by the outlines of the English theatres as we know them. It is well to remember that Burbage, "the first builder of theatres," was not only a carpenter and builder (performing thus the function of the architect) but was something of an artist as well[3]. It would be strange in-

[1] Cf. Chambers, *Mediaeval Drama*, vol. II, pp. 186–9.
[2] Cf. chap. XIII.
[3] Cf. Mrs C. C. Stopes, *Burbage and Shakespeare's Stage* (1913), p.108.

deed if a man of Burbage's interests did not know something of Vitruvian theories and of Continental opinion in regard to theatrical architecture. It would be even stranger if theatres were in England constructed on the same plan as the Continental neo-Vitruvian theatres were they not the product of the same impetus to theatrical construction.

That these early theatres of England were recognized as built after classical models would, however, seem to be attested by the drawing of the Swan Theatre and the accompanying comment of 1596 hereafter discussed[1]. The words of the Reverend John Stockwood in his sermon preached at "Paules Crosse" on August 24, 1578, are even more convincing:

I know not how I might with the godly learned especially more discommende the gorgeous Playing place erected in the Fieldes, than to terme it, as they please to have called it, a Theatre, that is, even after the manner of the old Theatre at Rome, a show place of al beastlie and filthy matters[2].

That the stages of the Elizabethan theatres were divided into two parts is well known from the persistent discussions of the last fifteen years in regard to the "apron" stage and in regard to the functions of the outer and inner stages. But the fact has generally been forgotten that this division of the stage was but following the ancient division of the stage and was one of the fundamental principles followed by the Renaissance artists in stage construction[3].

---

[1] Cf. chap. XIII.   [2] Mrs Stopes, *op. cit.* p. 26.

[3] Cf. the descriptions of Philander, p. 23, and of Serlio, pp. 33, 34. Note also the comment of Barbaro (p. 192, 1567 ed.), "Podium quid sit iam diximus, nostri parapettum, & poggium uocant in fronte scenae, cuius inferior pars ad orchestram pertinens, est pulpitum." That the terms *scena, proscenium, podium, pulpitum,* and *orchestra* brought confusion to the Renaissance scholars is frequently demonstrated. Cf. Scaliger, *Poetices,* p. 36. Note also the theatre drawings of Caesariano.

As to the actual evidence for the use of scenes in the Elizabethan public theatres there is little that can be added to that cited by Reynolds and Graves and Feuillerat. But the significance of the borrowing by the Office of the Revels of a blue linen cloud[1], supposedly from a public theatre (or more probably from a "private" theatre), must be emphasized, for the possession of part of the regular equipment of a neo-Vitruvian stage implies much more than it records. Professor Reynolds's argument in regard to the use of trees on the stage adds evidence to the same point. However, the evidence which seems to me most significant is that of the Revels accounts which indicate, as I have said, that certain performances were only partially provided by the Revels with the necessary scenic adornments[2]. It seems an almost inevitable inference that these companies possessed part of the stage equipment necessary.

As to the use of "machines" we have the proof of the plays themselves that thunder and ghosts and heavenly beings and the exposure of interior scenes were regularly provided on the stage. The discussion of the influences at work to limit and define the use of these machines I shall postpone until the next chapter[3].

That scenes and machines were known on the English stage much earlier than has generally been accepted is the conclusion toward which all the evidence points. At what date they were introduced we thus far have lacked the evidence to decide. But that the progress in stage spectacle was the result of the attempt to adorn the academic and the court stages appropriately seems evident, and that the progress of stage spectacle was until almost the middle of the seventeenth century practically unmodified by the demands of the public theatre seems likewise to be true. Nevertheless no considera-

[1] Cf. p. 112. [2] Cf. pp. 108, 109.
[3] Cf. discussion on pp. 132–140.

tion of stage spectacle can ignore the fact that the English theatre was apparently sharing with all of western Europe the effect of the Vitruvian revival, and that the English theatres—both "private" and "public" —were such theatres as resulted everywhere from the new interest in the theatres of the ancients.

CHAPTER X

DRAMATIC CRITICISM

ONE other source of information concerning the Elizabethan theatre remains to be considered, one upon which scholars have been wont to depend perhaps over-much—the literary criticism of the period. It is, of course, to be remembered that the art criticism of the Elizabethan period was almost altogether literary criticism for the reason that the arts other than literature were still of exotic growth, and criticism follows creation. There was, indeed, in the literary criticism of the late sixteenth century in England a not inconsiderable body of dramatic criticism. But the art of the theatre, and in particular the scenic art of the theatre, was yet too foreign to find adequate critical exposition save where it touched the realm of dramatic criticism. Those questions of dramatic structure which are most closely allied to questions of scenery and spectacle were, however, discussed,—the questions of dramatic *genre*, of the origins of drama and theatre, of unity of place, of the bringing of the gods into the play and the theatre, of the use of thunder, of death on the stage, of the presentation of interior scenes. As matters of stage mechanism these questions can be translated into questions of type of scenery, of methods of varying a necessarily static scene, of the use of the *deus ex machina*, of the use of trap-doors, of the production of thunder, of the use of the *eccyclema* or the *exostra*. And even a study necessarily not exhaustive reveals the fact that these questions were pertinent to the presentation of contemporary plays.

Practically all of the early critics of the Renaissance

as well as of the succeeding "Age of Classicism" were much concerned with the question of dramatic types. For the most part they would have accepted Higgins's definitions in the English *Nomenclator* of *tragedy* as "a loftie kind of poetrie, shewing the rufull end of noble personages, and their fal from felicitie," "personages," it may be noted, in whose fall even the gods and the spirits from hell were alike interested; and of *comedy* as "a base kind of poetrie which endeth troublesome matters merrilie." With his definition of *satire* as "a nipping kind of poetrie, taunting and sharplie shewing men their faults" there would perhaps have been less general agreement, for the Elizabethans as well as the critics of the seventeenth century were much confused by the idea of *satire* in this sense and in that sense in which the early classical writers used it to indicate a dramatic *genre* the name of which was derived from its actors, the satyrs. The adjectives *satiric* and *satyric* especially came to be used uncomprehendingly[1]. On the other hand, confusion between the satyric and the pastoral drama was pronounced, and at last the sylvan drama became the rustic drama, the satire became the pastoral. The types of poetry were discussed by Ascham, Lodge (on the authority of "Donate the grammarian"), Webbe (who appended the Horatian canons to his *Discourse*), Sidney, and Harrington.

But it was in Puttenham's *Arte of English Poesie* that the first logical account of the origin of theatres was attempted, and the account is of considerable importance. Puttenham explained:

Satyres were first vttered in their hallowed places within the woods where they honoured their gods vnder the open heauen, because they had no other housing fit for great assemblies. The old comedies were plaid in the broad streets vpon wagons or

---

[1] See the *New English Dictionary*.

carts vncouered, which carts were floored with bords & made for remouable stages to passe from one streete of their townes to another, where all the people might stand at their ease to gaze vpon the sights. Their new comedies or ciuill enterludes were played in open pauillions or tents of linnen cloth or lether, halfe displayed that the people might see. Afterward, when Tragidies came vp they deuised to present them vpon scaffoldes or stages of timber, shadowed with linen or lether as the other, and these stages were made in the forme of a *Semicircle*, wherof the bow serued for the beholders to sit in, and the string or forepart was appointed for the floore or place where the players vttered, and had in it sundrie little diuisions by curteins as trauerses to serue for seueral roomes where they might repaire vnto & change their garments and come in againe as their speaches & parts were to be renewed. Also there was place appointed for musiciens to sing or to play vpon their instruments at the end of euery scene, to the intent the people might be refreshed and kept occupied. This maner of stage in halfe circle the Greekes called *theatrum*, as much to say as a beholding place, which was also in such sort contriued by benches and greeces to stand or sit vpon, as no man should empeach anothers sight. But as ciuilitie and withall wealth encreased, so did the minde of man grow dayly more haultie and superflous in all his deuises, so as for their *theaters* in half circle, they came to be by the great magnificence of the Roman princes and people somptuously built with marble & square stone in forme all round, & were called *Amphitheaters*, whereof as yet appears one among the ancient ruins of Rome, built by Pompeius Magnus....

This account is continued by a description of the magnitude and skill of contrivance noted in the amphitheatre of Pompeius Magnus and by a description of exhibitions other than plays which were shown in these amphitheatres[1].

The account of Puttenham is interesting because it

---

[1] Cf. Gregory Smith, ed., *Elizabethan Critical Essays* (1904), vol. II, pp. 37–9. Puttenham's work was published in 1589.

shows the attempt to differentiate the origins of the dramatic *genres*, because it shows an interest in the classical theatre, because it attempts to explain the relation of the theatre to the amphitheatre, and because it shows a significant dependence upon classical authority. Horace and Pliny were probably the sources of part of the information here used, but the important letter of Cassiodorus to Symmachus dealing with the history of the theatre seems to me to have been perhaps the chief source of Puttenham's information. The works of Cassiodorus had been published by Fornerius in Paris in 1579, and the information contained in this letter was constantly thereafter used by students of antiquity[1].

[1] For an account of editions of Cassiodorus's works, 1579, 1656, 1663, 1679, 1729, see Teuffel and Schwabe, *History of Roman Literature*, vol. II, p. 531, § 483. The extract from the letter to Symmachus here quoted is from the 1729 edition, Epistle 51 of Book IV:

"Fecerunt Antiqui locum tantis populis parem, ut haberent singulare spectaculum, qui mundi videbantur habere dominatum. Sed quia nobis sermo probatur esse cum docto, libet repetere, cur Antiquitas rudis legatur haec moenia condidisse. Cum agricultores feriatis diebus sacra diversis numinibus per lucos vicosque celebrarent, Athenienses primum agreste principium in urbanum spectaculum collegerunt: Theatrum Graeco vocabulo visorium nominantes, quod eminus astantibus turba conveniens sine aliquo impedimento videatur. Frons autem theatri scena dicitur, ab umbra luci densissima, ubi a pastoribus inchoante verno diversis sonis carmina cantabantur. Ibi actus musicus, & prudentissimi saeculi dicta floruerunt. Sed paulatim factum est, ut honestissimae disciplinae improborum consortia fugientis, verecunda se exinde consideratione subtraherent. Tragoedia ex vocis vastitate nominatur; quae concavis repercussionibus roborata, talem sonum videtur efficere, ut pene ab homine non credatur exire. Erigitur autem in hircinos pedes; quia si quis inter pastores tali voce placuisset, capri munere donabatur. Comoedia a pagis dicta est. Comus enim pagus vocatur: ubi rustici gestientes, humanos actus laetissimis carminibus irridebant. His sunt additae horcistarum (*a*) loquacissimae manus, linguosi digiti, silentium clamosum, expositio tacita, quam Musa Polymnia reperisse narratur: ostendus homines posse & sine oris affatu suum velle declarare. Musae vero Eoa lingua quasi ὁμούσιαι dicuntur, quod invicem sicut virtutes necessariae sibi esse videantur. His levium pennarum acumina ideo in

The famous account of the theatre of Pompeius Magnus in the *Natural History*[1] of the elder Pliny had, however, an early and lasting effect on Renaissance writers and can never be ignored.

The question of the unity of place was the question of dramatic criticism which was ultimately to over-shadow all others in its importance in its relation to the scenic representation of the drama. The gradual evolving during the Renaissance of the definite rule demanding unity of place as a result of the extension and mis-

fronte pinguntur, quoniam earum sensus celeri cogitatione subvectus res altissimas intuetur. (*b*) Pantomimo igitur, cui a multifaria imitatione nomen est, cum primum in scenam plausibus invitatus advenerit, assistunt consoni chori diversis organis eruditi: tunc illa sensuum manus oculis canorum carmen exponit; & per signa composita, quasi quibusdam literis, edocet intuentis aspectum; in illaque leguntur apices rerum; & non scribendo facit, quod scriptura declaravit. Idem corpus Herculem designat, & Venerem; foeminam praesentat, & marem; Regem facit, & militem; senem reddit, & juvenem; ut in uno credas esse multos, tam varia imitatione discretos. Mimus etiam, qui nunc tantummodo derisui habetur, tanta Philistionis cautela repertus est, ut ejus actus poneretur in literis; quatenus mundum curis edacibus aestuantem laetissimis sententiis temperaret. Quid acetabulorum tinnitus? Quid dulcissimi soni referam varia percussione modulamen? Quod tanta gratia jucunditatis accipitur, ut inter reliquos sensus auditum sibi ad munus summum tunc homines aestiment fuisse collatum; ut aetas subsequens miscens lubrica Priscorum inventa traxit ad vitia; & quod honestae causa delectationis repertum est, ad voluptates corporeas praecipitatis mentibus impulerunt. Hos ritus Romani, sicut caeteras culturas, ad suam Rempub. utiliter trahentes, aedificium alta cogitatione conceptum magnanimitate mirabili condiderunt. Unde non immerito creditur. (*c*) Pompejus hinc potius Magnus fuisse vocatus. Et ideo sive masculis pilis contineri, sive talis fabrica refectionis studio potuerit innovari, expensas vobis de nostro Cubiculo curavimus destinare; ut & vobis acquiratur tam boni operis fama, & nostris temporibus videatur Antiquitas decentius innovata."

That this letter was considered as authoritative and was quoted by Philander before the publishing of the works of Cassiodorus must also be remembered. Cf. above, p. 23.

[1] See particularly Bk xxxvi, chap. xxiv.

interpretation of Aristotle's allusion to the duration of time in tragedy as compared with epic poetry, I have already discussed. Whether the Greeks, however, observed the unity of place in the drama as the gradually attained custom derived from the continuous presence of the chorus on the stage throughout the performance, as Professor Cunliffe believes, or whether the general conditions of the Greek stage led to the observance, as Professor Friedland believes, it seems quite certain that the stage of the Italian Renaissance with its fixed architectural scenery implied an adherence to this principle almost of necessity[1].

In English drama, consciously or unconsciously, the principle of the unity of place seems to have been followed before the time of the building of the public theatres. Professor Boas, indeed, says that he knows of no instance of a play before this date which violates the rule, and he notes a very interesting justification of the observance of unity of place as theatrically convenient in Nicholas Grimald's dedicatory letter to Gilbert Smith prefixed to his *Christus Redivivus* of 1543, in which he says: "Loca item, haud usque eo discriminari censebat: quin unum in proscenium, facilè & citra negocium conduci queant[2]."

The dedicatory letter prefixed to George Whetstone's *Promos and Cassandra* in 1578 gave the first clear expression of the basis of the rule in the essential conditions of reality. Whetstone confessedly based his arrangement of his history into two comedies on the demands of decorum and defended the dignity of plays by reference to the ancient Romans, who

heald these shows of suche prise, that they not only allowede the publicke exercise of them, but the graue Senators themselues countennaunced the Actors with their presence.

[1] See on this point also Professor Bond's introduction to his *Early Plays from the Italian.* [2] Boas, *op. cit.* p. 28.

After discussing foreign plays he made his all-important pronouncement:

The *Englishman* in this quallitie, is most vaine, indiscreete, and out of order: he fyrst groundes his worke on impossibilities: then in three howers ronnes he throwe the worlde: marryes, gets Children, makes Children men, men to conquer kingdomes, murder Monsters, and bringeth Gods from Heauen, and fetcheth Diuels from Hel[1].

It will be noted that Whetstone finds the basis for the undesirability of running through the world and thus violating the unity of place, in the fact that it cannot be done in three hours. His is the true argument for unity of time as demanded for verisimilitude, and for unity of place as a corollary of unity of time. It is significant, too, that Whetstone comments on the English violation of decorum in bringing "Gods from Heauen" and in fetching "Diuels from Hel."

In Sidney's *Apology* (composed *c.* 1583 and published 1596) is found the amplified statement of the rules for unity of time and place, together with the attack upon the English stage for its violation of these rules which has been made the text for almost innumerable discourses on the lack of scenery on the Elizabethan stage. In spite of its too frequent repetition, it must again find place here as perhaps the most important contribution to our knowledge of the subject. After praising *Gorboduc* as the chief ornament of the English drama, Sidney explained the disappointment which he yet felt:

...yet in troth it is very defectious in the circumstaunces; which greeueth me, because it might not remaine as an exact model of all Tragedies. For it is faulty both in place, and time, the two necessary companions of all corporall actions. For where the stage should alwaies represent but one place, and the vttermost time presupposed in it should be, both by *Aristotles* precept

---

[1] Cf. Smith, *op. cit.* vol. i, p. 59.

and common reason, but one day, there is both many dayes, and many places, inartificially imagined. But if it be so in *Gorboduck*, how much more in all the rest? where you shal haue *Asia* of the one side, and *Affrick* of the other, and so many other vnder-kingdoms, that the Player, when he commeth in, must euer begin with telling where he is, or els, the tale will not be con-ceiued. Now ye shal haue three Ladies walke to gather flowers, and then we must beleeue the stage to be a Garden. By and by, we heare newes of shipwracke in the same place, and then wee are to blame, if we accept it not for a Rock. Vpon the backe of that, comes ovt a hidious Monster, with fire and smoke, and then the miserable beholders, are bounde to take it for a Caue. While in the meantime two Armies flye in, represented with foure swords and bucklers, and then what harde heart will not receiue it for a pitched fielde?[1]

And Sidney added what I fancy is the key to the situation when he said, "And doe they not know, that a Tragedie is tied to the lawes of Poesie, and not of Historie? not bound to follow the storie[2]...." For as Professor Friedland has pointed out, it is difficult to achieve the unities in the process of transforming Italian *novella*, chronicles, and English tales into dramas. It seems probable that these sources from which the Eliza-bethan writers drew their dramatic material were ac-countable for the violation of the rules, just as it is pro-bable that the earlier dramas reflected the observance of the unities in the dramas which served as sources for them. But the fact that increasing freedom in regard to the observance of the unity of place is to be noted after 1576 when the public theatres were coming to their dominance in things dramatic is to be carefully con-sidered.

Certainly the poets of the later Elizabethan period accepted the violation of the rules as usual. Ben Jonson, avowed classicist, defended the rules and satirized the

[1] Cf. Smith, *op. cit.* vol. i, p. 197.   [2] *Ibid.* p. 198.

violence being done them. In the prologue to *Every Man in his Humour* he bade his audience anticipate his play as one,

> Where neither *Chorus* wafts you ore the seas;
> Nor creaking throne comes downe, the boyes to please;
> Nor nimble squibbe is seene, to make afear'd
> The gentlewomen; nor roul'd bullet heard
> To say, it thunders; nor tempestuous drumme
> Rumbles, to tell you when the storme doth come[1].

Thus we see the popular play of the period with its changing place, its *deus ex machina*, its lightning and thunder effected by the "nimble squibbe" and the "roul'd bullet."

Again in the dialogue prefixed to *Every Man out of his Humour*, Jonson ridiculed the changing scene of the contemporary drama:

> *Mitis.* ...but what's his *Scene*?
> *Cordatis.* Marry, *Insula Fortunata*, Sir.
> *Mit.* O, the fortunate Island? masse, he has bound himselfe to a strict law there.
> *Cor.* Why so?
> *Mit.* He cannot lightly alter the *Scene*, without crossing the seas.
> *Cor.* He needs not, hauing a whole Iland to run through, I thinke.
> *Mit.* No? how comes it then, that in some one Play we see so many seas, countries, and kingdomes, past ouer with such admirable dexteritie?
> *Cor.* O, that but shewes how well the Authors can trauaile in their vocation, and out-run the apprehension of their auditorie.

But against the servile acceptance of the rules and the mockery of those who failed to observe them was raised the voice of Shakespeare, frankly denying the possibility of verisimilitude on the stage and recognizing

---

[1] References unless otherwise indicated are to W. Bang, *Ben Jonson's Dramen*, printed from the folio of 1616 (1905).

dramatic art as by its very nature stimulating the minds of the audience to imagination and demanding as the condition of its effective presentation the illusion so attained[1]. The same challenging appeal is made in several plays, but it finds perhaps its most eloquent expression in the prologue to *Henry V*:

> O For a Muse of Fire, that would ascend
> The brightest Heauen of Inuention:
> A Kingdome for a Stage, Princes to Act,
> And Monarchs to behold the swelling Scene.
> Then should the Warlike *Harry*, like himselfe,
> Assume the Port of Mars, and at his heeles
> (Leasht in, like Hounds) should Famine, Sword, and Fire
> Crouch for employment. But pardon, Gentles all:
> The flat vnraysed Spirits, that hath dar'd,
> On this vnworthy Scaffold, to bring forth
> So great an Obiect. Can this Cock-Pit hold
> The vastie fields of France? Or may we cramme
> Within this Woodden O, the very Caskes
> That did affright the Ayre at Agincourt?
> O pardon: since a crooked Figure may
> Attest in little place a Million,
> And let us, Cyphers to the great Accompt,
> On your imaginarie Forces worke.
> Suppose within the Girdle of these Walls
> Are now confin'd two mightie Monarchies,
> Whose high, vp-reared, and abutting Fronts,
> The perillous narrow Ocean parts asunder.
> Peece out our imperfections with your thoughts:
> Into a thousand parts diuide one Man,
> And make imaginarie Puissance.
> Think when we talke of Horses, that you see them,
> Printing their proud Hoofes i' th'reciuing Earth:
> For 'tis your thoughts that now must deck our Kings,

[1] I have cited the authority of Jonson and of Shakespeare in this chapter as expressing the Elizabethan theories of stage practice even where the actual words written belong to the seventeenth century.

> Carry them here and there: Iumping o're Times;
> Turning th'accomplishment of many yeeres
> Into an Howre-glasse, for the which supplie,
> Admit me *Chorus* to this Historie[1].

And as if to complement Jonson's description of the voyaging authors, Shakespeare promised in the prologue to the second act of *Henry V*, that while the playhouse must remain for a time as at Southampton, where the scene is now transported,

> there must you sit,
> And thence to France shall we conuey you safe,
> And bring you backe; charming the narrow seas
> To giue gentle Passe: for if we may,
> Wee'l not offend one stomacke with our Play[2].

A third discussion of dramatic criticism that involved that of the use of theatrical apparatus was the discussion pertaining to the *deus ex machina*. In the passage already cited from Whetstone the impropriety was suggested of too frequently bringing the gods from heaven and the devils from hell. Webbe in annexing the Horatian canons of the *De Arte Poetica* to his *Discourse* interpreted the dictum of Horace:

> It fytteth not to bring in the personnes of Gods but in verie great matters. *Cicero* sayth, when the Tragedy wryters cannot bring theyre matters to good passe, they runne to God[3].

And the ironic reference of Jonson to the creaking throne which "comes downe the boyes to please" has already been instanced, while the fact that Jonson's follower, Mayne, found special ground for praise of Jonson in that "no hard plot / Call'd downe a God

---

[1] Quoted from the 1623 folio as published in the *Bankside Shakespeare* (1892).

[2] *Ibid.* ll. 496–500.

[3] Smith, *op. cit.* vol. I, p. 293.

t'untie th'unlikely knot[1]" would seem to indicate Jonson's conscious adherence to the classical rule.

Professor Cunliffe in his thesis on *The Influence of Seneca on Elizabethan Tragedy* noted particularly the comparative absence of the gods descending from the skies, while he commented on the frequency with which spirits from below ascended to the stage, attributing this custom to the prevailing influence of Seneca. Whether or not the Elizabethan writers were deterred from giving proportionate representation to the gods who descended in the machine, because of a fear of violating the classical precept or because of the positive influence of Seneca in raising ghosts and furies as accessories in rousing pity and fear, it is at least certain that the gods descending from heaven were sufficiently familiar to cause the heavens above the stage to be confused with the *deus ex machina*, so that in Higgins's *Nomenclator* in 1584 the English equivalent of *machina* was given as "The skies or coūterfit heauen ouer the stage, from whence some god appeared or spoke."

And Professor Reynolds, studying the plays of the period, summed up their theatrical needs:

the plays demand a stage with at least three doors leading to it, a balcony, trap-doors, and devices in the "heavens" for the lowering and raising of actors and properties[2].

Vitruvius spoke of "when the gods enter to sudden claps of thunder," and he undoubtedly referred to the stage practice which expressed the classical conception of thunder as an accessory of divinity, and of Jove as hurling thunderbolts at whom he would destroy. The idea of rousing pity and fear by spectacle, I have already

[1] Quoted from the collection *Jonsonus Virbius*, published in 1638, printed in the Gifford-Cunningham edition of Ben Jonson's *Works* (1875), vol. IX, p. 452.

[2] Cf. G. F. Reynolds, "William Percy and his Plays," in *Modern Philology*, vol. XII, pp. 241 *sq.*

spoken of, as a result of the interpretation of Aristotle's warnings in regard to the matter. In the English drama there is the usual strange mingling of Christian and pagan conceptions in matters where a people with Christian theology for a background of thought in regard to the supernatural has undertaken to follow pagan dramatic tradition. When a play such as *The Birth of Hercules* has been adopted from its classical original, the strictly classical use of thunder has accompanied the play into the English theatre. Thunder signifying the miraculous birth of Hercules is heard, and thunder anticipates the approach of Jupiter to announce the Jovian fatherhood of Hercules to the distressed Dromio[1].

But since Jupiter and other pagan gods rarely appeared in the Elizabethan drama, the suggestion of divine wrath (Christian or pagan) was frequently made by the use of thunder alone. Shakespeare, in his treatment of the storm in *King Lear*, expressed most perfectly the interpretation which developed as a sort of modified classicism. When Lear takes leave of Goneril, he says:

> I do not bid the thunder-bearer shoote
> Nor tell tales of thee to high-undying Ioue[2].

And during the storm Kent says,

> The wrathful skies
> Gallow the very wanderers of the darke.

To which Lear replies:

> Let the Great Goddes
> That keepe this dreadfull pudder o're our heads
> Finde out their enemies now. Tremble thou Wretch,
> That hast within thee Undivulged Crimes
> Unwhipt of Justice[3].

---

[1] Cf. edition in *Malone Society Reprints* (1911), stage directions at close of Act IV and opening of Act V.

[2] *Bankside Shakespeare*, 1623 folio text, ll. 1514, 1515.

[3] *Ibid.* ll. 1693–7.

In such fashion divine wrath is expressed, and Jove hurls his thunderbolts even though he is not visible. And as a stage device thunder and lightning have to this day retained their usefulness in exciting pity and terror.

That the mechanical devices for representing thunder and lightning were those of Serlio and were also reminiscent of those of Pollux is made clear by Jonson's "rolled bullet" and "nimble squib," though the drums were also used to herald the coming storm, as Jonson's words indicate, and as the stage directions in *The Birth of Hercules*, "ye drums for thunder[1]," make sure.

But certainly the Elizabethan dramatist put his greatest confidence in the representation of death on the stage as the supreme means by which to rouse pity and fear. Professor Cunliffe proved that the bloody stage of Senecan tragedy was definitely accepted in the English drama. It seems to me that it is important to recognize, however, the constant clash in English practice between the classical observance of the decencies on the stage and the acceptance of the full horror of a bloody stage. It must be remembered that the Elizabethans were perfectly familiar with the classical prohibition of death on the stage and particularly with the Horatian statement of this prohibition. Webbe's translation of this rule was as follows:

In a Comedie it is [not] needful to exhibit all the actions openlie, as such as are cruell, vnhonest, or ougly; but such thynges may better be declared by some meete and handsome wordes, after what sorte they are supposed to bee done[2].

It must also be remembered that the Greek dramatists were familiar to the early scholars of England, that Greek dramas were early acted in the universities, and

[1] Cf. stage directions at close of Act IV. In this connection see the words of Barbaro, p. 25.

[2] Smith, *op. cit.* vol. 1, p. 293.

that with the majority of the early dramatists university men, it is impossible to conceive of the English drama uninfluenced by the devices of the Greek drama. Furthermore, as I have already pointed out, it is quite certain that Pollux's *Onomasticon* was early known, and the theatrical terms there defined must have given early English classical scholars, as they have given succeeding generations of scholars, the chief suggestions in regard to the Greek stage with which to piece out the much-interpreted description which Vitruvius gave. Likewise the scholia of the Greek dramas were patiently and curiously studied. It is, therefore, probable that the English drama exhibited customs reminiscent of the Greek theatre long after authors and public alike had become unconscious of their source. And in this connection the influence of the *Poetices* of Scaliger with its description of the machines of the Greek theatre taken from Pollux must be reckoned as particularly important.

Because the question of the treatment of death on the stage was of such overwhelming importance, and because it was so closely related to the whole question of the treatment of interior scenes on a stage primarily intended to represent public actions, the methods used on the Greek stage have much interest for students of the English stage of the Renaissance. I quote from Professor Flickinger's *The Greek Theater and its Drama*:

Being unable actually to represent an interior scene the Greek playwrights gladly availed themselves of several substitutes. The most common of these was the messenger's speech....Another substitute was found in the cries of characters murdered behind the scenes....A third method consisted in throwing open the doors in the background and revealing a scene of murder done within[1]....

If it were desired to disclose to the audience the corpse of someone who had just been done to death behind the scenes,

[1] R. C. Flickinger, *The Greek Theater and its Drama* (1918), p. 241.

perhaps with the murderers still gloating over their crime, or to set any similar view before the faithful eyes of the spectators, the simplest device was to fling open the appropriate door of the scene-building and thus to display the desired objects or persons close behind the opening....But the ancient commentators often speak of a contrivance which was used to bring a supposedly interior scene out of the opened doors and more fully into the view of the audience. This device is sometimes described as "turning" or "revolving" (στρέφειν) and sometimes as being "rolled out" (ἐκ, "out" + κυκλεῖν, to "wheel"). And though eccyclema (ἐκκύκλημα) was used as the generic term, I am persuaded that there were in fact two types of machines[1]....

That Renaissance scholars, however, confused or identified the *eccyclema* and the *exostra* would seem to be established by the description in the *Poetices* and that in the *Nomenclator*. Scaliger says in listing the machines of the theatre:

Tertium ἐγκύκλημα nominabant: alii ἐξώστραν. Erat haec sedes sublicis elata, strata longuriis, super quibus sella. Destinabatur locus is ea recitanda, quae secretò patrata essent in aedibus. qualia in Œdipode Sophoclis, Plauti Amphitryone, & Casina & aliis[2].

The definition given by Higgins in the *Nomenclator* reads:

exostra. Cic. ἐγκύκλημα, ἐξώστρα, Machina lignea, qua quae intus geruntur aut fiunt, versatione rotarum spectatoribus ostenduntur. A vice or gin of wood, wherwith such things as are done within out of sight, are shewed to the beholders by the turning about of wheeles.

The use of the messenger's speech as a means of informing the audience concerning deaths which had taken place off the stage it is not in place to discuss here,

---

[1] Flickinger, *op. cit.* pp. 284, 285. Cf. also Haigh, *Attic Theatre* (1898), pp. 229–36, for discussion and full record of scholia on the *eccyclema*.

[2] Cf. the *Poetices*.

nor the use of the cries of the dying. But that the devices for disclosing interior scenes, particularly those revealing death which had taken place off the stage, were incorporated as characteristic features of English Renaissance tragedy seems an indisputable conclusion when its frequent "discoveries" are considered. Undoubtedly a curtain or scene drawn often revealed the tragic spectacle. But certain stage directions cannot easily be explained in this fashion. Thus *The Misfortunes of Arthur* directs that "The breathlesse body of Mordred in Armour as he fell is brought upon the Stadge[1]," and the Second Part of *Henry the Sixth*, in the 1623 folio (l. 1848) directs "Bed put forth," a variation from the quarto reading (l. 1226), "Warwicke drawes the curtaines and showes Duke Humphrey in his bed[2]." Of this latter instance Mr Appleton Morgan writes:

At line F. 1848 of the Second Part of this play there occurs the stage-direction "Bed put forth"; which expresses the actual poverty and meanness of the stage for which Shakespeare wrote. At that point the spectators have been asked to imagine a stately audience room in King Henry's palace. The dead body of Duke Humphrey is to be visited; Warwick says to the assembled court "Enter his chamber, view his lifeless corpse"; a bed is brought in[3]....

The stage so managed, Mr Morgan calls "a stage that was comic in its practical disabilities."

Another interesting instance of the use of some such device as the *eccyclema* or *exostra* is found in *Richard the Third*. The 1597 quarto reads (l. 167), "Enter Lady Anne with the hearse of Harry the 6," while the 1623 folio (ll. 171, 172) reads, "Enter the Coarse of Henrie sixt with Halberds to guard it, Lady Anne being the

[1] Cf. Cunliffe, *Early English Classical Tragedy*, p. 286.

[2] The references are to the *Bankside Shakespeare*.

[3] Cf. Introduction to the Third Part of *Henry the Sixth*, *Bankside Shakespeare*, p. iii.

Mourner." Such instances could be multiplied end-lessly[1], and it seems to me clear that they indicate the use of some stage mechanism—probably a car pushed out from one of the stage doors. It seems equally certain that the suggestion for such a machine is more apt to have come from the Greek dramas, from the definitions in Pollux or from their re-working in Scaliger, and from the earlier scholia of Aristophanes and the other Greek dramatists, all of which sources of information were known to English scholars, than to have arisen independently and spontaneously. The use of such a device, in fact, seems to me to prove a studied acceptance of the classical stage as a model, rather than any meagreness and poverty of either ideas or apparatus, to have been characteristic of the early English stage.

That the *exostra* functioned in Greek comedy is shown in Aristophanes's *Acharnians*, where Euripides is wheeled out, probably on a trundle couch shoved through the door, and also in his *Women at the Thesmophoria*. Since this device is explained in the scholia of Aristophanes and is indicated in the text as well, the ancient use of a machine for exposing interior scenes of all sorts must early have been known to English dramatists, and it was apparently accepted[2]. For it was not only where the tendency to wallow in horrors was carefully concealed under a show of classical tenderness for the susceptibilities of the audience by the use of devices for revealing what had been carefully concealed that the Elizabethan dramatists and the seventeenth century dramatists alike made use of this means of ex-

[1] The long "List of Stage Directions Illustrating the Use of the Curtains and the Inner Stage in Plays Acted 1576–1642," compiled by Professor Thorndike and published in his *Shakespeare's Theater*, pp. 433–44, will illustrate this fact.

[2] Note that Scaliger instances the *Amphitruo* of Plautus as well as the *Oedipus* of Sophocles to illustrate the use of this machine.

posing to the view of the audience a scene from an invisible interior.

To collect the scattered information that goes to make up the total of our knowledge of the contribution of spectacle to the English stage during the sixteenth century is to discover the extent of the classical forces at work: Vitruvius known in the fifteenth century and regarded as authoritative in the sixteenth; the second edition of the *Onomasticon* dedicated to Linacre and certainly familiar to the later sixteenth century scholars also, as the *Nomenclator* shows; English scholars, courtiers, and churchmen participating in the scholarly and artistic life of Italy; dramatic presentations promoted in the grammar-schools, in the universities and inns of court, and at court, the production of classical plays preceding that of native dramas; private and public theatres built apparently after the neo-Vitruvian models accepted on the Continent; dramatic criticism concerning itself with the principles of dramatic structure most closely bound up with the principles of theatrical representation and confessedly based on classical authority. But such a review shows more than the scholarly nature of the origins of dramatic spectacle on the English stage. It shows the enjoyment of the scenic representation of the drama to have been for the most part an aristocratic privilege throughout the century, and in the early years of the century to have been the privilege of the courtly circle and those who imitated the court in their pleasures. It shows artists and workmen brought from Italy and elsewhere to serve the court. It shows scenic representations growing luxurious in the presence of royalty whether at the universities or in the inns of court or at the court itself. And finally it shows the scenery and the other aids to spectacle in dramatic representations to have been those characteristic of Italian court representations.

Vitruvius, Pollux, Cassiodorus, Aristotle, Horace, and Pliny were alike called upon as ultimate authorities by the scholars and critics of the stage, but Italian artists and Italian workmen gave the practical knowledge necessary, and the courtly circle in England during the Renaissance witnessed a drama performed in the manner of the ancients as it was interpreted by Italian artists. So much seems certain, though for the years before Elizabeth we have only conjecture and circumstance to offer as excuse for conviction. Concerning the stage during the reign of Elizabeth we have such proof as circumstantial evidence can afford. Of the seventeenth century we can speak with the assurance of definite knowledge.

PART III
STAGE DECORATION IN ENGLAND
1600–1650

CHAPTER XI

PROGRESS IN THE THEORY OF ARCHITECTURE
AND PERSPECTIVE

THE first half of the seventeenth century witnessed
on the Continent and in England as well an un-
paralleled development in the technique of stage scenery,
a modification of theatrical architecture by which the
stage of the permanent theatre was adapted to the exhibition of scenes, and a great increase in the number and
popularity of public theatres. The consequence was that
by the end of this half-century the public, like the court,
had developed a taste for theatrical spectacle which it
was both possible and profitable to satisfy. It is of the
causes that contributed to the establishing of these conditions that I purpose to treat.

In the first place, the study of Vitruvius continued
as in the sixteenth century. The Italian translation of
Daniello Barbaro was republished in Italy in 1629 and
1641, a Spanish translation was published in 1602,
another edition of the German translation of Rivius in
1614, another edition of the French translation of Martin in 1618, and the De Laet Latin edition at Amsterdam
in 1649[1]. This last edition was based on the text and
notes of Philander, but it incorporated also excerpts
from the notes of Barbaro and included part of the
Vitruvian lexicon of Bernardino Baldi, the *Elements of
Architecture* (in Latin) of Henry Wotton, the works of
Alberti on painting and sculpture, extracts from the
comments of Salmasius on Solinus, and odds and ends

---

[1] Again I have relied primarily on the list of editions compiled by
Gwilt and published in his edition of Vitruvius already referred to.

of other diverse material more or less relevant. While it does not furnish the most valuable text for the practical architect, this edition, constituting a sort of variorum edition, does gather together many of the sources upon which the Renaissance artists were most wont to depend, and it is, therefore, extremely valuable to the student of the history of artistic theory.

Along with these editions of Vitruvius must be ranked in importance the *De Verborum Vitruvianorum Significatione* of Bernardino Baldi, published in 1612, and the *Elements of Architecture* of Henry Wotton, published in 1624, both commentaries on the nomenclature of Vitruvius.

In the second place, the optical sciences were entering upon a period of very rapid development, and perspective, which seems during this time to have been regarded as one of the curiosities of optical illusion, received its proportionate attention. It was an era of special progress in the invention of optical instruments, among them the telescope and the microscope, and an interest in all matters concerning light and vision was roused in scientists, artists, and unlearned public alike[1].

In England the scientific spirit of inquiry is amply proved to have existed in regard to these matters by the records of the activities of such men as Wotton, Bacon, Evelyn, and Wren[2]. Wren is said to have invented an instrument for perspective drawing[3]. We are told that

[1] Cf. Florian Cajori, *History of Physics* (1889), p. 37, for a record of these inventions.

[2] The diaries, letters, and informal records of the times are our chief authorities in regard to the activities of these forerunners of the Royal Society. It is interesting to remember that it was not until 1614 that Roger Bacon's *Perspectiva* was first printed at Frankfurt.

[3] Cf. *Philosophical Transactions of the Royal Society*, vol. iv, pp. 898, 899, "The Description of an Instrument invented divers years ago by Dr Christopher Wren, for drawing the Out-lines of any Object in Perspective."

Wotton at the age of twenty "proceeded Master of Arts; and at that time read in Latine three Lectures *de Oculo*," wherein he described the form, the motion, and the "curious composure" of the eye. On this occasion also he "fell to dispute this Optique Question, Whether we see by the Emission of the Beams from within, or Reception of the Species from without[1]." Sir Francis Bacon in his *New Atlantis* proposed

Perspective Houses, where wee make demonstrations of all Lights, and Radiations: And of all Colours....Also all Colouration of Light; all Delusions and Deceits of Sight...[representing] things neare as a-farr off; and things A-farr off as Neare. Making Faigned Distances[2]....

Such possibilities of optical illusion could not be disregarded in any consideration of art, and of painting in particular. The descriptions of perspective painting by Vitruvius and Pliny were often taken as the departing points for criticism or analysis. Ben Jonson in *Timber*, writing *De Progressione Picturae*, said:

Picture took her feigning from poetry; from geometry her rule, compass, lines, proportions, and the whole symmetry.... From the optics it drew reasons, by which it considered how things placed at a distance and afar off should appear less; how above or beneath the head should deceive the eye, &c. So from thence it took shadows, recessor, light, and heightnings[3].

Artists interested themselves in demonstrating these possibilities. Foreign travellers in England commented particularly on the portrait of Edward VI "perspec-

---

[1] *Reliquiae Wottonianae*, collected by Izaak Walton, and prefixed by a life of Sir Henry Wotton (1672), b 2, b 3.

[2] Cf. Francis Bacon, *New Atlantis* (edited by A. B. Gough, 1915, probably written in 1623–4), pp. 41, 42.

[3] Jonson, *Works*, vol. ix, pp. 186, 187, No. cxxi of *Timber*. Jonson's marginal reference is to Pliny, xxxv, 25, 26, but as later editors have pointed out, his section or chapter references are erroneous. Vitruvius is also cited.

tively painted" which was to be seen at Whitehall and which must be viewed from a certain angle if the likeness were to be perceptible. They commented also on tables to be seen at St James's with pictures "perspectively rather than artistically painted[1]." "Perspectives" were added to walks in gardens and were painted outside the windows of rooms to feign an outlook which was non-existent[2]. Artists exhibited "perspectives" as artistic curiosities, and Evelyn notes particularly those of Stenwyck and Reeves, concerning the latter of whom we hear much in other years from Pepys, who bought from him "perspective glasses[3]." Some of these "perspectives" were arranged to be viewed through a small hole in the protecting box. For instance, Evelyn writes in 1655:

Was shew'd me a pretty perspective and well represented in a triangular box, the great church of Harlem in Holland to be seene thro' a small hole at one of the corners and contriv'd into an handsome cabinet. It was so rarely don that all the artists and painters in town flock'd to see and admire it[4].

Interest in the uncomprehended and delight in the marvels inexplicably achieved by science are permanent characteristics of the unlearned public. Therefore the popular enthusiasm for the curiosities of optical illusion was not to be disregarded during the seventeenth century. And anyone familiar with Ben Jonson's comedies and masques will not need to be reminded of this in-

[1] Cf. W. B. Rye, *England as Seen by Foreigners in the Days of Elizabeth and James the First* (1865), p. 280; Paul Hentzner, *Travels in England during the Reign of Queen Elizabeth* (Cassell's Library, 1892), p. 32.

[2] Cf. John Evelyn, *Diary* (ed. Wheatley-Bray, 1879), under dates February 27 and March 1, 1644–5, for typical entries concerning perspectives so used.

[3] *Ibid.* under dates January 2 and February 15, 1648–9, and May 10, 1652.

[4] *Ibid.* under date February 5, 1655–6.

terest as his characters constantly revealed it. Further-more, the timeliness of such works as *News from the New World Discovered in the Moon* and the *Masque of Augurs* must be apparent.

The public exhibition of "motions" is proved by licences granted by the Master of the Revels, who in 1624 also granted a licence "to sett forth a Showing Glass, called the World's Wonder[1]." Mirrors and per-spective glasses—every means of distorting reality and deceiving the sight—came to be of great interest. With-out this interest the history of the stage would, however, have been very different.

At a time when interest in optics was so generally manifest, it was to be expected that it would be reflected in those works on perspective which dealt altogether or in part with the question of theatrical perspective. Among the more important contributions to this special-ized subject was that of Guido Ubaldi, who in Book VI of his *Perspectiva* discussed stage scenery and established the scientific foundations for the later technical stage work of Sabbatini. The experiments and practices of others are said to have been fashioned in Ubaldi's work into a theory having permanent value because of the sure foundation of geometry which he gave it. He studied scientifically the problems of perspective "re-lief," established methods of determining the proper inclination of the stage, the arrangement and propor-tions of the "houses"; and to use the words of Poudra,

Il passe ensuite à la perspective sur la toile du fond, ce qui ne présente plus de difficultés, puisque ce plan est un tableau, il indique ensuite les moyens de dessiner les droites appartenant à des faces de maisons qui ne seraient ni parallèles, ni perpendicu-laires au plan de la scène, ou dans des plans non perpendiculaires entre eux comme seraient des maisons pentagonales ou héx-

[1] J. Q. Adams, ed., *The Dramatic Records of Sir Henry Herbert* (1917), p. 47.

agonales ou autres, et même des temples ronds, et même terminées par des droites non horizontales ou verticales.

As late as the time of Dr Brook Taylor this work of Ubaldi was regarded in England as authoritative, and on it was based Taylor's work[1].

In 1611 or 1612, *La Perspective* of Salomon de Caus, a French engineer, was printed in London. This work included a discussion of scenography, its description of theatrical scenes based on that of Vitruvius[2].

In 1625 the *Prospettiva Pratica* of Pietro Accolti was published, a work which is said to be the logical successor to that of Serlio in its explanation of theatrical perspective. It seems to have been considered as authoritative in the period in which it was written.

Between 1642 and 1649 the three volumes of Du Breuil's *La perspective pratique* were published, and in 1651 a second and much improved edition of the first volume[3]. In this work Du Breuil, so Poudra says, discussed the perspective of the theatre and explained the two methods of changing scenes—by means of the drawn scene and the turning machine. This fact is interesting in any consideration of the French stage, but Du Breuil's work must also be considered interesting in any study of the English stage, because of the fact that it was twice translated into English, which translations went through several editions[4].

---

[1] Poudra, *op. cit.* pp. 185 *sq.* Cf. also T. H. Fielding, *Synopsis of Practical Perspective*, p. 16.

[2] Poudra gives the date of publication as 1612, Larousse (*Grand Dictionnaire Universel*) as 1611.

[3] Poudra, *op. cit.* pp. 271 *sq.*

[4] I have seen only the edition (evidently much abridged) published as "The Practice of Perspective: Or, an Easy Method of Representing Natural Objects according to the Rules of Art....Written in *French* by a Jesuit of *Paris*; since translated into *German* by Ch. Reubold and into English, by Rob. Pricke. And now a Second Time into the same Language, by E. Chambers, F.R.S. Third Edition, 1743."

During this period appeared also certain works wholly devoted to the technique of the theatre, the best known of which is that of Nicola Sabbatini, *Pratica di fabricar Scene e Machine ne' Teatri*, published at Ravenna in 1638. From Malone onward English scholars have instanced this work as a landmark by which to estimate the relative progress of the English stage and the Italian[1].

Sabbatini's confessedly based his work on that of Ubaldi, and the reader is insistently referred to the sixth book of Ubaldi's work for a knowledge of the fundamental theory on which Sabbatini built his super-structure of practical directions for the building and adorning of the stage.

Perhaps the most significant fact about this work of Sabbatini's is its division into two books, the first of which deals with the scenes for plays, while the second deals with the scenes and machines necessary to the intermedia. The first book, therefore, describes the usual static scenery familiar in the Italian representation of plays in the sixteenth century, while the second describes the means whereby changes of scene are secured and other spectacular effects produced. This arrangement of the matters for discussion illustrates one of the fundamental principles apparent in the history of the stage: the shifting or changing of scenes was a spectacular device, desired because of its showy and startling possibilities. Early changes of scene were in no way induced by a dramatic change of place. The idea of a necessary relation between a change of scene and a change of place was, indeed, a late development in the history of the scenic stage.

In general, the first book of Sabbatini's work explains

1 Nicola Sabbatini, *Pratica di fabricar Scene e Machine ne' Teatri* (Ravenna, 1638). The title-page of this edition bears the words, "Re-stampa di nouo coll' Aggiunta del Secondo Libro."

the same style of stage that was described by Serlio, an inclined scaffold four feet high in front and rising one half inch for each foot of stage depth, with "houses" arranged and built according to the demands of perspective. The first houses are placed at least three feet back from the front of the stage. They are usually constructed on a wooden frame covered with canvas which has been dipped in size and then painted. Like Serlio, Sabbatini emphasizes the fact that the horizon must be fixed well back of the stage, so that even the remoter houses shall be of considerable size.

Certain additions or developments are, however, noted that are absent in Serlio's work. At a distance of one foot from the front of the scaffold there is to be erected a screen or parapet four and a half feet high, which shall serve as a means to hide from the sight of the observers the working of the trap-doors and other stage devices, and at the same time afford a place from which lights may be hung when desired. Furthermore the "telaro" of the middle prospect must extend far enough beyond the sides of the last two houses to keep the stage picture continuous. The heavens are built above the stage either as one continuous expanse or in such fashion that they may be broken. A cloth is used to cover the heavens and is painted in perspective. Thus Sabbatini gives us an indication of the use of the railing provided in English theatres of this period, indicates the possible genesis of foot-lights, and explains the back-cloth and the heavens.

Like Serlio, Sabbatini advises against the use of figures painted in the scenes, while he emphasizes the value of chimneys, cornices, and similar means of giving variety to the scene, and he gives detailed instructions for the designing of all these parts according to perspective. However, he adds instructions for the aerial perspective which was not dealt with by Serlio. He insists that at the outset decision be made as to the direction from which the light is to come, and that all shadows and shadings be appropriately represented; he also explains how to paint the houses and the heavens so that they will seem to fade into the desired distance at the rear of the stage. Likewise the painting of the houses which represent temples and other elaborate structures must be done with careful regard to the perspective view of their parts. This emphasis on light and shadow and on the aerial perspective by which the effect of distance is obtained represents clearly a more developed technique.

Sabbatini suggests but does not advise the use of three or more streets on the stage instead of the one street usually found. The streets may be made to issue from a common point or from various points, but in either case the result is apt to be houses so small as to lack effectiveness. This suggestion is interesting in view of the number of post-Restoration plays in England which demanded intersecting walks.

However, the permanent value of Sabbatini's work lies in its exposition of the experimental methods by which scenes were shifted and machines and other spectacular devices operated. He regards as established the necessity for changing the scenes in intermedia. But since the effectiveness of such changes is dependent on the suddenness with which the change is realized by the audience, Sabbatini at the outset of this discussion explains three methods of distracting the attention of the audience. Someone in the back of the room may attract attention to himself by disorderly conduct. Or there may be a pretence that part of the spectators' seats have fallen down. Or drums may be beaten and instruments sounded, a method generally to be preferred, since the first two methods sometimes cause undesirable alarm among the spectators.

The front houses, Sabbatini explains, must always remain fixed, even though the other houses are changed, for the whole mechanism of the stage would be revealed if there were to be any alteration of the front houses. But since the whole stage is rendered artistically inconsistent if the front houses remain while the others are changed, it is preferable to construct instead of the front houses an arch adorned with columns and statues. Inside this arch the houses may then be arranged. Thus additional beauty is gained for the scene, the effectiveness of the perspective is increased, and the mechanism of the shifting scenes remains hidden. It is desirable that this arch be constructed separately from the scaffold, as is the screen or parapet in front of the scaffold.

Three methods of effecting changes of scene are described. But it must be remembered that in any scenes which are to be changed there may be no projections such as chimneys or shop-fronts. If the first method of changing the scenes is to be used, the usual two-sided frames are constructed, but the painted canvas covers are made separate from the frames. The frames may then be covered and uncovered at will with these pieces of canvas variously painted. If the second method is to be used, the two-sided houses are built as usual, but additional houses are built and placed inside the houses visible at the beginning of the performance. When a change of scene is to be effected, a house concealed within the first house is slipped over the second, one concealed within the second is slipped over the third, in the fashion illustrated. The third method requires the construction of the scenes with a wooden top and base in the shape of an isosceles triangle. These scenes may then be turned about by means of a crank attached to the axis which projects under the stage.

The middle perspective or back-scene may be opened

by constructing it in two parts, which can then be drawn off to either side of the stage.

Various other spectacular effects and the methods of their achievement are also described. When it is desired to have a disappearing scene, the houses which are to disappear are preferably built of wood and built in

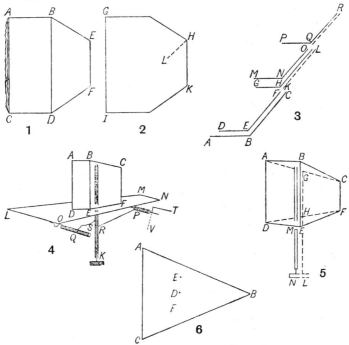

FIG. 8. THE METHODS OF SHIFTING STAGE SCENERY

From Sabbatini, *Pratica di fabricar Scene e Machine ne' Teatri*, 1638

1 and 2, First Method ; 3, Second Method ; 4, 5, 6, Third Method

sections. An iron bar run through iron holders on the back of the scene-sections holds the sections in place, and when the bar is suddenly removed, the scene is demolished. Both sides of such sectional scenes should be painted, so that the effect of ruins may be secured if possible when the scene vanishes.

Transformation scenes are also easily arranged. A man may be transformed into a rock or a rock into a man by simply raising or lowering the rock through an opening in the floor in front of the man.

A scene on fire may be provided if due care is exercised. It would seem that the triangular scenes are here considered preferable. A cloth wet in aqua-vitae is spread over the side of the scene not exposed to the audience, a man stationed near each scene applies a torch, the triangles are quickly revolved, and the buildings appear to be burning.

An inferno may be presented by the judicious use of smoke and flames emitted through trap-doors on the stage.

A sea may be constructed on the stage in various ways. A cloth may be painted to resemble the sea and ropes then sewn under the cloth, the ends of the ropes projecting on each side. Workmen may then seize these ends and shake the sea into appropriate billows, great care always being exercised to let the waves recede and advance in orderly and natural fashion. Or the sea may be represented by a row of painted cylinders with curved sides, each cylinder having its crank handle attached, by means of which it may be turned. If a tempestuous sea is to be presented, thin boards painted black, with crest-like silvered tops, may be placed between the cylindrical waves, and a man stationed beneath each board may raise and lower it as the rage of the sea demands. A ship may be made to ride the sea if a board painted and cut out to resemble a ship is made to run in a groove among the waves, a man stationed below being responsible for its heaving with the billows. The man underneath the sea may also be responsible for working the oars of a galley attached to a stick which he holds, and he may make a boat turn round if it is properly constructed and well adjusted in a cylinder.

The heavens constitute an important part of the stage

effects for intermedia. In general, an arched effect is to be secured in the constructing of the heavens. Movable clouds are variously managed. A man stationed in the heavens and holding a pole, to the far end of which is attached a cloud, may be responsible for certain effects, while machines and engines are responsible for other, more complicated changes. The machines are of two sorts: those that descend directly and those that descend and advance toward the front of the stage at the same time. These machines are usually, of course, merely seats for the gods or heroes or masquers, raised and lowered by a simple arrangement of pulleys and ropes. "Paradise" may be constructed in an opening in the heavens in which are placed eight or ten concentric circles or polygons of wood, each a foot wide and covered with cloth, the whole painted according to the requirements of aerial perspective. Dawn and like effects may be arranged in similar fashion.

Lightning and thunder are also provided for. Boards a foot wide, in each of which is cut a zig-zag rift, may be placed in the heavens. The edges of the rifts may be covered with gold leaf if desired. When a candle is placed behind each board, and the rift in the board opened and closed quickly, the effect is that of lightning. For the accompanying thunder a thirty-pound ball of iron or stone is to be rolled down an uneven set of steps fixed in a channel constructed in the chamber above the heavens.

Sabbatini gives many interesting suggestions as to the lighting of the stage. Lights may be hung along the parapet, he notes, or arranged in the arch if the arch is provided. But difficulties are always present. Both oil lamps and torches have their disadvantages, and if the lights are arranged in the heavens, they interfere with the machines, while if they are hung from the parapet, they are too low for satisfactory light. If they are within the houses, they interfere with the changing of the scenes. But all these methods are worthy of consideration. If a quick transition from light to darkness or darkness to light is to be effected, a device is suggested by which shades over the lights are raised and lowered at will.

The stage curtain may be managed on a roller or may be raised and lowered by pulleys and ropes.

I have summarized at length this work of Sabbatini because of the key which it affords us to the methods

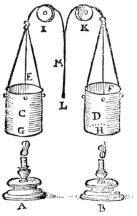

FIG. 9. From Sabbatini, *Pratica di fabricar Scene e Machine ne' Teatri,* 1638

by which certain spectacular effects in the English masques and court plays must have been attained. But as I have already indicated, this work also affords us a basis upon which we may estimate the comparative development of the English stage. It is evident that the problems of perspective, of the invisible and inaudible change of scene, of the proper lighting of the stage, and of the most effective management of machines and other devices to startle and surprise the audience were the ones with which the stage artist was wrestling.

The greatest contribution to architectural progress in England during this period was the translation of Serlio's work into English in the *Five Books of Architecture*, the translation being made at the instigation of one Robert Peake in 1611. Whether or not he was the actual translator is uncertain, since the initials "B.W." appear at the close of the work. At the end of the second book are the words:

Here endeth the second Booke of Architecture, entreating of Perspectiue Arte; translated out of Italian into Dutch, and out of Dutch into English, at the charges of Robert Peake, for the benefit of the English Nation; and are to be Sold at his house neere Holborne Conduit, under the Sunne Tauerne. 1611.

Since a Robert Peake was sergeant-painter to James I at this period, holding the office with John De Critz, a Fleming, it is to be presumed that it was to this Robert Peake that we owe this English translation. It is important to note, too, that the translation was not made directly from the Italian but from the Dutch, and since Vasari in his chapter "Of Divers Flemings" records the translation of Serlio "into the Teuton tongue" by Pieter Koeck, we may presume that it was the work of this Flemish artist that was translated. The fact that De Critz was a Fleming may have been influential. The work was dedicated to Prince Henry[1].

[1] Vasari, *op. cit.* vol. IX, p. 267. The question of responsibility for the English translation is complicated by the fact that the sons of Robert Peake, the painter, were, according to the *Dictionary of National Biography*, print-sellers, with a shop near Holborn Conduit, though the younger Robert Peake was, according to this same authority, born in 1592, and hence was only nineteen years old when the Serlio was published. The dedication to Prince Henry sounds rather like the address of an older officer in its reference to the childhood of the prince:

"To the High and Mightie Prince, Henry, Prince of Wales.

Sir, No vaine ambition of mine own Desire, much less presumption of my none Desert, incited me to present this Volume to your Princely view; but rather, the gracious Countenance, which (euen from your

I have already summarized[1] the pertinent sections of this work, and there is no need to repeat that summary here, but I wish particularly to emphasize the importance of the translation as affording us a knowledge of the current stage terms of the period and of the manner of their use.

Childehood) you haue euer daigned to all good Endeauours, inuited Mee also (after so many others) to offer at the high-Altar of your Highnesse fauour, this new-Naturalized Worke of a learned Stranger: Not with pretence of Profit to your Highnesse (who want not more exquisite Tutors in all excellent Sciences) but, under the Patronage of your powerfull Name, to benefite the Publicke; and conuay vnto my Countrymen (especially Architects and Artificers of all sorts) these Necessary, Certaine, and most ready Helps of Geometrie: The ignorance and want whereof, in times past (in most parts of this Kingdome) hath left vs many lame Workes, with shame of many Workemen; which, for the future, the Knowledge and vse of these Instructions shall happily preuent, if the euent but answere (in any measure) to that Hope of mine, which alone both induced this Desire and produced this Designe: Wherein I must confesse my part but small, sauing my great aduenture in the Charge, and my great Good-will to doe Good. All which, together with my best Seruices, I humbly prostrate at your Princely feete, as beseemes

Your Highnesse

most humble Seruant

ROBERT PEAKE."

[1] Cf. above, pp. 32–4.

CHAPTER XII

THE WORK OF INIGO JONES AND HIS CONTEMPORARIES IN ENGLAND

MOST of the history of the development of a technique in the decoration of the English dramatic stage during the period from the death of Elizabeth to the Restoration centres about the work of Inigo Jones, but the number of excellent artists in England, both foreign and native, was increasing, and the purchase of art collections abroad gave added impetus to the interest at court in artistic matters. Among the foreign artists at the court of James were Constantino de' Servi[1] and the sergeant-painter De Critz (or Decretz), who was succeeded in office by his son[2]. In 1625 Gentileschi worked in England, it is said. The visit of Van Dyck in 1620 marked the beginning of a new influence, and in 1632 he returned to establish himself in England. Rubens, too, had a special significance in England through his visits there, through the purchase of his entire cabinet by Buckingham in 1626, and through the later purchase of his work to adorn the new banqueting-hall in Whitehall[3].

Nicholas Lanier, who occasionally designed scenery for the court masques, seems to have been particularly relied on as the artistic agent of the court. He acted in 1627 or 1628 as the agent for the purchase by Charles of the collection of the Duke of Mantua, and

[1] Cf. Reyher, *op. cit.* pp. 76, 77.

[2] *Dictionary of National Biography*, article on "De Critz."

[3] Cf. Reyher, *op. cit.* p. 344. For a summary of the artistic interests at the court of Charles, cf. Dorothea Townshend, *Life and Letters of Mr Endymion Porter* (1897), pp. 144–8.

even during the Commonwealth he passed between Flanders and England with pictures and musical instruments[1].

In 1635 Charles established the first public institution of art, the Museum Minerva; and in 1648 Sir Balthazar Gerbier, who is known also to have designed scenery for masques, was responsible for the founding of the "Academy of Foreign Languages and All Noble Sciences and Exercises[2]."

In spite of this more general interest in matters of art which thus developed, the architectural history of the period is, as I have said, concentrated about Inigo Jones. And what is true of architectural history in general is peculiarly true of the history of stage scenery. Jones was one of the earliest of the English architects to go to Italy to study, and from Italy he apparently went to the court of Denmark. Soon after the accession of James I to the throne of England, his queen, Anne of Denmark, seems to have been instrumental in causing Jones's return to England, where he soon was responsible for the management of the spectacle that was to characterize the Stuart court, his first work being in connection with the *Masque of Blackness* in 1604–5. About 1613 Jones returned to Italy, and in 1614 he is known to have been again in that country, while on one of these journeys he also visited France. In 1615 he returned to England to assume the duties of Surveyor of His Majesty's Works, which he executed until 1643, when he was put out of office for loyalty to the King's cause. At his death in 1652 his plans and designs went to his pupil, assistant, and relative, John

[1] Cf. *Dictionary of National Biography*, article on "Nicholas Lanier," and Reyher, *op. cit.* pp. 77, 78.

[2] Cf. Barry's lecture "On the History and Progress of the Art," in *Lectures on Painting*, by the Royal Academicians (Barry, Opie, and Fuseli), Wornum ed. 1848, for a record of these early academies.

Webb, whom he expected to be his successor in office, it would seem[1].

Of Jones's dependence on classical authorities no further proof is needed than the taunts of Ben Jonson, for it will be remembered that it was the part of Vitruvius Hoop that gave such offence to the "Surveyor of the King's Works" that the Master of the Revels had it struck out from *The Tale of a Tub*. But Jonson's more famous *Expostulation with Inigo Jones*, written apparently to commemorate the quarrel that separated the supreme writer of masques from their supreme designer, is even better known and is more definite in its implications[2]:

> Master Surveyor, you that first began
> From thirty pounds in pipkins, to the man
> You are: from them leap'd forth an architect
> Able to talk of *Euclid*, and correct
> Both him and *Archimedes*; damn *Archytas*,
> The noblest inginer that ever was:
> Control *Ctesibius*, overbearing us
> With mistook names, out of Vitruvius;
> Drawn *Aristotle* on us, and thence shewn
> How much Architectonice is your own:
> Whether the building of the stage, or scene,
> Or making of the properties it mean,
> Vizors, or antics[3]....

[1] The accounts of Jones's life are numerous, though based on scanty information. Generally reckoned as authoritative are Peter Cunningham, *A Life of the Architect, Inigo Jones*, published for the Shakespeare Society, London, 1848; R. Blomfield, *A History of Renaissance Architecture in England*, vol. I, pp. 88–122; and the same writer's articles in the *Portfolio* for 1889, beginning on pp. 89, 113, and 116. Cf. also Reyher, *op. cit.* pp. 76, 77.

[2] Reyher, *op. cit.* pp. 192–200, gives an unprejudiced account of the relations of Jonson and Jones and of the famous quarrel between them. For the records of the suppression of Vitruvius Hoop's part, cf. Adams, *Dramatic Records of Sir Henry Herbert*, pp. 19, 34, 54.

[3] Jonson, *Works*, vol. VIII, pp. 109–13.

That Jones was a careful student of the Italian authorities on architecture is also convincingly proved. His annotations on the Vicenza theatre of Palladio and Scamozzi have already been quoted[1], and Blomfield testifies to the evidence given by Jones's copy of Palladio of his careful comparison of Palladio's work with that of Serlio, Vignola, Scamozzi, and others[2]. Mr Keith says also: "Again and again among the drawings of Inigo Jones we find studies in architectural design based on the precepts of Serlio where book and folio of that author are marginally cited as authority," while, according to the same writer, John Webb's copy of Serlio exists still with its carefully written translations and annotations[3].

Yet even Mr Keith says:

Although it is true that the introduction of movable scenery had revolutionized stage design by the time that Inigo Jones began his theatrical work at the court of James I, thus greatly lessening the value of Serlio's treatise as a text-book on the art, nevertheless, in certain of the architectural scenic compositions of Inigo Jones, Serlio's influence is plainly visible, while a woodland setting designed by Inigo for the pastoral of "Florimene" was obviously inspired by the "Satirical" scene in Serlio. Moreover, completely movable scenery was not employed by Inigo Jones in every instance[4]....

This assumption that Jones entered upon his work in England fully equipped with an adequate technique by which to achieve changes of scene and other spectacular effects has been made by many other careful scholars. The well-known designs for *Florimène* and

---

[1] Cf. above, pp. 56, 57.

[2] Cf. *Portfolio* (1889), p. 117; also Cunningham, *Life of Inigo Jones*, pp. 16, 17.

[3] *The Builder*, vol. cvii, p. 312.

[4] For the complete discussion of this point, see *The Builder*, vol. cviii, pp. 331–3.

Salmacida Spolia have, indeed, led the majority of students to accept them as typical of all of Jones's work rather than as the representatives of the final period of Jones's experiments in stage scenery, experiments which were continuous from 1605 until 1640[1].

As a matter of fact, a study of the masques in chronological order reveals quite clearly the stages of progress in these experiments. The first ballet at the court of James of which we have record was presented January 1, 1604, and was in reality but the last of the "entertainments" which had been features of the Elizabethan court. The next was Samuel Daniel's masque, the *Vision of Twelve Goddesses*, presented by the Queen and her ladies on January 8, of the same year. The scenery for this masque was distributed throughout the hall in the old pageant fashion, a cave and temple at one end of the hall and a mountain at the other. It is interesting to note that Sybilla used a "perspective" glass through which to view the goddesses as they appeared, but the significant fact to be remembered is the distributed scene of the masque[2].

Then in 1605 Ben Jonson and Inigo Jones worked together to prepare for Twelfth Night the *Masque of Blackness*, and as Reyher indicates, there was at once

[1] For excellent accounts of the designs for Inigo Jones's later work, see W. J. Lawrence, "The Mounting of the Carolan Masques," in *The Elizabethan Playhouse*, vol. 1, pp. 99 *sq.*, and Blomfield, *History of Renaissance Architecture in England*, vol. 1, pp. 91 *sq.* Reyher, *op. cit.* pp. 332–83, in a chapter dealing with "La Mise en Scène," gives the only complete account of the setting of both the early and the late masques.

[2] Cf. Reyher, *op. cit.* pp. 355–7. For a complete bibliography of texts and comments covering all the English masques, cf. also Reyher, pp. 519–32. In the following pages I have referred to specific texts for the masques only in cases where I have quoted directly from them. I have not attempted to give a complete list of the masques but only to isolate for observation such masques as show innovations and experiments in spectacular devices and hence reveal the stages of scenic progress.

established the principle of the concentrated scene arranged on a stage built at one end of the hall. That this masque attempted to show the very latest fads in scenic effects no one can doubt after reading its descriptions, and it is particularly interesting to note the stress placed on conformity to the demands of perspective. Because of its peculiar importance in the history of the technique of the stage, I quote parts of the description of the scene essential to the understanding of the scenic effects provided:

First, for the scene, was drawn a *landtschap* (landscape) consisting of small woods, and here and there a void place filled with huntings; which falling, an artificial sea was seen to shoot forth, as if it flowed to the land, raised with waves which seemed to move, and in some places the billows to break, as imitating that orderly disorder which is common in nature.

The Masquers were placed in a great concave shell, like mother-of-pearl, curiously made to move on those waters and rise with the billows; the top whereof was stuck with a chevron of lights....On sides of the shell did swim six huge sea-monsters, varied in their shapes and dispositions, bearing on their backs the twelve torch-bearers, who were planted thereon in several graces; so as the backs of some were seen; some in purfle, or side; others in face; and all having their lights burning out of whelks, or murex-shells.

These thus presented, the scene behind seemed a vast sea, and united with this that flowed forth, from the termination or horizon of which (being the level of the State, which was placed in the upper end of the hall) was drawn by the lines of perspective, the whole work shooting downwards from the eye; which decorum made it more conspicuous, and caught the eye afar off with a wandering beauty: to which was added an obscure and cloudy Night-piece, that made the whole set off.

Much later in the masque,

...the Moon was discovered in the upper part of the house, triumphant in a silver throne, made in a figure of a pyramis.

Her garments white and silver, the dressing of her head antique, and crowned with a luminary or sphere of light: which striking on the clouds, and heightened with silver, reflected as natural clouds do by the splendor of the Moon. The Heaven about her was vaulted with blue silk, and set with stars of silver, which had in them their several lights burning[1].

It will be noted that in this masque as in the sixteenth century Italian court performances a painted curtain or "scene" concealed the stage until the beginning of the performance. This curtain is here described as a "landtschap" or landscape, a term which is usually used in a definite sense when it occurs in stage descriptions to signify a country scene painted on a curtain or shutter[2]. Here the curtain falls to reveal the scene, which is carefully constructed according to the demands of perspective, the State being taken as the point of sight, but there is absolutely no suggestion of a change of scene.

It will also be noted that the "heavens" here constructed over the stage were decorated after the fashion of the roofs and halls where earlier the pageant-like masques had been seen. Vitruvius had devoted an entire book of the *De Architectura* to a discussion of astronomy as one of the necessary studies of the architect, and the most luxurious works of the architect were adorned with astronomical designs throughout the Renaissance. But until the concentrated scene was established as the

[1] Jonson, *Works*, vol. VII, pp. 3–20.

[2] It will be noted that Jonson here uses the Dutch form. According to the *New English Dictionary*, the word was first introduced into English in Haydocke's translation of Lomatius in 1598. The sense usually given to the word in the seventeenth century is recorded in the 1632 edition of Cotgrave's *Dictionarie of the French and English Tongues*: "Paisage; Paisage, Landskip, Countrey-worke; a representation of fields, or of the countrey, in painting, &c." Cf. the use of the word in Townshend's *Albion's Triumph*, however (p. 177 below), where the painting described includes buildings.

standard, the building of the heavens as part of the masque stage was, of course, impossible. Accordingly it is from this time on that we find great emphasis placed on the heavens and their moving clouds and spectacular adornments as features of the masques.

The indulgence in a multitude of lights was undoubtedly the effect of the Italian influence of Serlio and his followers. But the origin of the "night-piece," mentioned here and also in the work of Mahelot in the French theatre of this period and continuing in popularity throughout the century, is not certain[1].

In 1606 Jones was responsible for the scenery for the *Masque of Hymen*, in which, though there is no change of scene in a technical sense, variety is added to the spectacle by the use of a machine and by experiments with the heavens. When the scene was drawn to "discover" the stage, there was seen "the machine of the spectacle," a great globe which turned to reveal the masquers. This globe seems to have been a *machina versatilis*, which like the *scena versatilis*, was the object of Jones's experiments about this time. The other new and significant features in the decoration of the masque were two great statues "feigned of gold," bearing up the clouds, "which were of relievo, embossed, and tralucent as naturals: to these a cortine of painted clouds joined, which reached to the utmost roof of the hall." The clouds opened to reveal the three regions of the air, and from the middle region, "two concave clouds from the rest thrust forth themselves (in nature of those Nimbi, wherein by Homer, Virgil, &c. the gods are feigned to descend) and these carried the eight ladies...who, as the engine moved, seemed also to bow

---

[1] There are some references to night-pieces that seem to indicate that they were representations on the flat or curtain at the back of the stage of the stars and clouds of night; but the whole matter is uncertain.

themselves[1]." The emphasis on the construction of the heavens, the figures at the sides of the stage presumably anticipating the arch structure, the interest in the engineering feats, the citing of classical authority for clouds bearing their burdens of divinity, are all significant features of the record of this masque.

Campion's masque presented at Whitehall on Twelfth Night, 1607, in honour of the marriage of Lord Hayes, introduced interesting devices, though the descriptions of the masque are ecstatic rather than clarifying. There were two stages erected, the higher one for the scene, the lower one for dancing, a "double veil" or curtain about the upper stage concealing the scene. A minor feature of the decoration, but one interestingly reminiscent of Serlio, was the "artificial Battes and Owles" "plac't on wyre," and "continually mouing" about the house of Night. But the clear description of the "transformation" device gives more important information in regard to the structure of the stage. The outstanding feature of the decoration was the group of "nine golden trees of fifteene foote high, with armes and braunches very glorious to behold." When the transformation was to occur,

That part of the stage whereon the first three trees stode began to yielde, and the three foremost trees gently to sincke, and this was effected by an Ingin plac't under the stage. When the trees had sunke a yarde they cleft in three parts, and the Maskers appeared out of the tops of them, the trees were sodainly conuayed away, and the first three Maskers were raysed againe by the Ingin....

The trees advanced in threes to be thus transformed, and it would seem that three trap-doors and only three had been arranged[2].

Jonson's *Masque of Beauty*, presented at court in

---

[1] Jonson, *Works*, vol. VII, pp. 43–73.
[2] Campion, *Works* (ed. Vivian, 1909), pp. 57–76.

1608, is interesting because of the zeal shown for "motions." A floating island on a sea moved forward, a throne on the island had "a circular motion of its own," while the steps to the throne had a "motion contrary." The whole effect is rather dizzying, but it seems to have been much admired, and Jonson specifically credits the "motion" to the King's master-carpenter, though he notes the inadequate aid given by the painters. Aside from the motions the interest in the masque centred about the moon riding in a silver chariot, that, "drawn by virgins, was seen to ride in the clouds...with the sign Scorpio, and the character, placed before her." The marks of Jones's work are missing, and the carpenter's substitute "motions" are inadequate[1].

The Hue and Cry after Cupid, a masque presented at court on the occasion of the Lord Viscount Hadding-ton's marriage in 1608, written by Jonson and designed by Jones, is generally reckoned among the most magnificent and costly of masques. For the purpose of this study it is important as indicating certain hitherto unrecorded scenic devices. There were two pilasters at the side of the scene, "and over head two personages, Triumph and Victory, in flying postures, and twice so big as the life, in place of the arch, and holding a garland of myrtle for the key." As Reyher points out, this reference to the arch is the first indication we have of its habitual use[2].

Furthermore it is recorded that "on the sudden, with a solemn music," a bright sky broke forth from the clouds, and "there were discovered first two doves, then two swans, with silver geers, drawing forth a triumphant chariot." Later, as Vulcan cries, "Cleave, solid rock! and bring the wonder forth," "with a loud

[1] Jonson, *Works*, vol. VII, pp. 23–39.
[2] *Ibid.*, pp. 85–102. Cf. Reyher, *op. cit.* p. 360.

and full music," the cliff which was the chief adornment of the stage, "parted in the midst, and discovered
an illustrious concave, filled with an ample and glistering
light, in which an artificial sphere was made of silver,
eighteen foot in the diameter, that turned perpetually."
This parting of the scene to reveal what was interior
to it represented the initial stage of Jones's experiments
with the *scena ductilis*, on which he was finally to base
his method of scene-shifting. But it must be noted that
Jones here used loud music in the prescribed fashion
to distract the attention of his audience while the scene
was being opened.

Jonson's *Masque of Queens*, presented at Whitehall
a year later, gave credit to the architect: "The device
of their attire [that of the masquers] was Master Jones's,
with the invention, and architecture of the whole scene,
and machine." This masque clearly showed that Jones
was consciously experimenting with the *machina versatilis* (for the classical name is used), as well as with
other stage mechanisms.

The part of the scene which first presented itself was an ugly
Hell; which flaming beneath, smoked unto the top of the roof,
[but] on the sudden was heard a sound of loud music, as if many
instruments had made one blast; with which not only the hags
themselves, but the hell into which they ran, quite vanished,
and the whole face of the scene altered, scarce suffering the
memory of such a thing; but in the place of it appeared a
glorious and magnificent building, figuring the House of Fame,
in the top of which was discovered the twelve Masquers, sitting
upon a throne triumphal, erected in form of a pyramid and
circled with all store of light.

Afterward "the throne wherein they sat, being *machina
versatilis*, suddenly changed; and in the place of it appeared Fama Bona." The masquers as they descended
seated themselves in three chariots drawn respectively
by eagles, griffons, and lions, and were driven around

the stage. Thus we see the flaming hell described by Sabbatini, as well as the significant *machina versatilis*[1].

Daniel's *Tethys' Festival, or the Queen's Wake*, performed at Whitehall in 1610, was one of the works the design of which was most enthusiastically credited to Jones. The masque shows Jones battling with the problem of changing scenes and particularly with the problem of concealing the mechanism of the change. The curtain was drawn "at the sound of a loud musick," and the scene was revealed, the scene being

a port or haven, with bulworkes at the entrance, and the figure of a castle commanding a fortified towne: within this port were many ships, small and great, seeming to lie at anchor, some neerer and some further off, according to perspective.

The haven and the ships were thus evidently painted on the back scene while the side scenes or houses represented the bulwarks with the castle and fortified town.

However, the chief value of the description of the scene of this masque lies in what follows:

When suddenly, at the sound of a loud and fuller musique, Tethys with her nymphes appeares, with another scene, which I will likewise describe, in the language of the architector who contrived it, and speakes in his own mestier to such as are understanders and lovers of that design. First, at the opening of the heavens, appeared three circles of lights and glasses, one within another, and came downe in a straight motion five foote, and then began to move circularly; which lights and motion so occupied the eyes of the spectators, that the manner of altering the scene was scarcely discerned; for in a moment the whole face of it was changed, the port vanished, and Tethys with her nymphes appeared in their severall cavernes, gloriously adorned.

[1] Jonson, *Works*, vol. VII, pp. 103–45. Reyher, *op. cit.* pp. 364, 365, comments on the use for the first time of the "*decor successif*," but the use of the term suggests a consciousness of the relation of setting and *locale* which seems to me an anachronism.

This method of dazzling the eyes of the spectators was evidently effective, for it was the usual method thereafter adopted by Jones for concealing a change of scene. Yet later in the same masque we are merely told that "Sodainely appeares the queenes majesty, in a most pleasant and artificial grove, which was the third scene," and we are left unsatisfied as to the means adopted for concealing the change. In this masque we are assured of a definite shifting of the scenes, however, probably after the fashion described by Sabbatini[1].

The experiments with the *scena ductilis* with which Jones concerned himself at this time were manifest particularly in a masque of Prince Henry's, written by Jonson and produced January 1, 1611, *Oberon, the Fairy Prince*. The wording of the description is significant:

The *first face* of the scene appeared all obscure, and nothing perceived but a dark rock, with trees beyond it, and all wildness that could be presented; till, at one corner of the cliff, above the horizon, the moon began to shew....

Suddenly Silenus says:

> See! the rock begins to ope,
> Now you shall enjoy your hope:
> 'Tis about the hour, I know.

There the whole scene opened, and within was discovered the frontispiece of a bright and glorious palace, whose gates and walls were transparent.

Again Silenus cries:

> Stay! the cheerful chanticleer
> Tells you that the time is near:—
> See, the gates already spread!
> Every Satyr bow his head.

There the whole palace opened, and the nation of Faies were discovered, some with instruments, some bearing lights, others singing; and within afar off in perspective, the knights masquers

[1] Cf. Somers, *Collection of Tracts* (1809 ed.), vol. II, pp. 192–9.

sitting in their several sieges: at the further end of all, Oberon, in a chariot, which, to a loud triumphant music, began to move forward, drawn by two white bears.

The chariot moved "as far forth as the face of the scene," and ultimately the dancers "dance into the work," and "the whole machine closed." Thus it is made clear that the stage was arranged with two front scenes or shutters, which were pulled off one at a time, the rock scene to reveal the palace, and the palace to reveal the whole stage arranged as the fairy kingdom[1].

The *Lords Masque*, written by Campion, and presented on the occasion of the marriage of the Count Palatine and Lady Elizabeth in 1613, was magnificent and costly, and the motions of stars and lights were works of wonder. But only two new technical devices appear. The first of these was the division of the scene laterally into two parts, hidden by two separate curtains, which were drawn to reveal first the lower part of the scene and then the heavens. This division must have marked the beginning of a new system in the arrangement of the heavens, and it certainly forecast the sky-borders with which the later stage was provided in lieu of the more compact arched heavens of the early stage. The masque also showed, however, another experiment in changing the scene, for "from the side of the Scene appeared a bright and transparent cloud, which reached from the top of the heavens to the earth:—the cloude brake in twaine, and one part of it (as with a winde) was blown overthwart the Scaene." The under part of the scene vanished, and when the cloud lifted, the change was revealed. Another change of scene is recorded, but its method is not explained[2].

[1] Jonson, *Works*, vol. VII, pp. 165–81.
[2] Campion, *Works*, pp. 89–100. Beaumont's *Masque of the Inner Temple and Gray's Inn* of 1613 (H. A. Evans, *English Masques*, 1897, pp. 88–99), says also, "The fabric was a mountain with two descents

Jonson's *Vision of Delight,* presented at court in 1617, reveals the same characteristics of Jones's work: the scene changed first while a cloud and a machine claimed the interest of the spectators, and changed again "to a loud music" by the drawing of a scene and the opening up of the back scene. The masque is specially interesting, however, because of the first scene, which was "A Street in Perspective of fair buildings," a departure which marked the tendency in certain masques to approach in their setting the setting regularly used in tragedy and comedy[1].

No further notable advances in technique are apparent in the masques until after 1624. The scenery designed by Jones for Jonson's *Neptune's Triumph for the Return of Albion,* a masque said never to have been played because of the ambassadorial jealousies aroused in connection with its proposed presentation in 1624, was used for the performance of *The Fortunate Isles and their Union,* performed on Twelfth Night, 1626[2]. Though the description given by Jonson does not make quite clear the mechanism of the stage, it at least shows that further experiments were being attempted. The scene opens to reveal the island of Delos, with the masquers arranged on it. "The Island moves forward, then recedes." Afterward "the first prospective of a maritime palace, or the house of Oceanus, is discovered, with loud music. And the other above is no more seen." Then "the second prospect of the sea is shown, to the

and severed with two traverses." A comparison of the work of Constantino de' Servi in 1613 for Campion's *Masque at the Marriage of the Earl of Somerset,* and of the work of Nicholas Lanier in 1617 for Jonson's *Masque of Lethe* (or *Lovers Made Men*), with the work of Jones shows how far in advance of other artists his experiments in the technique of changing scenes had taken him at this time.

[1] Jonson, *Works,* vol. VII, pp. 281–95.

[2] Evans, *English Masques,* pp. 171, 172; Mary Sullivan, *Court Masques of James I* (1913), pp. 134, 135.

former music," and finally, "the fleet is discovered, while the three cornets play[1]." It would seem that Jones was here experimenting with the *scena ductilis* in a method the exact reverse of that in earlier use. Evidently he opened up the full stage at first, and then shut off part of it by drawing together the halves of the scene of the maritime palace. Whether he opened up the scene again to reveal the "second prospect of the sea," or whether this was another scene drawn in front of that of the maritime palace is not clear, but the first arrangement would seem probable, especially since the fleet is later introduced into the scene.

Succeeding masques do not vary widely as far as their technique is concerned. But the increasing number of machines introduced is noteworthy, and hills or other objects rising through the floor of the stage and then suddenly dropping out of sight are more and more frequently employed. In Jonson's *Chloridia*, presented in 1630, however, the "further prospect" (apparently the back scene), changes, though the rest of the stage remains fixed.

In 1631 Inigo Jones and Aurelian Townshend collaborated in designing and devising two masques, *Albion's Triumph* and *Tempe Restored*, the first of which is peculiarly interesting, first because of its revelation of the current interest in architecture and in engineering feats, and secondly because of its insistence on the glories of ancient Roman life as Britain's inheritance from its Roman past. As to the first of these causes of interest: "the ornament that went about the Scene" was further adorned by red velvet curtains that hung from the crown in the centre and were draped around the pilasters at the side of the stage, while

at the foot of the pillasters, on each side, stood two Women, the one yong, in a watchet Robe looking vpwards, and on her

[1] Jonson, *Works*, vol. VIII, pp. 21–38.

head, a payre of Compasses of gold, the poynts standing towards Heaven: the other more ancient, and of a venerable aspect, apparreled in tawney, looking downewards; in the one hand a long ruler, and in the other, a great paire of iron Compasses, one poynt whereof, stood on the ground, and the other touched part of the ruler. Above their heads, were fixt, compertiments of a new composition, and in that over the first, was written *Theorica*, and over the second *Practica*, shewing that by these two, all works of Architecture and Ingining have their perfection[1].

But the second and major cause of interest in this masque is its careful record of the royal amusements of a Roman emperor[2]. The first scene represented a Roman atrium. The attention of the spectators being directed to Mercury, who is "Re-assum'd into Heaven in Pompe," "The scene changed into the Forum of the City of Albipolis, and Albamastus triumphing, attended like a Roman Emperor, is seene a farre off to passe in pomp." Then the scene "is turned into an Amphitheater, with people sitting in it," and "such kind of pastimes as Victorious Emperors were wont to present as spectacles to the People, are heere produced for Anti-Maskes upon the stage." Another interval of cloud and machine, and the scene becomes a "pleasant Grove of straight Trees," while finally the "Scene is varied into Landscipt, in which was a prospect of the King's Pallace of *Whitehall*, and part of the Citie of *London*, seene a farre off," this last undoubtedly a tribute paid by Jones to his own continuance of the classical traditions of Great Britain in the plans for the new palace at Whitehall. There is no indication of the technique by which these scenic results are achieved.

[1] Aurelian Townshend, *Poems and Masks* (ed. Chambers, 1912), pp. 57–78; Reyher, *op. cit.* p. 362.
[2] It will be recalled that one of the standing jokes of antiquarians is the work of Jones in proving Stonehenge the remains of a Roman temple.

Tempe Restored was chiefly remarkable for the machines and the spectacular use of lights which it displayed, but we note also "flying in the air." The author comments on its great scene:

This sight was of the difficulty of the Ingining and number of persons the greatest that hath been seene here in our time. For the apparitions of such as came down in the ayre, and the *Choruses* standing beneath arrived to the number of fifty persons all richly attired, shewing the magnificence of the Court of England[1].

Carew's *Coelum Britannicum*, presented in 1633, is particularly interesting because again the Roman antiquity of Britain is stressed. When the curtain went up, it

discovered the Scaene, representing old Arches, old Palaces, decayed walls, parts of Temples, Theatres, Basilicas and Thermae, with confused heaps of broken Columnes, Bases, coronices, and Statues, lying as under ground, and altogether resembling the ruines of some great city of the ancient Romans, or civiliz'd Brittaines.

The feature of this masque was a great hill which rose up and covered the scene, and "This strange spectacle gave great cause of admiration, but especially how so huge a machine, and of that great height, could come from under the Stage, which was but six foot high." The method of changing the scenes in this masque is not clear, but it is evident, as Reyher points out, that the "great hill" was used to conceal an unusually elaborate change of scenery, and the final effects of the masque are attained while the attention of the spectators is attracted by descending and ascending clouds and a

[1] Townshend, *Poems and Masks*, pp. 79–99. Cf. Chambers's note on the indebtedness of this masque to the *Ballet comique de la Royne* of Baltasar de Beaujoyeulx, presented at the court of Henry III of France in 1582, Jones rather than Townshend probably being responsible for the borrowings. Cf. also Reyher, *op. cit.* pp. 201, 374.

PLATE IV

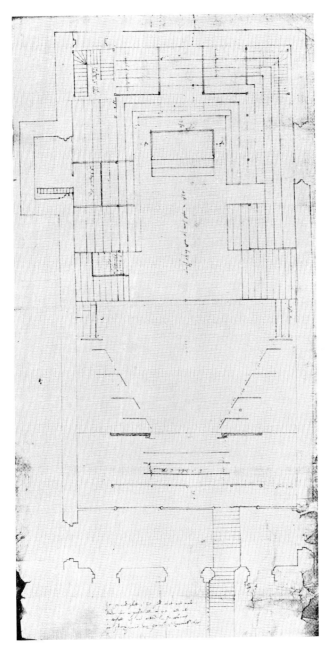

INIGO JONES'S PLAN
Showing the Arrangement of the Stage and Hall on the
Occasion of the Presentation of *Florimène*, 1635

great cloud that finally passes "overthwart" the scene, "leaving nothing behind it but a serene Skye." It is likewise evident that flat scenes were not yet in use, and that Jones was still at work on methods of concealing changes of scene[1].

The masques of the succeeding years are those of the period when experiments were in the process of full realization. From the records of dramatic performances we know that in 1635 when *Florimène* was performed at court, the two-sided or angular scene was still in use, and that in 1636 at Oxford the series of "shutters" or wings were used, presumably for the first time. Of the method by which the changes were effected, there-fore, in the great masques between 1630 and 1640, it is only possible to say that the technique which we happen to have described for plays rather than masques leads us to suppose that at some time about 1635 or 1636, Jones made the great change from the angular side-scene to the flat side-scene, and that the greater number of changes that it was possible to arrange in this way is the cause of increased variety in the masques[2].

Two masques it is important to note for other reasons than their contribution to theatrical technique: Thomas Heywood's *Love's Mistress*, or, *The Queen's Masque*, acted three times at court in 1636, and then publicly acted "by the Queen's Comoedians" at the Phoenix in Drury Lane, and Nabbes's *Microcosmos* presented in the Salisbury Court playhouse and there only. These masques indicate one of the means by which the taste for spectacle in the drama was being formed in the general public and indicate the gradual democratizing of spectacle, the culmination of which came only after the Restoration. There is little indication of scenery in

[1] Thomas Carew, *Poems* (ed. Hazlitt for the Roxburghe Library, 1870), pp. 195–235. Cf. Reyher, *op. cit.* pp. 367, 368.
[2] Cf. below, pp. 188, 189.

the text of *Love's Mistress*, but Heywood addressed himself to the reader, acknowledging the new scenes designed for it when it was the second time presented at court on the King's birthday. He explained,

> I cannot pretermit to give a due Charracter to that admirable Artist, Mr. *Inego Jones*, Master surveyor of the King's worke, &c. Who to every Act, nay almost to every Sceane, by his excellent Inventions, gave such an extraordinary Luster; upon every occasion changing the stage, to the admiration of all the Spectators; that, as I must Ingeniously confesse, It was above my apprehension to conceive, so to their sacred Majesties, and the rest of the Auditory[1].

Of Nabbes's *Microcosmos*, described as "A Morall Maske, presented with generall liking, at the private house in Salisbury Court," we have knowledge because of the description in the text. A significant statement is made: "Within the arch a continuing perspective of ruines, which is drawne still before the other scenes whilst they are varied." This latter statement indicates a distinct advance in technique, for it anticipates the curtain of the modern stage dropped to conceal the mechanism of the change of scene and makes unnecessary the loud music, the dazzling "motion" of lights, the clouds thrown "overthwart" the scene, the machine let down—all the devices employed to distract the attention of the audience[2].

In 1638 William Davenant was appointed poet-laureate. Immediately before and after this date he, working usually with Inigo Jones, was responsible for

---

[1] Cf. Thomas Heywood, *Dramatic Works* (1874), vol. v, pp. 81–160, for complete text.

[2] Cf. *Old English Plays*, New Series (ed. A. H. Bullen), *The Works of Thomas Nabbes*, vol. ii, pp. 161–218. Professor Thorndike, *op. cit.* p. 192, includes this among masques the text for which contains no indication of shifting scenery, but this statement must be due to some oversight.

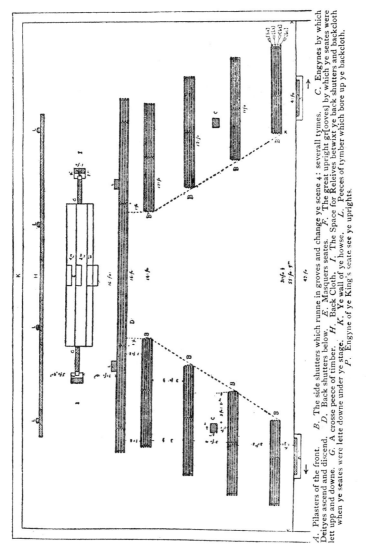

A. Pilasters of the front. B. The side shutters which runne in groves and change ye scene 4: severall tymes. C. Engynes by which Deityes ascend and discend. D. Back shutters below. E. Masquers seates. F. The great upright gr[ooves] by which ye seates were lett upp and downe. G. A crosse peece of timber. H. Back Cloth. I. The Space for Releives betwixt ye back shutters and backcloth when ye seates were lette downe under ye stage. K. Ye wall of ye howse. L. Peeces of tymber which bore up ye backcloth. P. Engyne of ye King's seate see ye uprights.

FIG. 10. DESIGN BY INIGO JONES FOR THE STAGING OF THE MASQUE "SAL-MACIDA SPOLIA." From Reyher's reproduction from Lansdowne MS. 1171

Ground platt of a sceane where ye side peeces of ye sceane doe altogither change with ye back shutters comparted by ye sceane of ye King and Queens Majesties Masque of Salmacida Spoila in ye new masquing howse Whitehall 1640.

the masques at court which, at least on the side of
spectacle, brought the Carolan masque to an appropriate climax. Fortunately we have the original drawings of Jones for the last of these great masques, *Salmacida Spolia*, presented in 1640[1]. These drawings have
been so frequently published as to make them familiar
to all students of the stage. But certain points remain
to be stressed. The stage is divided by the back shutters,
so that the part of the stage in front of the shutters is
complete in itself. The back and side shutters run in
grooves and in this masque provide four complete
changes of scene. But when the back shutters are
opened up, the stage extending to the back cloth is
revealed, and here are arranged the masquers' seats,
which are let down under the stage when not in use, and
the scenes in relief, the "relieves" which never completely gave way to flats. In the flats or shutters of the
front stage, the *scena ductilis* achieved its ultimate triumph.

In this masque the stage is no longer overcast by
solidly constructed heavens, but each of the flat scenes
is overlapped by a cloud depending from the roof and
moving in a groove also.

Before discussing the technique which is shown in
the plays of this period, the scenery for which is described in the texts of the plays themselves or of which
we know by the account of an eye-witness, it is necessary to consider the significance of the masque
technique as it developed, and this we can do only if we
recall certain well-known facts in regard to the seventeenth century conception of the function of the masque.
Bacon's essay *Of Masques and Triumphs* has long formed
the basis of such knowledge:

These Things are but Toys, to come amongst such serious
obseruations; but yet, since Princes will haue such Things, it

[1] William Davenant, *Dramatic Works* (*Dramatists of the Restoration*,
1872), vol. II, pp. 301–31.

is better they should be Graced with Elegancy than Daubed with Cost. *Dancing to Song*, is a Thing of great State, and Pleasure....It is true, the *Alterations* of *Scenes*, so it be quietly and without Noise, are Things of Great Beauty and Pleasure; for they feed and relieue the eye, before it be full of the same Object. Let the *Scenes* abound with *Light*, specially *Coloured* and Varied[1].

It is evident that the central idea is that masques are princes' toys, and that their value lies in their ability to delight the senses; consequently the value of changing scenes is found in the relief from weariness and satiety which they afford the eye of the beholder.

The same idea was incorporated in the sneers of Jonson's *Expostulation with Inigo Jones*:

> What is the cause you pomp it so, I ask?
> And all men echo, you have made a masque.
> I chime that too, and I have met with those
> That do cry up the machine, and the shows;
> The majesty of Juno in the clouds,
> The peering forth of Iris in the shrouds;
> The ascent of lady Fame, which none could spy.
> Not they that sided her, dame Poetry,
> Dame History, dame Architecture too,
> And goodly Sculpture, brought with much ado
> To hold her up: O shows, shows, mighty shows!
> The eloquence of masques! what need of prose,
> Or verse, or prose, t'express immortal you?
> You are the spectacles of state, 'tis true,
> Court-hieroglyphics, and all arts afford,
> In the mere perspective of an inch-board;
> You ask no more than certain politic eyes,
> Eyes that can pierce into the mysteries

[1] This essay "Of Masques and Triumphs" was printed first in the 1625 edition and was not reprinted in the 1638 Latin edition. Cf. *A Harmony of Lord Bacon's Essays, etc.*, 1597–1638 (Arber's *English Reprints*, 1871), pp. xxxii, xxxiii, and text on pp. 539, 540.

Of many colours, read them, and reveal
Mythology, there painted on slit deal.
Or to make boards to speak! there is a task
Painting and carpentry are the soul of masque[1].

The same idea of the function of masques was incorporated by Daniel in his defence of masques in his preface to the *Vision of Twelve Goddesses*:

Seeing also that these ornaments and delights of peace are in their season, as fit to entertain the world, and deserue to be made memorable as well as the grauer actions,—both of them concurring to the decking and furnishing of glory and Maiestie, as the necessary complements requisit for State and Greatnesse.

Likewise in the preface to *Tethys' Festival* he explained that

shewes and spectacles of this nature, are usually registered among the memorable acts of the time, being Complements of State, both to shew magnificence and to celebrate the feasts to our greatest respects,

the amplification of which statement is found in the study, *Court Masques of James I*, by Mary Sullivan, published in 1913. Daniel added another statement often quoted, "But in these things wherein the onely life consists in shew; the arte and inuention of the Architect giues the greatest grace, and is of most importance."

Davenant also justified masques in similar fashion:

Princes of sweet and humane natures have ever, both amongst the ancients and moderns in the best times, presented spectacles and personal representations, to recreate their spirits wasted in grave affairs of State, and for the entertainment of their nobility, ladies, and courts[2].

The stupendous cost of the masques, their importance as state functions, the emphasis on spectacular rather than literary and dramatic elements, the consequent

[1] Cf. above, p. 163.
[2] Davenant, *op. cit.* vol. II, p. 265, in preface to *Britannia Triumphans*.

exaltation of the architect's contribution,—all these factors entered inevitably into the forming of a taste for spectacle at court. And the gradual acquaintance with court spectacles gained through the presentation of masques elsewhere than at court, particularly in the public theatres, influenced. unmistakably the trend of theatrical history in England[1].

As I have said, however, so far as the masques were concerned, changes of scene were part of the princely toys, decorative and productive of wonder, able to startle and surprise, affording a sure relief from ennui in their variety. Accordingly they were prized. And because they were prized, it was worth the Master Surveyor's time and effort to achieve a technique that was suitable, and this he did on the basis of classical instructions by experiments with the *scena ductilis* and the *scena versatilis*, the latter of which he finally discarded as unworkable as a means of changing the scene. It remains to be seen whether the same technique was being applied to representations of the regular drama that was being applied to the masque, and whether the same signs of experiment appear.

It is, however, in connection with a dramatic representation at Oxford in August, 1605, that we first hear of Jones's experiments with moving scenery, for it will be remembered that the *Masque of Blackness* of that year contains no possible indication of change of scenes. But in August a contemporary account makes it certain that Jones had determined on an experiment with the *periaktoi*, and it was peculiarly appropriate that the

---

[1] Reyher, *op. cit.* pp. 497, 498, has formulated a very interesting "Liste des principales pièces où se trouvent insérés des Masques." Cf. A. H. Thorndike, "Influence of the Court Masque on the Drama, 1608–15," in *Publications of the Modern Language Association*, N.S., vol. VIII, pp. 114–20; also C. W. Wallace, *The Children of the Chapel at Blackfriars*, 1597–1603 (1908), p. XII.

experiment should be made in Oxford and in connection with a Latin tragedy. The description as given by Stringer follows:

I found the Earles of Worcester, Suffolk, and Northampton with the Lord Carye, who had been to view St. Marie's and Christ Church....They (but especially Lord Suffolk) utterly disliked the stage at Christ Church, and above all, the place appointed for the chair of Estate, because it was no higher, and the King so placed that the auditory could see but his cheek only; this dislike of the Earle of Suffolk much troubled the Vice-chancellor and all the workmen, yet they stood in defence of the thing done, and maintained that by the art perspective the King should behold all better than if he sat higher. Their Chancellor also, after his coming, tooke part with the University, and on the Sunday morning the matter was debated in the Councill-chamber. In the end, the place was removed, and sett in the midst of the Hall, but too far from the stage, viz. 28 foote, so that there were many long Speeches delivered which neither the King nor any near him could well see or understand. The stage was built close to the upper end of the Hall, as it seemed at the first sight. But indeed it was but a false wall fair painted and adorned with stately pillars, which pillars would turn about, by reason whereof, with the help of other painted cloths, their stage did vary three times in the acting of one Tragedy. Behind the foresaid false wall there was reserved five or six paces of the upper end of the Hall, which served them to good uses for their houses and receipt of the actors, &c.

The tremendous gravity with which the perspective view of the stage was debated by the university authorities and the court makes clear the importance attached to perspective, just as did the account of the *Masque of Blackness*. But the innovation was evidently the changing of the scene, and that the *scena versatilis* was chosen for the experiment is clearly shown. But in what fashion the "other painted cloths" helped to vary the scene we are uncertain.

That this innovation was to be reckoned as a "rare device" rather than as an expression of the logical necessity arising from a change of place may be inferred from the additional information given by Stringer:

For the better contriving and furnishing of the stages, seates, and scaffolds in St. Marie's and Christ Church, they entertained two of his Majestie's Master Carpenters, and they had the advice of the Comptroller of his Works. They also hired one Mr. Jones, a great Traveller, who undertooke to further them much, and furnish them with rare devices, but performed very little, to that which was expected. He had for his pains, as I heard it constantly reported, £50[1].

When it is remembered that the *periaktoi* were regularly called *machines*, the significance of Jones's continued experiments in the masques of 1606 and 1609, and the use of the term *machina versatilis* in the *Masque of Queens* must become apparent. But it is important to note that the experiment was begun in connection with a regular dramatic representation, and not with a masque, and that it was begun under circumstances conducive to classical researches. However, there can be no doubt that Jones was familiar with the two methods of changing the scene described by Servius, and it seems to me an inevitable conclusion from the study of the masques and plays that he tried first the *scena* or *machina versatilis* and then the *scena ductilis*, upon which he finally worked out a perfect system of scene-shifting. Nor does it seem to me that there can be any doubt that the same interest in adding "rare devices" to plays and masques alike recommended him to the grateful attention of the court.

On the occasion of the King's visit to Cambridge in 1619 plays were again represented, and Chamberlain wrote to Sir Dudley Carleton that the hall in Trinity

[1] Cf. Nichols, *Progresses of King James* (1828), vol. I, pp. 530 *sq.*

"was so well ordered for room, that above 2,000 persons were conveniently placed." Of the method of the presentation of the plays we know almost nothing[1].

But of the visit of King, Queen, and court to Oxford in August, 1636, and of the plays there performed, we fortunately possess adequate record. The record is peculiarly interesting because it throws light on the matter of the introduction of flat scenes running in grooves, such as characterized the latest masques at the court of Charles I. Anthony à Wood is the authority for our knowledge of the whole period of the royal visit, and I quote from his account of the play presented on the evening of August 29 in Christ Church hall:

It was intituled "Passions Calmed," or "The Settling of the Floating Island," made by Strode, the Orator, and performed by the Scholars beyond expectation. It was acted on a goodly stage, reaching from the upper end of the Hall almost to the hearth place, and had on it three or four openings on each side thereof, and partitions between them, much resembling the desks or studies in a Library, out of which the Actors issued forth. The said partitions they could draw in and out at their pleasure upon a sudden, and thrust out new in their places according to the nature of the Screen, whereon were represented Churches, Dwelling-houses, Palaces, &c. which for its variety bred very great admiration. Over all was delicate painting, resembling the Sky, Clouds, &c. At the upper end a great fair street of two leaves that opened and shut without any visible help. Within which was set forth the emblem of the whole Play in a mysterious manner. Therein was the perfect resemblance of the billows of the Sea rolling, and an artificial Island, with Churches and Houses waving up and down and floating, as also rocks, trees and hills. Many other fine pieces of work and Landscapes did also appear at sundry openings thereof, and a Chair also seen to come gliding on the Stage without any visible help. All these representations, being the first (as I have been informed) that

[1] Nichols, *op. cit.* vol. i, pp. 48–50.

were used on the English stage, and therefore giving great content. I have been therefore the more punctual in describing them, to the end that posterity might know that what is now seen in the Play-houses at London belonging to his Majesty, and the Duke of York, is originally due to the invention of Oxford Scholars.

As to the accuracy of this final statement there may be some doubt, since we know that Inigo Jones was present to assist in the representation of these plays. It is therefore highly probable that the most expert architect of his time was more than an inspiration to these "Oxford Scholars" in their invention, if such it was. Whether or not it was at this time that the side scenes were first represented as flats which, running in grooves, could be drawn off, one after another, to reveal the successive changes of scene is not clear. But there is this much to be said for the truth of the assertion: The pastoral *Florimène* played at court the year before used the old angular side scenes. We know that in 1640 the masque of *Salmacida Spolia* used this complete system of flats or drawn scenes. Therefore 1636 is at least a plausible date for their introduction. But the point to be stressed, a point more important than the exact date at which a technical advance was made, is that the plays presented at the university were again showing exactly the same type of scenic representation that was being used in the masques at court. And it is likely that they even showed a slight technical advance over the masques.

Wood also describes the play given in Christ Church hall on the succeeding night, Cartwright's *Royal Slave*, of which he says:

It contained much more variety than that of "Passions calmed." Within the shuts were seen a curious Temple, and the Sun shining over it, delightful forests also, and other prospects. Within the great shuts mentioned before, were seen villages, and men visibly appearing in them, going up and down, here and there, about their business. The Interludes were represented with as much variety of scenes and motions as the great wit of Inigo Jones (well skilled in setting out a Court Masque to the best advantage) could extend unto. It was very well pen'd and acted, and the strangeness of the Persian habits gave great content.

The additional questions raised by this account cannot well be answered in this place, but it must be noted that painted figures were evidently introduced in the back flat; and that interludes, such as were known in the Italian court plays and which were directly connected in the mind of the writer with masques, were shown in connection with the play.

According to the usual custom, these plays were acted within a few days of their first presentation for the benefit of the university and "strangers" who wished to see them. *The Royal Slave*, however, had a further history which seems to me significant. Wood records:

In November following, the Queen sent to the Chancellor that he would procure of Christ Church the Persian attire of the Royall Slave and other apparell wherein it was acted, to the end that she might see her own Players act it over again, and whether they could do it as well as 'twas done by the University. Whereupon the Chancellor caused the Cloathes and Perspectives of the Stage to be sent to Hampton Court in a Waggon, for which the University received from her a letter of thanks....The Chancellor desired of the King and Queen that neither the Play, or Cloaths, nor Stage, might come into the hands and use of the common Players abroad, which was graciously granted[1].

Why the chancellor should fear that the "stage" or scenes, as well as the play and costumes, might fall into the hands of the common players is not apparent unless

[1] Anthony à Wood, *History and Antiquities of the University of Oxford* (1792–6), vol. II, pp. 407–14.

they were at this time presenting plays with scenes and presumably presenting court plays with the scenes used at court after they were discarded there. Some such arrangement is certainly suggested by the chancellor's request and the gracious granting of the request.

The texts of these two university plays as they have come down to us include enthusiastic descriptions of the scenes, but of the technique used to accomplish the changes of scene there is no indication. For our knowledge of technique we are, therefore, altogether dependent on Wood. And the use of the term "Appearance" to describe the scenes in *The Royal Slave* has been the subject of speculation among scholars from Malone to Professor Thorndike. However, it seems impossible to doubt the general accuracy of Wood's description, a description which has generally been overlooked.

As to the court performances of plays other than masques we have little information. Unfortunately the records of the Office of the Revels under James, Charles I, and Charles II are either lost or unedited. While certain writers, notably Malone and Chalmers, saw the office book of Sir Henry Herbert for the period 1622–42, and have left us valuable excerpts in their works, we have no such body of knowledge on which to draw for these late reigns as is furnished in the dramatic records of the reigns of Edward VI, Mary, and Elizabeth, edited by Professor Feuillerat. Professor Adams has done all students of the subject a service in gathering together such evidence as is available in his *The Dramatic Records of Sir Henry Herbert*, but the record is inevitably inadequate and incomplete.

Seemingly because we lack the necessary information upon which to base a conclusion as to the manner of setting forth the court drama during the Stuart period, there has come about an assumption that the plays of the Jacobean and Carolan courts were in general not furnished with the spectacle with which the plays at the court of the parsimonious Elizabeth were provided. Yet we know that the court masques during this period attained an unprecedented splendour. We know, too, that the visits of the King and court to the universities were made the occasions for the elaborately spectacular presentation of plays. We know that certain plays were presented at court not only with scenes but with changing scenes, and that Inigo Jones had made experiments extending over a period of thirty-five years in perfecting his methods for effecting such changes of scene in court performances. Occasionally Sir Henry Herbert has noted the fact of the scenes in connection with his licensing of the play, but such notices always are entered for some reason entirely aside from any interest that may or may not have attached to the mere fact that scenes were used.

The plays in connection with which Sir Henry recorded the use of scenes are *The Faithful Shepherdess* in January, 1633–4, *Florimène* in 1635, and *Cleodora* in 1640. The reason for the specific mention of scenes is given in every case:

On Monday night, the sixth of January and the Twelfe Night, was presented at Denmark-house, before the King and Queene, Fletchers pastorall called *The Faithfull Shepheardesse*, in the clothes the Queen had given Taylor the year before of her own pastorall.

The scenes were fitted to the pastorall, and made by Mr. Inigo Jones, in the great chambre, 1633[1].

Which is to say that the clothes or costumes were old, given by the Queen to Taylor, the Yeoman of the Revels, to use on this occasion, but that the scenes were made specially to fit the new pastoral.

[1] Adams, *Dramatic Records of Sir Henry Herbert*, pp. 53, 55, n. 3.

The entries for *Florimène* and *Cleodora* are even more explicit in indicating the reason for the mention of scenes:

The pastoral of *Florimene*, with the descriptions of the sceanes and interludes, as it was sent mee by Mr. Inigo Jones, I allowed for the press, this 14 of Decemb. 1635. The pastorall is in French, and 'tis the argument only, put into English, that I have allowed to be printed[1].

On Thursday the 9 of Aprill, 1640, my Lord Chamberlen bestow'd a play on the Kinge and Queene, call'd *Cleodora*, Queene of Arragon, made by my cozen Abington. It was performed by my lords servants out of his own family, and his charge in the cloathes and sceanes, which were very riche and curious. In the hall at Whitehall.

The King and queen commended the generall entertaynment, as very well acted, and well set out.

It was acted the second tyme in the same place before the king and queene[2].

It may be said that there is no indication in the text of *The Faithful Shepherdess* or of *Cleodora* that scenes were provided.

On the contrary, certain plays recorded without comment by the Master of the Revels are known from other sources to have been provided with scenes. A case in point is Cartwright's *Royal Slave*, described merely as an "Oxford play, written by Cartwright. The king gave him forty pounds[3]." Yet a warrant exists for payment of £154 for "alterations, reparations, and additions which were made unto ye scene, apparell, and propertyes[4]" of this play, the scenes for which we know from Wood were obtained from Oxford. Another case is that of *Aglaura*, acted in 1638, first at Blackfriars,

[1] Adams, *op. cit.* p. 41; cf. also p. 55.
[2] *Ibid.* p. 58.   [3] *Ibid.* p. 57.
[4] C. C. Stopes, "Shakespeare's Fellows and Followers," in *Sh. Jahr.*, vol. XLVI, p. 91.

and afterwards at court. The statement made in Aubrey's *Brief Lives* in regard to this play in the article on Sir John Suckling has been responsible for much of the misapprehension concerning the pre-Restoration stage. The statement says: "When his Aglaura was [acted], he bought all the cloathes himselfe, which were very rich....He had some scaenes to it, which in those dayes were only used at masques[1]."

In like fashion entries for certain masques have been preserved, but only rarely any notice of scenes, which we know to have been "the soul of masque."

We, therefore, may choose to believe that at the court of James and Charles a lavish use of spectacle was made for masques and picked dramatic performances, but was frugally withheld from the majority of plays; that the lack of information as to the usual scenic representation of the drama at court argues the drama meagrely adorned; that the accidentally preserved records of scenes for certain plays represent practically the complete record of such scenes. Or we may believe that the court drama of Elizabeth, adorned with whatever of scenery and spectacle the sixteenth century afforded, was followed by the court drama of James and Charles, adorned with such devices as the progress of architectural theory and the ingenuity of Inigo Jones could devise; that the taste for spectacle must have been as manifest in the presentation of plays as masques; that the extant records of scenes for plays are but preserved by chance and are merely indicative of the means used to adorn the drama at court; that these dramatic performances probably as much excelled those of the court of Elizabeth as the masques of James and Charles excelled the pageant-masque and entertainment of Elizabeth.

[1] Aubrey, *Brief Lives* (ed. A. Clark, 1898), vol. ii, p. 244.

CHAPTER XIII

SPECTACLE IN THE THEATRES

THE significance of the technique developed for the shifting of scenes and the management of spectacle on the stage is to be found in the final incorporation of these devices in the permanent theatres. As I have already said, one of the outstanding features of the seventeenth century was its manifest interest in theatre building. Molmenti, for instance, in his work on Venice lists eighteen theatres built during the seventeenth century[1]. But even more important than the number of theatres constructed was the tendency to modify the Vitruvian model to a theatre with a stage more fitted to the use of perspective scenery as it had been evolved during the sixteenth century. Accordingly the theatre at Parma, completed in 1618 or 1619, becomes of supreme importance, for it marked the adoption of the great central proscenium arch, a fusion of the entrances of the Palladian stage into one. The result was a stage on which scenery could be arranged back of the central opening or arch as it was on the temporary stages of the banqueting-halls and masking-houses.

The next step forward was the introduction of movable scenes in the theatre, which is said to have occurred first in the case of the Teatro di San Cassiano in Venice, rebuilt in 1637, the first public opera-house. And the fact of its being an opera-house needs to be considered[2].

[1] P. G. Molmenti, *Venice* (trans. H. F. Brown, 1906–8), *The Decadence*, vol. I, p. 155 note.

[2] For the history of this theatre, cf. Molmenti, *Venice, The Golden Ages*, vol. II, p. 28, and *The Decadence*, vol. I, p. 154.

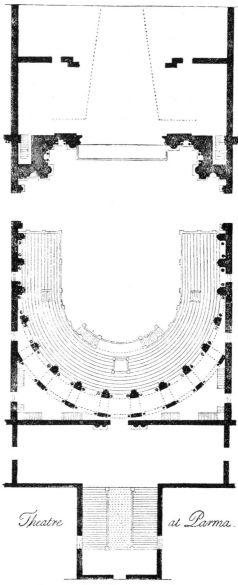

Theatre at Parma.

FIG. 11. THE THEATRE AT PARMA
From George Saunders, *A Treatise on Theatres*, 1790

The last invention of importance in Italy was that made by Giacomo Torelli, who introduced "a device for shifting the scenes by means of a lever or winch." The date of this invention is uncertain, but it is supposed to have been used first in the Teatro di SS. Giovanni e Paolo, which was built in 1639[1].

Evelyn, in 1644, wrote from Rome of Bernini,

a Florentine sculptor, architect, painter, and poet, who, a little before my coming to the citty, gave a publiq opera (for so they call shews of that kind) wherein he painted the scenes, cut the statues, invented the engines, compos'd the musiq, writ the comedy, and built the theater[2].

And in 1645 he wrote from Venice of attending the opera, where he saw "variety of sceanes painted and contrived with no lesse art of perspective, and machines for flying in the aire, and other wonderful motions," and he recorded the fact that "the sceanes changed thirteen times[3]." It is, however, essential to recognize the fact that these spectacular achievements were those of opera.

At any rate, we have in Italy a single-arched proscenium front, movable scenery introduced and habitually used for public operatic performances, and a more nearly perfected mechanism for changing scenes than Sabbatini's descriptions prophesied.

In France the influence of these new theatrical interests was felt also. The court theatre, the Petit Bourbon, and the single permanent public theatre, the Hôtel de Bourgogne, ceased to be adequate. The latter was,

---

[1] Molmenti, *Venice, The Decadence*, vol. 1, p. 158. Molmenti in a note on the subject of Torelli's invention quotes: "'Giacome Torelli da Fano inventò il moversi delle scene coll' arzano, e fece quattro famosi teatri in Parigi, Parma, Venezio, e Fano.' Museo Civico, Cod. Cicogna, 2991, fasc. ii. fol. 30."

[2] Evelyn, *op. cit.*, under date of November 19, 1644.

[3] *Ibid.*, Ascension Week, 1645 (vol. 1, p. 245).

on the demand of the actors in 1631, refurbished after the Italian fashion. The new Théâtre du Marais was erected in 1634. And Cardinal Richelieu caused to be erected a model theatre particularly adapted to the display of changing scenes and machines[1]. The introduction of Italian opera about 1645, and finally the bringing of the famous Torelli from Italy through the influence of Cardinal Mazarin made for the extensive and rapid development of spectacle[2].

That the French theatre made such rapid progress after 1630 was thus apparently due to the two cardinals who were successively in power. Cardinal Richelieu was jealous for his supremacy in all things and was not content to suffer Italian excellence in theatrical matters to go unchallenged. Cardinal Mazarin was an Italian who when occasion offered introduced Italian methods of presenting opera and operatic spectacle.

Fortunately we have indisputable evidence as to the scenes in the French public theatre in the notations of certain decorators at the Hôtel de Bourgogne after 1633 of things necessary to be provided, together with a valuable set of their drawings for the stage settings of certain plays. These records have recently been published by Professor H. C. Lancaster under the title of *Le mémoire de Mahelot, Laurent, et d'autres décorateurs de l'hôtel de Bourgogne et de la Comédie-Française au XVIIe siècle*. The first entries are those of Laurent Mahelot for 1633, 1634. Concerning these entries Professor Lancaster comments:

Dans les notices de quelques pièces [*Diane, Ménechmes, Visite differée, Amaranthe*], où la scène représente des "maisons et

---

[1] Cf. Bapst, *op. cit.* pp. 180–91; also Brander Matthews, *A Study of the Drama* (1910), p. 60, for plan of the Richelieu theatre, and frontispiece depicting the stage of that theatre during a performance.

[2] For a history of ballet and opera in France, cf. Bapst, *op. cit.* pp. 193–211, particularly the account of the 1642 performance of *Le mariage d'Orphée et d'Eurydice* at the Théâtre du Marais.

rues" ou une forêt, le système indiqué est déjà moderne, car, quoique l'espace idéal de la pièce soit plus grand que celui de la scène, et qu'on représente des endroits dans une forêt assez éloignés les uns des autres, il n'y a pour le spectateur qu'un seul tableau. Mais les décors décrits dans la plupart des notices sont plutôt disposés comme au moyen-âge, quoique rapetissés pour la salle de l'Hôtel. La scène se divise en compartiments, dont chacun fait un tableau complet. L'action de la pièce passe d'un compartiment à un autre et le spectateur obligeant tâche de n'en voir qu'un seul à la fois[1].

The records of Michael Laurent cover a period after 1678, and Professor Lancaster discusses the change that took place between the time of Mahelot and that of Laurent, a change from the *décor simultané* or mediaeval stage, to the classic or modern stage. He points out that two methods of effecting this change were possible: shutting off part of the scene (as Mahelot did occasionally), or eliminating all the scene save one compartment, which must then be made to fill the stage. Whether or not any such logical and gradual change took place, the records after 1678 leave no room for doubt that the single pictures on the stage completely superseded the earlier incongruities of the setting. The influences that brought about this change, according to Professor Lancaster, were the study of Greek and Latin drama, the example of Italian drama, and the popularity of the pastoral[2].

It is not in place here to discuss the probable supplementing of such influences by the classical and neo-

---

[1] Cf. p. 34. In this connection Bapst, *op. cit.* p. 187, says: "Les décors à perspective régulière et perfectionnée que *Mirame* avait inaugurés furent appliqués à toutes les pièces montées avec luxe à la fin du règne de Louis XIII et sous Louis XIV, telles que *Psyché, la Toison d'or, Andromède, Circé,* c'est-à-dire, aux pièces dites 'a machines,' comme aux représentations de la cour. Le théâtre français proprement dit, celui qui se jouait à l'Hôtel de Bourgogne, ne profitera que bien plus tard de ces essais de mise en scène."

[2] Lancaster, *op. cit.* pp. 41, 42.

classical architectural theory that dominated the discussion of stage-technique. Nor is it necessary here to discuss the reasons for the tardy giving up of the mediaeval methods on the French stage. But it is necessary to note that every account of scenery on the English stage which has been preserved goes to prove that the English stage was directly indebted to the Italian stage for its inspiration in matters of spectacle, as was the French stage.

Yet no one can deny the increasing influence of France in English dramatic affairs after the accession of Charles I in 1625 and the bringing of a French queen to the English throne. The royal favour shown the French comedians in London in 1635 is proved by various documents[1], and it is unquestioningly accepted that the English drama was directly influenced by the French. Probably, however, the most important modification of the English stage tradition was to come, after the Restoration, from the strict classicism that developed under the French Academy. The Academy, founded in 1635 by order of the French king and under the direct leadership of Cardinal Richelieu, found its opportunity in the famous controversy waged about the *Cid* in 1636, and thereafter defined and enforced conformity to classical theories of the drama. Professor Spingarn sums up this movement:

it was through the offices of Chapelain, seconded by the authority of Cardinal Richelieu, that it [the rule of unity of time] became

---

[1] Adams, *Dramatic Records of Sir Henry Herbert*, pp. 60–2, and for the records of the less favoured players of 1629, pp. 59, 60. Adams, *Shakespearean Playhouses*, pp. 420–4, gives an account of the temporary theatre in Drury Lane occupied by the players in 1635. Cf. also A. H. Upham, *French Influence in English Literature* (1908), pp. 372–402, and Dorothea Canfield Fisher, *Corneille and Racine in England* (1904), pp. 1–18 especially, for interesting facts concerning the relationship between the French and the English drama at this period.

fixed in the dramatic theory of France. In a long letter, dating from November, 1630,...Chapelain sets out to answer all the objections made against the rule of twenty-four hours. It is sustained, he says, by the practice of the ancients and the universal consensus of the Italians; but his own proof is based on reason alone....By 1635 he had formulated the whole theory of the three unities and converted Cardinal Richelieu to his views. In 1636 the famous *Cid* controversy had begun. By 1640 the battle was gained, and the unities became a part of the classic theory of the drama throughout Europe[1].

This theory did not go unchallenged, for as Professor Lancaster notes, as early as 1632, De Rayssiguier in his preface to the translation of Tasso's *Aminta* said: "la plus grande part de ceux qui portent le teston à l'Hôtel de Bourgogne veulent que l'on contente leurs yeux par la diversité et changement de la face du théâtre[2]." And it is interesting to see that the conflict between the desire for conformity and propriety and the desire for variety was thus early recognized, for it was this conflict that was to be felt as the result of French influence in the English post-Restoration theatre.

The first half of the seventeenth century saw in England as elsewhere a great increase in the number and popularity of theatres. This fact is clear from Professor Adams's list of London playhouses, which shows eight new public theatres to have been erected between 1600 and 1629[3]. The building of a new court theatre, the Cockpit-in-Court, he assigns to 1632 or 1633. Be-

[1] Spingarn, *op. cit.* pp. 209, 210.

[2] Lancaster, *op. cit.* p. 42. An article also by Professor Lancaster, "The Three Unities of French Classical Drama," in the *Publications of the Modern Language Association*, vol. XVI, pp. 307–15, proves that in 1630 "the three unities had become sufficiently strong in France to elicit the explanations of their opponents, even when they were unable to overcome the expression of their hostility."

[3] Cf. Adams, *Shakespearean Playhouses*, frontispiece showing map of London and list of playhouses.

cause the history of this court theatre throws the light of important facts upon the whole question of theatrical architecture during this period, it may be well to review the knowledge that now is in the possession of students in regard to this matter.

Though the question of the possible attendance of royalty upon individual performances in the public playhouses has been from time to time contested by scholars, it is generally conceded that royal visits to the playhouses were not established as a custom until after the Restoration. Masques and plays were presented before the court in the great hall of the palace where the ruler was then in residence or in a specially built banqueting-hall or masking-house[1]. Contemporary references to performances in the Cockpit used to be considered as referring to the Cockpit or Phoenix playhouse, and any obvious inconsistencies were explained away. Then came new discoveries which seemed to have an important bearing upon the question of the royal interest in dramatic performances.

In 1913 Mr Hamilton Wright Bell published an account of his discovery, among the drawings of Inigo Jones and John Webb now in the Worcester College library, of plans for a small theatre of octagonal shape, with a stage into which five "prospects" opened. The stage projected five feet beyond the proscenium wall, was four and a half feet above the level of the pit, and was surrounded by a low railing eighteen inches high. As distinguishing features Mr Bell noted a permanent arched proscenium, a classic façade, and pedestals flanking the central doors. Such a theatre whenever built and whether built by Jones or not certainly reveals the typical neo-Vitruvian characteristics[2] and

[1] Cf. Reyher, *op. cit.* pp. 332–48; Adams, *Shakespearean Playhouses*, pp. 384–91.

[2] Hamilton Bell, "Contributions to the History of the English Playhouse," in the *Architectural Record*, vol. xxxiii, pp. 263 *sq.*

is distinctly reminiscent of the Olympic Theatre of Palladio.

In 1917 Professor Adams, on the basis of a representation of the court Cockpit in John Fisher's Survey of Whitehall made between 1660 and 1670, identified this theatre as the court theatre, the Cockpit-in-Court, which he thinks was erected about 1632 or 1633. In this connection Professor Adams proved that

at times throughout the reign of James dramatic performances were given in the Cockpit; but the auditorium was small, and the performances must have been of a semi-private nature. The important Court performances, to which many guests were invited, were held in the Great Hall[1].

However, Professor Adams thinks a new theatre must have been erected to be used solely as a playhouse, and not as an amphitheatre. "A speech spoken to their two excellent Majesties, at the first Play play'd by the Queenes Servants, in the new Theater at Whitehall," written by Thomas Heywood and published in 1637, furnishes the chief evidence as to the date of this theatre[2]. I quote this speech here since not only its date is of interest but also its content, for it gives assurance of the interest felt in ancient theatres and in theatres as serving the royal pleasure:

When *Greece*, the chiefe priority might claime
For Arts, and Armes, and held the eminent name
Of Monarchie; They erected divers places,
Some to the Muses, others to the Graces.
Where Actors strove, and Poets did devise
With tongue and pen, to please the eares and eyes
Of Princely Auditors; The time was, when
To heare, the rapture of one Poets pen,
A Theater hath beene built, By the fates doome,
When the Empire was removed from thence to *Rome*

[1] Adams, *Shakespearean Playhouses*, pp. 392, 393.
[2] *Ibid.* pp. 391–400.

The potent *Caesars* had their *Circi*, and
Large Amphitheaters: in which might stand
And sit, full fourscore thousand, all in view,
And touch of voice: this great Augustus knew.
Nay *Rome*, its wealth, and potency injoy'd,
Till by the barbarous Gothes these were destroy'd.
But may this structure last, and you be seene
Here a spectator with your Princely Queene,
In your old age as in your flourishing prime,
To out-strip *Augustus* both in fame and time[1].

The whole question of a royal theatre and of the identity of this drawing discovered by Mr Bell is, however, complicated, it seems to me, by Mr William Grant Keith's discovery in 1917 of another drawing of a theatre by Inigo Jones[2]. Mr Keith, it may be said, fails to find any indication of Jones's work in the drawing of which Mr Bell wrote his account and thinks it rather to have been the work of John Webb.

The theatre plan discovered by Mr Keith is inserted in Jones's copy of Palladio, which seems to have been owned by him as early as 1601. The theatre plan is much like that of Serlio as far as the stage is concerned, though it seems to have resulted from experiments in modifying the plans of the Teatro Olympico at Vicenza. A single arched opening, placed several feet back on the stage, leads to the rear stage. A marginal note indicates that Jones desired to make this opening still greater. Along with the drawing of the theatre is sketched an "elevation of a scena, having a central arched opening in which a set of scenery is represented in position in a street scene sketched in perspective." "The plan of the rear stage," Mr Keith comments, "terminating as it does with the second pair of side

---

[1] Heywood, *Dramatic Works*, vol. VI, p. 339.
[2] W. G. Keith, "A Theatre Project," in the *Burlington Magazine*, vol. XXI, pp. 61 *sq*., 105 *sq*.

PLATE V

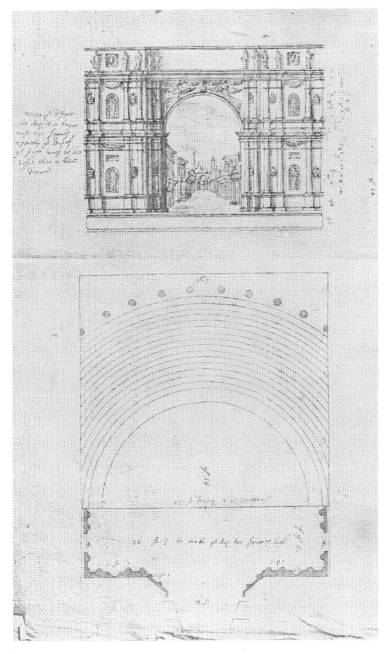

THEATRE PLAN DISCOVERED BY W. G. KEITH IN INIGO JONES'S
COPY OF PALLADIO
Reproduced with the kind permission of Mr W. G. Keith and the
Burlington Magazine

scenes, makes it difficult to arrive at the precise type of scenic arrangement intended," but he adds that the scenes, being of the angle-shaped kind, tend to prove the theatre of early origin. Taking into consideration all the evidence, Mr Keith concludes that this theatre was the work of Inigo Jones soon after he returned from Italy to his work as Surveyor. It is, of course, quite possible that the project for such a theatre would have been of interest to both architect and court at that period. But Mr Keith's most interesting conclusion, a conclusion dependent on fixing an early date for the drawing, is that Jones, who was evidently interested particularly in the stage of his theatre, evolved for himself the idea of the single-arched proscenium, with its consequent advantaging of scenic effects, and that he worked independently and with no knowledge of the Teatro Farnese at Parma, which was not finished till 1618 or 1619.

It is at once evident that whether or not this theatre plan discovered by Mr Keith was ever put into execution, it represents a type of theatre in advance of the Cockpit plan identified by Professor Adams in that it provides for scenery back of the central arched opening. Furthermore, it directly precedes in its characteristic structure the post-Restoration theatres of Christopher Wren.

The puzzle as to the date and sequence of these drawings must remain unsolved until someone who has the opportunity to study again the original drawings of Jones and Webb can offer a solution. But it is of the greatest significance that among these drawings are plans for two theatres which show unmistakably the influence of the same forces that were determining the structure of the Continental theatres. It comes to seem highly improbable that while the master surveyor and his assistant were designing theatres of the neo-classical sort, the public theatres should have been built of entirely different and independent design. Furthermore, it is to be considered that the Surveyor of the King's Works would in all probability have had some part in the construction of the public theatres. It is only necessary to recall the work of Wren and Vanbrugh to be assured of the participation of the office in similar undertakings.

That the spectacular representation of the drama was coming to be considered as possible in the public theatres as well as at court is indicated in many ways. Mr W. J. Lawrence in his "The Origin of the English Picture-Stage," dates the certain presentation of plays with movable scenes from the period 1637 to 1640[1]. But it must be noted that in every case in which we are certain that plays were presented with movable scenes, they were shown at Blackfriars, the Phoenix (or Cockpit), or Salisbury Court. Of these three theatres we know from Wright's *Historia Histrionica*, that they were called private houses, and that "they were all three built almost exactly alike for form and bigness." They were rectangular theatres, and the stages must have been such as admitted of the use of movable scenes even though they were not built primarily for such exhibitions.

It will be recalled that the whole history of the sixteenth century theatre in Italy reveals the development of theatre structure along two lines. On the one hand, the description of the Greek and Roman theatres by Vitruvius and other classical authorities gave rise to the Palladian theatre, to the type of theatre exemplified at Vicenza. It was essentially a non-scenic theatre, and even when scenery was added, it could be added only as Barbaro and other commentators of the period added the *periaktoi* to their classical theatres, introducing them immediately behind the stage entrances. In similar

[1] *Elizabethan Playhouse*, Second Series, pp. 120–47.

fashion Scamozzi introduced the scenic runways or per-spectives back of the stage entrances, but he made these additions to the theatre on the occasion of a royal visit.

On the other hand, the necessity for adapting the Vitruvian theatre to the space provided for court enter-tainments, together with emphasis on the Vitruvian suggestions for the spectacular representation of the drama that seemed fitting for courtly performances, re-sulted in the theatre of Serlio, a rectangular theatre with a stage adapted to the exhibition of perspective scenery.

In the theatre at Parma these two types of theatre were fused into one. But that they were both interesting for some reason or other to Inigo Jones and his as-sistant, John Webb, is proved by the existence of the two plans discovered by Mr Bell and Mr Keith re-spectively. That both types of theatre were represented in the English theatres of the period is, therefore, at least a plausible theory, and it is possible that the dis-tinction always made between the public theatres and the private theatres rested on this fundamental differ-ence in type. But such theories can only be proved or disproved by a careful review of the dramas acted be-tween 1576 and 1640 on the basis of the particular theatres in which they were acted. The significance given to the use of the various stage entrances by both Vitruvius and Pollux must be taken into account in determining whether or no the two types of stage could and did persist together[1]. But such a study is not possible here, and no decision is therefore to be reached.

That the English theatre was, however, showing the same signs of architectural progress that were revealed

[1] Nabbes's *Covent Garden* (1632) in its very classical administration of the middle, left, and right "scoenes" or entrances makes certain the fact that there was a desire to experiment with the classical method. Thorndike, *op. cit.* p. 129, comments on this play but does not consider the experiment of much significance.

on the Continent appears certain. As far as the question of the prevalence of scenery on the public stage before the Restoration is concerned, there seems to be little advantage to be gained from a discussion of facts already well known to every student of the English stage[1]. Yet certain points not usually emphasized seem worthy of stress. The foreigners who visited the English theatres in the late sixteenth and early seventeenth centuries made no comment as to differences in structure between English and Continental theatres. On the other hand, the De Witt account of the London theatres about 1596 specifically called the four theatres *amphitheatra*, and singling out the Swan as the most noteworthy, commented that "its form seems to approach that of a Roman structure[2]." That classical features

[1] Cf. above, "Introduction," for a list of recent contributions to the discussion of the subject. Of particular importance in showing the growing tendency to spectacular representations of the drama in the public theatres through the influence of court representations is Graves, *The Court and the London Theatres during the Reign of Elizabeth.* However, Mr Graves fails to make certain distinctions which seem to me essential. The discussion of the use of the word *scene* (pp. 15, 16) assumes that Florio and Palsgrave were describing the contemporary stage, whereas their definitions bear distinct indications of being derived from a common original, the definition given by Cassiodorus beginning "Frons autem theatri scena dicitur" (cf. above, p. 125, note); this definition was accepted on the authority of Cassiodorus throughout the period under consideration. Mr Graves also includes in his discussion of theatres during the reign of Elizabeth a considerable body of evidence dealing with the theatres during the reigns of James and Charles. Further, he does not make distinctions between the "public" and the "private" houses. And finally, he does not consider the Renaissance theory of dramatic representation in its inevitable influence on theatre building. The consideration of these points seems to me necessary to the just estimate of the influences that contributed to the theatre of the sixteenth and seventeenth centuries and to its constant growth and change.

[2] Cf. H. B. Wheatley, "On a Contemporary Drawing of the Swan Theater, 1596," in the *Transactions of the New Shakespeare Society,* 1887–92, Part II, pp. 215 *sq.*

were being stressed in those playhouses is indicated also by the constant emphasis on the types of columns pro-vided[1], for it was the "five orders" that particularly interested the architects of the period.

As to the permanent decorations of the stages of the theatres other than that furnished by columns, we know that they were painted in some fashion. The Fortune contract stipulated "that the said Peeter Streete shall not be chardged wth anie manner of pay(ntin)ge in or aboute the said fframe howse or Stadge or anie p^te thereof[2]," and descriptive phrases such as Gabriel Harvey's reference to the "painted stage" are often quoted. Furthermore Coryat, visiting Venice in 1611, wrote:

I visited one of their Play-houses where I saw a Comodie acted[3]. The house is very beggarly and base in comparison of our stately Play-houses in England: neither can their Actors compare with vs for apparell, shewes, and musick[4].

That certain structures and properties were long used on the public stage has been proved by the scholars to whose work I have so many times referred in these pages; that movable scenes were used in the private playhouses occasionally is proved by the undisputed instances of *Microcosmos*, *Aglaura*, and *Cleodora, Queen*

---

[1] Cf. *Henslowe Papers* (ed. W. W. Greg, 1907), p. 6, for stipulation in the Fortune contract that "all the princypall and maine postes of the said fframe and Stadge forwarde shalbe square and wrought palasterwise wth carved proporcōns called Setiers to be placed & sett on the Topp of every of the same postes"; and p. 20, for the agreement in rebuilding the Bear Garden (the Hope) "to make Turned Cullumes vppon and over the stage." See also Adams, *Shakespearean Playhouses*, pp. 246, 247.

[2] Cf. *Henslowe Papers*, p. 6.

[3] Coryat, *op. cit.* vol. II, pp. 16, 17.

[4] For additional information, cf. Graves, *op. cit.* pp. 68–70. Mr Graves does not quote the phrase in Coryat's description that seems to me most significant, "apparell, shewes, and musick," since *shewes* was regularly used for scenic representations.

of Arragon. That the possibility of using scenes in these playhouses was accepted in 1636 seems the inevitable conclusion from the request of the chancellor that the Oxford "stage" for *The Royal Slave* be not allowed to come into the possession of the common players. Thus the period fixed by Mr Lawrence for the certain introduction of movable scenes on the public stage, 1637–40, is, as he intended it, most conservative.

Mr Lawrence points out the fact that the civil wars and political struggles in England were responsible for the twenty years' delay that have made the historians of the English stage generally accept the backwardness of the English stage as an established fact. Yet, as he points out, such an assumption is assuredly disproved by the royal patent granted to Davenant March 26, 1639, to erect "a Theatre or Playhouse, with necessary tiring and retiring rooms, and other places convenient, …wherein plays, musical entertainments, scenes, or other like presentments may be presented." It was permitted "from time to time to act plays in such house so to be by him or them erected; and exercise music, musical presentments, scenes, dancing, or other the like," and it was declared lawful

to and for the said William Davenant, his heirs, executors, administrators, and assigns, to take and receive of such our subjects as shall resort to see or hear any such plays, scenes, and entertainments whatsoever, such sum or sums of money as is, are, or hereafter from time to time shall be accustomed to be given or taken in other playhouses and places for the like plays, scenes, presentments, and entertainments.

Mr Lawrence has stressed the fact that Davenant undoubtedly proposed under this patent to perform in the new house not only opera, but concerts as well.

However this may be, Davenant was forced in some way to relinquish his immediate rights under this patent, which he did in an indenture of October 2, 1639. That he did not renounce his rights altogether is proved by the fact that he again claimed these privileges after the Restoration[1].

The full significance of Davenant's proposed undertaking is perceived only when we recall that it was in 1637 that the opera in Venice, the Teatro di San Cassiano, was built with its movable scenes, and that it was in 1639 that Richelieu's theatre gave opportunity for great spectacular representations in France, while it was not until 1645 that Cardinal Mazarin introduced the first Italian opera into France[2].

The English stage was, therefore, keeping pace with the times when the political disturbances caused an interruption of nearly twenty years in the natural progress of theatrical events.

As for "machines" there was no question of their being adopted in the regular theatre at this time, for they were apparently accepted from the beginning in the theatres of England. However, they seem to have become during this period increasingly popular. It was not a period which brought to England any new body of critical doctrine affecting the representation of the drama. Instead it brought experiments which resulted in a more or less adequate technique in stage engineering as well as stage architecture. The public delight in spectacle and the means of ministering to that delight by the perfection of movable scenes and machines seem to have advanced together. Heywood's "Prologue to

[1] For a full account of the documents involved, cf. Adams, *Shakespearean Playhouses*, pp. 424–31. Cf. also Lawrence, *Elizabethan Playhouse*, Second Series, pp. 121–8, particularly the comment on the use of the word *opera* (p. 127 note).

[2] Cf. above, p. 198. The introduction of spectacle in the theatre in Richelieu's palace in 1630 is, of course, not to be forgotten, nor the prominence of the ballet before the introduction of Italian opera.

the Stage," printed with *The Royal King and the Loyal Subject* in 1637, probably told the exact truth:

To give content to this most curious Age,
The gods themselves we have brought downe to the Stage,
And figur'd them on Planets; made even Hell
Deliver up the Furies, by no spell,
(Saving the *Muses* rapture) further, we
Have traffickt by their helpe; no History
We have left unrifled, our Pens have been dipt
As well in opening each hid Manuscript,
As Tracts more vulgar, whether read, or sung
In our domesticke, or more forraigne Tongue:
Of Fairy Elves, Nymphes of the Sea, and Land;
The Lawnes and Groves, no number can be scan'd
Which we have not given feet to[1]....

Machines for the gods, machines for the furies and for the ghosts necessary to the tragedy of the time, thunder and lightning—all were more frequently used. Stage decencies were observed with as much show of blood as was possible by the use of "discoveries," which became increasingly popular. Repetition of instances illustrating the use of these devices is without value, for they are so frequent as to be accepted as a matter of course by all students of the stage.

The *exostra* also was becoming more familiar to the theatre-going public, as stage directions clearly show; yet its use has not been conceded by scholars in general. However, unless the words of the texts be specifically denied, it seems impossible to ignore the distinctions there made between stage directions clearly instructing that the curtains be drawn or the scene opened to reveal an interior scene and stage directions such as "Syllana drawn out upon a Bed as sleeping"; "Enter Violante in a Bed; Angelina and Dorothea sitting by her";

[1] Heywood, *Dramatic Works*, vol. VI, B 2.

"A Bed thrust out, the Palsgrave lying sicke on it"; "Enter the Admiral in his Bed"; "Enter Giovanni and Annabella lying on a bed[1]."

Indications are not wanting, however, that the conservative and rule-loving critics were commencing to express that scorn of popular delight in spectacle which it has always been the fashion of critics to decry.

Among the commendatory verses printed with Davenant's *The Just Italian* in 1630 was a poem by William Hopkins entitled "To my Friend M. D'Avenant, on his legitimate Poeme," which reviled the unappreciative public thus:

> Hence, giddy fooles; run to the noyse they make
> At *Paris*-garden; or your selues betake
> To the new Motion, the fine Puppet playes,
> And there adore. Commend the learned layes
> That make a din about the streets, or els
> Extoll the Iewes-trumpe, or the morris bells.
> There, your great heads may manage. Only let
> The wiser few, (whose blessed eares haue met
> The harmony that all the Muses make,
> And from those heauenly sounds assurance take,
> That thou sing'st the same tunes) admitted be
> To thy Seraphyck musicke, and set free
> To entertayne their soules in that high quire
> Which, not weak fooles, but such as Know, admire.

---

[1] Cf. *op. cit.* p. 57, where the use of the *eccyclema* is explicitly denied. Cf. however, R. Wegener, *Die Bühneneinrichtung des Shakespeareschen Theaters* (1902), p. 58, where a limited use of a "podium" on wheels is suggested. The stage directions instanced are taken from Richard's *Messalina* (1637–9), II; *Four Plays in One* (1647), *Triumph of Love*, IV, quoted by Thorndike, *Shakespeare's Theatre*, p. 437; *Hector of Germany* (c. 1613), I, i, Thorndike, p. 437; *Massacre at Paris* (n.d.), I, v, Thorndike, p. 440; *'Tis Pity She's a Whore* (1633), V, v, Thorndike, p. 443.

Similarly Thomas Carew wrote of this same play and the multitude that damned it:

> But thy strong fancies (raptures of the brayne,
> Drest in Poetique flames) they entertayne
> As a bold, impious reach; for they'l still slight
> All that exceeds Red Bull, and Cockpit flight.

And more explicitly defining the vulgarities that attracted the multitude, Jasper Mayne in *Jonson Viribus*, published in 1638, wrote "To the Memory of Ben Jonson" these words:

> Thy scene was free from monsters; no hard plot
> Call'd down a God t'untie th'unlikely knot:
> The stage was still a stage, two entrances
> Were not two parts o' the world, disjoin'd by seas.
> Thine were land-tragedies, no prince was found
> To swim a whole scene out, then o' the stage drown'd;
> Pitch'd fields, as Red-Bull wars, still felt thy doom;
> Thou laid'st no sieges to the music room[1].

It thus becomes apparent that the English public as well as the French was willing to barter correctness for interest, conformity for variety. But it must not be forgotten that the means for satisfying this taste of the vulgar public made manifest by its demands for spectacle in the public theatres had been evolved for the court by the most learned scientists and artists of the day.

[1] Printed in Jonson, *Works*, vol. IX, pp. 452, 453.

PART IV

STAGE DECORATION IN ENGLAND
AFTER THE RESTORATION

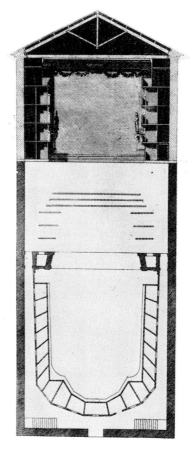

Celebre Teatro di Fano Architettura del Torelli Fano ec.

Scala di Palmi Romani

5 10 20 30 40 50 60 70 80 90 100

FIG. 12. THE TEATRO DI FANO OF TORELLI

From the *Pianta e Spaccato del Nuovo Teatro d'Imola*,
Architettura del Cavalier Cosimo Morelli, 1780

CHAPTER XIV

THE INCORPORATION OF SCENES IN
THE PUBLIC THEATRES

IN order to understand succeeding events in the English theatre it is necessary to consider the ideas of the function and characteristics of opera which prevailed during the middle years of the seventeenth century. As we have seen, the popularity of opera was growing by steps that were clearly marked: the first public opera-house built in Venice in 1637, a new theatre in which opera could be offered to the public proposed by Davenant in 1639, Italian opera introduced in France in 1645. Furthermore the progress of opera represented the progress of spectacle on the public stage. Evelyn, writing in 1644, explained the meaning of the word *opera*[1]; in 1645 he wrote more explicitly:

> This night...we went to the opera, where comedies and other plays are represented in recitative musiq by the most excellent musicians, vocal and instrumental, with variety of sceanes painted and contrived with no less art of perspective, and machines for flying in the air, and other wonderful motions; taken together it is one of the most magnificent and expensive diversions the wit of man can invent[2].

Likewise Sir John Reresby, writing of his travels in Italy during 1656 and 1657, described the events of the carnival season in Venice and noted particularly the "operas, which are usually tragedies, sung in music, and much advantaged by variety of scenes and machines[3]."

[1] See above, p. 197.   [2] See above, *ibid.*
[3] *Memoirs and Travels of Sir John Reresby, Bart.* (ed. by A. Ivatt, 1904), p. 58.

Of the beginnings of opera in England Dryden wrote in his essay *Of Heroic Plays*:

For heroic plays...the first light we had of them, on the English theatre, was from the late Sir William Davenant. It being forbidden him in those rebellious times to act tragedies and comedies, because they contained some matter of scandal to those good people, who could more easily dispossess their lawful sovereign than endure a wanton jest, he was forced to turn his thoughts another way, and to introduce the examples of moral virtue, writ in verse, and performed in recitative music. The original of this music, and of the scenes which adorned his work, he had from the Italian operas; but he heightened his characters, as I may probably imagine, from the example of Corneille and some French poets. In this condition did this part of poetry remain at his Majesty's return; when, growing bolder, as being now owned by a public authority, he revived his "Siege of Rhodes," and caused it to be acted as a just drama[1].

As a chronicle of events this record is valuable, but as an explanation of motives it is obviously inadequate, for the idea of producing opera was not a new one adopted by Davenant because of the exigencies of the times, but was rather one, as Mr Lawrence has pointed out, to which he held persistently from 1639 onward[2]. Furthermore opera demanded as essential conditions of its representation changing scenes, machines, and music. These Davenant proposed to give to the public in a great theatrical and financial adventure.

[1] *The Works of John Dryden* (Scott-Saintsbury ed., 1892), vol. IV, pp. 19, 20. Cf. also Aubrey, *Brief Lives*, art. on "Sir William Davenant."

[2] Cf. W. J. Lawrence, "The Origin of the English Picture-Stage," in *The Elizabethan Playhouse*, Second Series, pp. 121 *sq.* Dryden's explanation is the one accepted, however, by Professor Odell, who says (G. C. D. Odell, *Shakespeare from Betterton to Irving* (1920), vol. I, p. 6): "But Sir William Davenant, in 1656, by some exercise of influence, and especially by change of name from *play*, to *entertainment*, and *opera*, managed for a short time to regularise, more or less, performances on the public stage."

The remarkable fact about English theatrical history is its continuity, for in spite of the interruption of the years of exile and imprisonment which had been the fate of the Royalists, the drifting of the exiles back to England in the late years of the Commonwealth brought the revival of the same plans for theatrical progress that had seemingly been obliterated by war and Puritanism. In 1656 Davenant received permission in some way for the presentation of an opera[1]. As a matter of fact, this opera resolved itself into what was advertised on the bills as an "Entertainment at Rutland House, by Declamation and Musick: after the Manner of the Ancients." This entertainment was patterned after the entertainments by which the royal family was wont to be entertained at the houses of the nobility and in the royal palaces until the popularity of the more luxurious masque had caused it gradually to be superseded. This particular entertainment consisted of a prologue, two "declamations" in the nature of debates, and an epilogue, with music duly interspersed throughout[2].

That this entertainment was but one step toward the accomplishment of Davenant's original plan of producing opera is definitely indicated by the prologue, which thus reassured the audience:

Think this your passage, and the narrow way
To our Elisian Field, the OPERA:
Tow'rds which some say we have gone far about
Because it seemes so long since we set out.
Think now the way grown short, and that you light
At this small Inn, to bait, not stay all night.

[1] Cf. J. W. Tupper, *Introduction* to edition of *Love and Honour* and *The Siege of Rhodes* (1909), p. xxxviii, for account of record found in *Calendar of State Papers*, June, 1656.

[2] The text used is that in *The Works of S*^r *William Davenant*, printed for Henry Herringman in 1673. Cf. pp. 341 *sq*.

The first declamation or dialogue was "between Diogenes the Cynick, and Aristophanes the Poet, in Habits agreeable to their Country and Professions: who Declaim Against, and For Publik Entertainment by Morall Representation." Diogenes argued against assemblies "such as meet for recreation," and against heroic representations, music, scenes, and poetry, which were considered as the constituent elements of opera. But of particular interest in this study was his protest against scenes:

Would you meet to be delighted with Scaenes? which is, to be entertain'd with the deception of motion, and transposition of Lights; where, whilst you think you see a great Battel, you are sure to get nothing by the Victory. You gaze on imaginary Woods and Meadows, where you can neither fell nor mowe. On Seas, where you have no Ships, and on Rivers, where you catch no Fish.

Aristophanes replied, justifying "such as meet for recreation by Moral Representations," and in particular defending the use of scenes:

Is it not the fastest and shortest way to understanding, when you are brought to see vast Seas and Provinces, Fleets, Armies, and Forts, without the hazards of a Voyage, or pain of a long march?

The second declamation was between a Londoner and a Parisian concerning the comparative excellence of the two cities, and it is without special significance here.

Davenant, having in this *Entertainment* prepared the way for the next step in the execution of his design, did at last present an opera, *The Siege of Rhodes*, "made a representation by the art of prospective in scenes and the story sung in recitative musick[1]." So much of im-

---

[1] The text is that given by Professor Tupper. The preface "To the Reader" is found only in the texts of 1656 and 1659. The text of *The Siege of Rhodes* has been established by Professor Tupper on the basis of the 1663 edition, with which he has collated the other early editions.

portance is contained in the address "To the Reader"
prefixed to the edition of 1656 that I quote the pertinent passages at length:

I may receive disadvantage by this address design'd for excuses;
for it will too hastily put you in mind that errors are not far
off when excuses are at hand; this refers to our representation:
and some may be willing to be led to find the blemishes for it;
but would be left to their own conduct to discover the beauties,
if there be any. Yet I may forewarn you that the defects which
I intend to excuse are chiefly such as you cannot reform but
onely with your purse; that is, by building us a larger room; a
design which we began and shall not be left for you to finish,
because we have observ'd that many who are liberall of their
understanding when they would issue it out towards discovery
of imperfections, have not alwayes money to expend in things
necessary towards the making up of perfection.

It has been often wisht that our scenes (we having oblig'd
our selves to the variety of five changes, according to the ancient
dramatick distinctions made for time) had not been confin'd
to eleven foot in height, and about fifteen in depth, including
the places of passage reserv'd for the musick. This is so narrow
an allowance for the fleet of *Solyman* the Magnificent, his army,
the Island of *Rhodes*, and the varieties attending the siege of the
city, that I fear you will think we invite you to such a contracted
trifle as that of the Caesars carved upon a nut.

As these limits here have hinder'd the splendor of our scene,
so we are like to give no great satisfaction to the quantity of our
argument, which is in story very copious; but shrinks to a small
narrative here, because we could not convey it by more than
seven persons; being constrain'd to prevent the length of *recitative* musick, as well as to conserve, without incumbrance, the
narrowness of the place....

*   *   *   *   *   *

We conceive, it will not be unacceptable to you if we recom-
pence the narrowness of the room, by containing in it so much
as could be conveniently accomplisht by art and industry: which

wil not be doubted in the scenes by those who can judg that kind of illustration & know the excellency of Mr. *John Web*, who design'd and order'd it....

Thus Davenant reaffirmed his purpose of carrying to completion his original project for building a theatre suited to the exhibition of operatic spectacle. That the financial risks involved in such an undertaking were temporarily deterring him is evident.

But the apologetic words of the address are valuable otherwise than as a record of Davenant's plans, for they set forth certain ideals of scenic representation of the drama as they were then conceived. Five changes of scene were proffered and were explained on the basis of "the ancient dramatick distinctions made for time[1]." The later working out of this rule which permitted changes of scene between acts and not elsewhere found its justification not only in such extension of classical authority but also in the fact that scenes could be shifted with less disturbance at this time. But in spite of his explanation of the rule Davenant did not himself observe it with any strictness, for the scenes were made to appear more than once, and ten variations of scene are indicated in the course of the play.

That Davenant did not regard the scene as providing a place for the action is also shown in this preliminary address. Instead he referred to the scenes the excellence of which could be recognized by those "who can judg that kind of illustration." Professor Tupper in the authoritative *Introduction* to his edition of *Love and Honour* and *The Siege of Rhodes* discusses the function of the scenery in these early operas and points out the fact of its essential inconsistency as setting for action.

[1] The prologue to Nabbes's *Hannibal and Scipio* of 1635 explained:
> The places sometimes chang'd too for the Scene,
> Which is translated as the musicke playes,
> Betwixt the acts.

For instance, the first scene of *The Siege of Rhodes* includes a prospect of the city of Rhodes and its surroundings while the action takes place within the city. Professor Tupper adds that the scenery "is indeed an extension of the old method of indicating the place by posting its name over a door." Such an inference does not, however, seem to me to follow from the fact of the decorative and illustrative function of the scenery. But rather that it was added as decoration because decoration was an essential part of opera seems an inevitable conclusion in the light of Davenant's previous plans. Furthermore Davenant evidently believed that the popular interest in perspective was roused to the paying point, and his announcements of performances made their appeal to the public accordingly.

As we have seen, it was to John Webb that Davenant gave credit for the scenes which adorned his opera, and in two articles on "The Designs for the First Movable Scenery on the English Public Stage," published in the *Burlington Magazine* for 1914[1], Mr W. G. Keith has pointed out the significance of this fact. Moreover Mr Keith has identified among the drawings of Jones and Webb now at Chatsworth certain sketches for the scenes of *The Siege of Rhodes*, and he has discovered also two drawings among the Lansdowne MSS (no. 1171) which he believes represent the plan and section of the stage at Rutland House. We, therefore, have definite knowledge of this most important transition stage.

The stage lay, like that of *Salmacida Spolia*, entirely back of the proscenium by which it was framed. Like that of the stages for the late masques, too, the "Ornament which encompass'd the scene" made use of symbolic decorations, added a rich drapery, and included the title of the play in a central "compartiment."

---

[1] *Burlington Magazine*, vol. xxv, pp. 29 *sq.*, 85 *sq.*

Mr Keith describes the stage floor as "divided into two equal parts at the first line of the back shutters, the back part of the floor being sunk 4 inches below the level of the forepart." The side scenes were single flats fixed in place and hence remaining unchanged throughout the performance, while the back shutters were varied according to the demands of the action. When

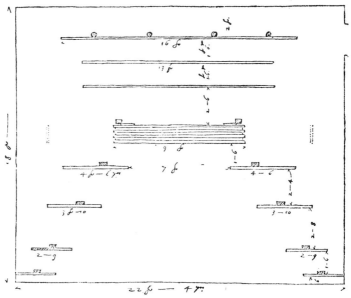

FIG. 13. JOHN WEBB'S PLAN OF THE RUTLAND HOUSE STAGE FOR "THE SIEGE OF RHODES." Reproduced with the kind permission of Mr W. G. Keith and the *Burlington Magazine*

the back shutters were drawn off, the "releive" scenes were visible on the back stage, while at the utmost limit of the stage was the back cloth. The side scenes receded at an angle of fifty degrees with the front line of the stage floor. The upper part of the stage was furnished with scenes suspended from the ceiling, these upper scenes matching those below. Such was the stage which in all its essentials carried over the characteristics of the stage of the court plays and masques of Charles I to the post-Restoration theatre.

The fact that Webb was chosen to design the scenery sufficiently proves the continuity of theatrical spectacle, for as Inigo Jones's assistant Webb had been in some part responsible for the scenery for the masques and plays at court before the wars, and as Inigo Jones's

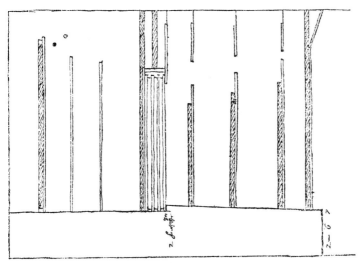

FIG. 14. SECTION OF RUTLAND HOUSE STAGE, SHOWING BACK AND FRONT STAGE. Reproduced with the kind permission of Mr W. G. Keith and the *Burlington Magazine*

heir he had inherited his plans and possessions. That he expected to fall heir also to Inigo Jones's place as Surveyor is indicated in a record preserved as "A Briefe of Mr. Webbs case." This brief cites as arguments in the case:

That he was brought up by his Unckle Mr. Inigo Jones upon his late Majestyes comand in the study of Architecture, as well that wch relates to building as for Masques Tryumphs and the like. That he was Mr. Jones Deputy and in actuall possession of the office upon his leaving London, and attended his Matie in that Capacity at Hampton Court and in ye Isle of Wight, when he received his Maties comand to designe a Pallace for Whitehal, wch he did untill his Maties unfortunate calamity caused him to desist[1].

It is quite possible that Davenant was, with Webb, expecting the appointment of Webb to the Surveyorship; but such expectations were doomed to disappointment, for Sir John Denham was ultimately made Surveyor, though Webb worked as his assistant and was given the reversion of the office. It was Webb and Davenant, however, who, working together, executed in the time of Charles II plans formulated in the time of Charles I, and it is due to them that the history of the theatre in England is continuous.

The perfect fulfilment of the plans so long maturing could not be hoped for until the time when there should be built a new opera-house or theatre admitting the use of elaborate spectacle. *The Siege of Rhodes* stopped short of being a complete success as opera, for the narrow stage prohibited the use of machines and limited the changes of scene to the back shutters. But one step led to another, and the next step was always eagerly anticipated by Davenant.

In 1658 Davenant undertook new ventures at the Cockpit in Drury Lane. There he produced a new opera, the theme of which was probably intended to allay any smouldering desire for repression which Cromwellian officers might feel toward the theatre. It was offered as

The Cruelty of the Spaniards in Peru; exprest by Instrumentall and Vocall Musick, and by the Art of Perspective in

[1] Quoted in J. A. Gotch, "The Original Drawings for the Palace at Whitehall, Attributed to Inigo Jones," in the London *Architectural Review*, vol. xxxi, p. 358, from *State Papers*, Domestic, Charles II, vol. v, p. 74.

Scenes, etc. Represented daily at the Cockpit in Drury Lane, at three afternoon punctually.

A note was appended to the effect that,

Notwithstanding the great expense necessary to scenes, and other ornaments in the entertainment, there is good provision of places made for a shilling. And it shall begin certainly at three afternoon[1].

In this opera, also, the scenery was regarded as illustrative, but the piece itself was narrative rather than dramatic in form. An interesting attempt at local colour is, however, to be noted in the scenery, from the Peruvian landscape, "a Lantdchap of the West-Indies," to the Spanish prison with its pictured tortures, which included an Indian prince being roasted at an "artificial fire" and basted by his Spanish conqueror. The general arrangement of the stage must have been similar to that of *The Siege of Rhodes*, the side flats continuing while the back shutters changed, for in the second entry while the sea and fleet are shown, two Indians enter "severally from the opposite side of the Wood, and gazing on the face of the *Scene*, fall into a Mimick Dance, in which they express the Argument of the Prospect by their admiration at the sight of the Ships."

The History of the Spaniards in Peru was followed by

The History of Sir Francis Drake: exprest by Instrumentall and Vocall Musick, and by the Art of Perspective in Scenes. The first part. Represented daily at the Cockpit in Drury Lane at Three afternoon punctually.

---

[1] The text of the operas which I have used is that in the 1673 edition of collected works (cf. p. 219, note 2). The title-pages of the original editions are given in the Maidment-Logan edition (Dramatists of the Restoration). The operas are published as parts of *The Playhouse to be Let*, where they are arranged in an order the reverse of that in which they originally appeared. Cf. 1673 ed. of *Works*, where they are found with *The Siege of Rhodes*, pp. 67–119, 1672 ed.

The stage arrangement for this opera remained essentially the same as that of previous productions, but the scenery became to a certain extent the setting for the action, and there was evident a more pronounced effort to reproduce the New World scenes with fidelity. Thus the first entry is distinguished by a scene in which

a Harbour is discern'd, (which was first discover'd by Sir Francis Drake, and called by him Port-pheasant) where two Ships are Moor'd, and Sea-Carpenters are erecting a Pinnace, whilst others are felling Trees to build a Fort. The narrowness of the entrance to the Harbour may be observ'd, with Rocks on either side, and out at Sea a Ship towing a Prize. And likewise, on the top of a high Tree, a Marriner making his Ken. This prospect is made through a Wood, differing from those of European Climats, by representing of Coco-Trees, Pines, and Palmitos. And on the Boughs of other Trees are seen Munkies, Apes, and Parrots.

Yet realism is not carried to excess, for the mariner here painted in his tree-top is addressed, and he replies from within.

In the fifth entry a "discovery" takes place after the fashion of the later plays. Rouse has entered and told to Drake the sad tale of an interrupted wedding and a stolen bride. As he bids him turn to behold the unhappy vision,

The Scene is suddenly changed to the former prospect of the rising of the Morning, and Venta Cruz; but about the Middle, it is vary'd with the discov'ry of a Beautiful Lady ty'd to a Tree, adorn'd with the Ornaments of a Bride, with her hair Dishevel'd, and complaining, with her hand towards Heaven: About her are likewise discern'd the Symerons who took her prisoner.

As Drake is about to go to the rescue of the lady, Pedro enters to announce that she is free, and "The Scene is suddenly chang'd again, where the Lady is vanisht, and nothing appears but that Prospect which was in the beginning of the Entry." Thus the rescue of the lady, which must have taken place while Drake was gazing on her in the midst of her captors, is announced, and the whole scene disappears. Whether the lady and her captors were painted on a flat and were revealed when the back shutters were partially drawn off, or whether pasteboard figures were introduced into the scene is not to be determined on the evidence of the text.

That these attempts at opera were crude was almost inevitable. But that they should have been undertaken at all is remarkable. Evelyn wrote on May 5, 1659:

> I went to visit my Brother in London, and next day to see a new opera, after ye Italian way, in recitative music and sceanes, much inferior to ye Italian composure and magnificence; but it was prodigious that in a time of such publiq consternation such a vanity should be kept up or permitted.

The reference is certainly to one of the Davenant operas, and it is worthy of note that Evelyn, who spoke with the authority of experience, recognized it as "after ye Italian way[1]."

It was, indeed, a strange time for theatrical adventuring. Cromwell had just died, the succession was uncertain, and party strife was rife. But as all the world knows, the king, Charles II, came back from his long sojourn abroad, and with his accession came the renewed protection of the theatres under the royal favour.

The temporary companies of actors which sprang up at the Restoration are without special significance for this study. The history of spectacle on the stage centres about the two companies formed under a royal grant of August 21, 1660. This grant gave to Thomas Killigrew and Sir William Davenant "power and authority to erect two companies of players" and also

> to purchase, builde and erect, or hire at their charge, as they shall thinke fitt, two houses or theaters, with all convenient

---

[1] Evelyn, *op. cit.*

roomes and other necessaries thereunto appertaining for the representation of tragydies, comedyes, playes, operas, and all other
entertainments of that nature, in convenient places: and likewise
to settle and establish such payments to be paid by those that
shall resort to see the said representations performed, as either
haue bin accustomely giuen and taken in the like kind, or as
shall be reasonable in regard of the great expences of SCENES,
musick and such new decorations as haue not been formerly
used[1].

Acting under this grant, Davenant's company, now
known as the Duke's company, began to play regularly
at the Salisbury Court playhouse on November 15,
1660; the King's company, under Killigrew, which had
evidently been playing at the Red Bull, moved on
November 8 to a theatre in Gibbon's Tennis Court,
Vere Street, Clare Market.

But Davenant was as usual looking ahead. The
agreement by which he "erected" the company which
began to play at Salisbury Court was a tripartite agreement of November 5, 1660,

between Sir Wm. Davenant of London, Kt. of the first part,
and Thomas Batterton, Thomas Sheppey, Robert Noakes,
James Noakes, Thomas Lovell, John Mosely, Cave Underhill,
Robert Turner, and Thomas Lilleston, of the second part; and
Henry Harris, of the citty of London, painter, of the third part.

This agreement provided for the management of the
company's affairs until Davenant should provide a "new
theater with *scenes*." But it further provided that on
one week's notice the company should join with Henry
Harris and other men and women whom Davenant
might provide "to performe such tragedies, comedies,
playes, and representations in that theater to be provided by him the said Sir William as aforesaid." It
was agreed also that in the distribution of the receipts

[1] Malone, *op. cit.* vol. III, pp. 249–51.

at the new house ten of the fifteen shares were to go to Davenant for various purposes, and that of the five remaining shares "the said Henry Harris is to have an equal share with the greatest proportion." Further it was agreed that the actors should become bound for £5000 as security for the fulfilment of their contract, and that Henry Harris should also become bound for a like amount within the week after notice of the company's removal to the new house had been given[1].

The identity of the Henry Harris here referred to has long been the subject of conjecture. Lowe formulated the accepted theory that he was the Harris who acted in *The Siege of Rhodes* at Davenant's new house, and who continued with the company in great reputation, becoming one of the managers after Davenant's death[2]. Whether or not Henry Harris was the actor Harris, it is clear that he was recognized in the agreement as a painter, that his engagement was not to begin until the new house with scenes was completed, that he was recognized as the third party to the contract, that separate provision for his bond was made, and that his relative share of the proceeds was guaranteed. A fact that seems to have escaped notice in this connection is that Henry Harris was appointed Yeoman of the Revels in 1660[3]. At any rate, it is certain that in this agreement Davenant was making provision for a theatre in which scenes were to be the distinguishing feature[4].

[1] Malone, *op. cit.* vol. III, pp. 257–63.

[2] R. W. Lowe, *Thomas Betterton* (1891), pp. 72–5.

[3] The patent is printed in *A Collection of Ancient Documents Respecting the Office of the Revels*, published by J. Halliwell-Phillips in 1870, p. 61, and the appointment dates from 1660. Cf. Adams, *Dramatic Records of Sir Henry Herbert*, p. 68, note 6.

[4] It is interesting to note that Davenant was to receive two shares "towards the house-rent, buildinge, scaffoldinge, and makeing of frames for *scenes*" and one other share "for provision of habitts, properties, and *scenes*," for the same division of work seems to persist in regard to

Meanwhile the performances at Salisbury Court took place with, it would seem, a minimum of scenery. John Tatham's *The Rump*[1] affords an interesting example of the plays written and produced at this time. Changes of place are frequent and occur without possible references to changes of scene. The play seems to feature the escape and pursuit of persons who flee through one stage door and re-enter by another, only to cross the stage and continue the mad chase in various exits and entrances. Also it gives interesting proof of the use of painted properties. When a bonfire is demanded, "A piece of Wood is set forth painted like a pile of Faggots and Fire, and Faggots lying by to supply it." When the rump is called for, "A Form is set forth," and "Racks are set out one turns the spit with Rumps on it." Dancing around the painted bonfire marks the closing scene.

Finally the new house was ready. Downes wrote in the *Roscius Anglicanus*:

His Company being now Compleat, Sir *William* in order to prepare Plays to Open his Theatre, it being then a Building in *Lincoln's-Inn Fields*, His Company Rehears'd the First and Second Part of the Siege of *Rhodes*; and the Wits at *Pothecaries-Hall*: And in Spring 1662, Open'd his house with the said Plays, having new Scenes and Decorations, being the first that e're were Introduc'd in *England*. Mr. *Betterton*, Acted Soly-man the Magnificent; Mr. *Harris*, *Alphonso*...Mrs. *Davenport*, *Roxolana*; Mrs. *Sanderson*, Ianthe: All Parts being Justly and Excellently Perform'd; it continu'd Acting 12 Days without Interruption with great Applause[2].

the making of scenes which apparently existed when the provision of scenes for court productions concerned both the Office of the Works and the Office of the Revels.

[1] John Tatham, *The Rump*, or *The Mirrour of the Late Times*, Acted Many Times with Great Applause, At the Private House in *Dorset-Garden*, 1660.

[2] John Downes, *Roscius Anglicanus* (Joseph Knight, ed. 1886), pp. 20, 21.

This statement of Downes as to the date of the opening of the new theatre has been generally discredited[1] because of the entry in Pepys's *Diary* for July 2, 1661: "took coach and went to Sir William Davenant's Opera; this being the fourth day that it hath begun, and the first that I have seen it." Succeeding entries in 1661 refer to the performances at the "Opera," and the scenery for *The Wits* and for *Hamlet* is particularly remarked. It is significant that the name of the "Opera" was thus applied to Davenant's house, for he had constantly looked forward to the production of opera, and the fact of a stage arranged for spectacle seems in the public mind to have been accepted as proof of the fulfilment of his plans. Whether or not it is significant in connection with the statement of Downes, it is true that in the autumn of 1662 Pepys adopts a new terminology; the Opera and the Theatre are thenceforth generally referred to as the Duke's House and the King's Theatre.

That the new theatre was but another step forward in the accomplishment of Davenant's purpose is evident from the prologue to the second part of *The Siege of Rhodes* played in the new house:

> But many Trav'lers here as Judges come;
> From *Paris*, *Florence*, *Venice*, and from *Rome*:
> Who will describe, when any Scene we draw,
> By each of ours, all that they ever saw;
> Those praising, for extensive bredth and height,
> And inward distance to deceive the sight
> When greater Objects, moving in broad Space,
> You rank with lesser, in this narrow Place,
> Then we like *Chess-men*, on a Chess-board are
> And seem to play like *Pawns* the *Rhodian* War.

[1] Cf. John Genest, *Some Account of the English Stage* (1832), vol. 1, p. 381, and succeeding writers. The other side of the argument is to be found in Knight's edition of Downes, *Introduction*, pp. xxiv, xxv.

Oh Money! Money! if the WITS would dress,
With Ornaments, the present face of Peace,
And to our Poets half that Treasure spare,
Which Faction gets from Fools to nourish War;
Then his contracted Scenes should wider be,
And move by greater Engines, till you see
(Whilst you Securely sit) fierce Armies meet,
And raging Seas disperse a fighting Fleet.
Thus much he bade me say; and I confess
I think he would, if rich, mean nothing less.

Certain it is that Davenant constantly looked forward to new adventures in spectacle[1].

Of the company under Killigrew, Wright records in his *Historia Histrionica*:

Yes, presently after the Restauration, the King's Players Acted publickly at the *Red Bull* for some time, and then Removed to a New-built Play-house in *Vere-street* by *Claremarket*. There they continued for a Year or two, and then removed to the *Theater Royal* in *Drury-lane*, where they made use of Scenes, which had been a little before introduced upon the publick Stage by Sir *William Davenant* at the *Duke's Old Theater* in *Lincoln's-Inn-Fields*, but afterwards very much improved, with the Addition of curious Machines by Mr. *Betterton*, at the *New Theater* in *Dorset-Garden*, to the great expence and continual Charge of the Players[2].

Meanwhile the patents were issued to Davenant and Killigrew under which they "and their heirs and assignees operated for over one hundred and eighty years in London[3]." The patents dated from January 15, 1663, and April 25, 1662, respectively.

That Killigrew likewise was interested in the idea of opera is evident from the entry made by Pepys in

[1] Cf. p. 29 of 1673 ed.

[2] J. Wright, *Historia Histrionica*, 1699. Reprinted in Lowe's ed. of Cibber's *Apology* (1889). Cf. vol. 1, pp. xxxi, xxxii.

[3] Cf. Odell, *op. cit.* vol. 1, p. 7.

his *Diary* on August 2, 1664, recording a visit to the King's House:

> I chanced to sit by Tom Killigrew, who tells me that he is setting up a Nursery; that is, is going to build a house in Moorefields, wherein he will have common plays acted. But four operas it shall have in the year, to act six weeks at a time; where we shall have the best scenes and machines, the best musique, and every thing as magnificent as is in Christendome; and to that end hath sent for voices and painters and other persons from Italy.

The entry is valuable as a record because of the definition of opera which is implied and because of the continued dependence on Italy here shown. That the plan was not to be successful is not of great importance in this study[1].

As a matter of fact, we know strangely little about the theatres of the post-Restoration period. Yet they seem to have been worthy of consideration. Monsieur de Monconys on May 22, 1663, visited the King's Theatre, and we have a record of his visit:

> L'apresdînée nous fûmes chez le Milord de Saint Alban; & de là à la Comedie dans la loge du Roi. Le Théâtre est le plus propre & le plus beau que j'aye jamais vû, tout tapissé par le bas de bayette verte; aussi-bien que toutes les loges, qui en sont tapissées avec des bands de cuir doré. Tous les bancs du parterre, où toutes des personnes de condition se mettent aussi, sont rangez en amphithéatre, les uns plus hauts que les autres. Les changemens de Théâtre & les machines sont fort ingenieusement inventées & executées.

On June 5, 1663, the same writer visited the Duke's House: "L'apresdînée je fus à la Comedie du Duc

---

[1] A very interesting summary of the early attempts at opera is given in the introduction to *The Siege of Rhodes* in the Maidment-Logan edition, vol. III, pp. 236–47; Professor Tupper in his introduction already referred to likewise gives a valuable history of opera and of the use of recitative.

d'York, où les changemens de Scene me plûrent beaucoup[1]."

Likewise Sorbière wrote of the King's Theatre in
1663: "Le theatre est fort beau, couvert d'un tapis
verd, & la scene y est toute libre, avec beaucoup de
changemens, & des perspectives[2]."

Richard Flecknoe, writing in 1664, *A Short Discourse of the English Stage*, commented with obvious inconsistency:

Now for the difference betwixt our Theaters and those of
former times, they were but plain and simple, with no other
Scenes nor Decorations of the Stage, but onely old Tapestry,
and the Stage strew'd with Rushes, with their Habits accordingly,
whereas ours now for cost and ornament are arriv'd to the height
of Magnificence; but that which makes our Stage the better
makes our Playes the worse perhaps, they striving now to make
them more for sight than hearing.

A few lines later he added:

For Scenes and Machines they are no new invention, our Masks
and some of our Playes in former times (though not so ordinary)
having had as good or rather better then any we have now.

Then he advanced the stock argument concerning the
advantage of scenes:

They are excellent helps of imagination, most grateful de-
ceptions of the sight, and graceful and becoming Ornaments of
the Stage, transporting you easily without lassitude from one
place to another, or rather by a kind of delightful Magick, whilst
you sit still, does bring the place to you. Of this curious Art the
Italians, this latter age, are the greatest masters, the *French*
good proficients, and we in England onely Schollares and
Learners yet, having proceeded no further then to bare painting,

---

[1] *Les Voyages de Monsieur de Monconys en Angleterre, et aux Pays-
Bas*. Suite de la seconde partie. 1695. Cf. p. 44.

[2] Samuel de Sorbière, *Relation d'une voyage en Angleterre* (1669 ed.),
p. 129.

and not arriv'd to the stupendous wonders of your great In-
geniers, especially not knowing yet how to place our Lights, for
the more advantage and illuminating of the Scenes[1].

Davenant addressed a "Poem to the King's Most
Sacred Majesty," presumably about 1663, in which he
proclaimed the glories of the English stage:

> If to reform the publick Mirrour (where
> The Dead, to teach their living Race, appear)
> May to the People useful prove, even this
> (Which but the object of your leisure is
> To respite Care, and which successively
> Three of our last wise Monarchs wish'd to see,
> And in a Century could not be wrought)
> *You*, in Three Years, have to perfection brought[2].

The evidence concerning the theatres is ample to
prove that they were admired by foreigners, that their
structure conformed to that of the neo-Vitruvian type,
and that their moving scenes elicited particular admiration. In spite of the depreciation of things English,
which has always been characteristic of English critics
and which is to be found in the comments of certain
critics of the theatre from Sidney onward, and in spite
of the frequently expressed desire to hark back to the
days of perfection now gone forever, which has always
characterized the criticism of the younger generation
by the older, it seems fairly safe to conclude that the
English post-Restoration theatres were beautiful structures, fitted with the spectacular devices then popular,
though not using the great spectacular machines of the
Salle des Machines. These machines were probably pro-
hibitive in their cost when they were to be used in a
theatre dependent on popular support.

---

[1] Richard Flecknoe, *A Short Discourse of the English Stage*, 1664, in
Spingarn, *op. cit.* vol. II, pp. 95, 96.
[2] Printed in *Madagascar and Other Poems* in 1673 ed., p. 269.

That it was Webb who was responsible for the designing of these first post-Restoration playhouses seems to me almost inevitable. It was Webb who worked with Davenant in designing the scenery for *The Siege of Rhodes*; it was Webb who designed the scenery for *Mustapha* in 1666, when it was played before the court in the Whitehall theatre[1]. It is known that he worked under Sir John Denham, who apparently did not himself perform many of the functions of his office as Surveyor. It was Webb who alone of the known architects of the period had had the necessary training and experience in theatrical affairs.

That perspective scenery was the attraction used by Davenant to attract the interest of the multitude to his theatrical adventures is certainly suggested by his epilogue to *The Playhouse to be Let*:

> This *Landtschap of the Sea*,—but by the way,
> That's an expression which might hurt our Play,
> If the severer Criticks were in Town;
> This Prospect of the Sea cannot be shown[2].

It is shown as well by the way in which the early operas and plays were advertised as represented by the art of perspective in scenes.

The popular interest in perspective is evidenced also in the record of other activities of the time. Perspectives added to gardens, perspectives painted and exhibited by popular artists, perspective glasses, perspective drawing as a fashionable accomplishment for ladies,—all are described again and again in the history of the time[3]. One of the popular entertainments of the

---

[1] Mr Keith comments on the drawings for this production in his article already instanced, *Burlington Magazine*, vol. xxv, pp. 85 *sq*.

[2] See above, p. 227, note.

[3] Pepys's accounts of his wife's attempts to learn this fashionable art are particularly amusing. Cf. his entry for April 26, 1669.

period was commonly known as *Paradise*[1]. It is to this entertainment that Prue refers in Wycherley's *The Gentleman Dancing-Master* when she complains that she is not allowed to go to the playhouse "nor to go to Punchinello, nor Paradise[2]." The description of 1661 which has come down to us is entitled "Paradise Transplanted and Restored in a Most Artfull and Lively Representation," and it records that

The Design, is a Model, or Representation of that Beautifull Prospect *Adam* had in Paradice when the whole Creation of *Animals*, were together subjected to his imperious eye, and from his mouth received their severel names, etc.

The show was evidently in the nature of a panorama, the musicians painted on the wall at the left of the door, a feast painted below stairs, even a group of aristocratic ladies painted as audience.

During the last half of the seventeenth century, too, the knowledge of architectural theory increased notably in England, so that the full record of treatises published on the subject cannot be easily compiled. However, certain noteworthy books must be mentioned. Palladio's *First Book of Architecture* was translated into English in 1663, Sir Balthazar Gerbier wrote his *Counsel and Advice to all Builders* in 1663 or 1664, Scamozzi's work was translated as *The Mirror of Architecture*[3], while Evelyn's translation of Freart's *Parallel between Ancient and Modern Architecture* in 1664 must be ranked with

[1] *Paradise Transplanted and Restored in a Most Lively Representation*...shown at Christopher Whiteheads...Written by I. H. Gent. London, 1661. Reprinted by Edwin Pearson, 1871.

[2] Whether the date of this entertainment can be used as evidence concerning the much disputed date of this play, which is generally believed to have been written some ten years after the date to which Wycherley assigned it (1661) is a matter which must depend on the date at which the entertainment ceased to be popular.

[3] I have seen only the third edition, which was published in 1636.

his own *Account of Architects and Architecture* of 1696–7 as important contributions to the art studies of the time.

Meanwhile the Great Fire of London had created an unpredecented opportunity for architectural progress in the rebuilding of the City, and Christopher Wren had been made deputy for Sir John Denham and had been put in charge of the work. On Denham's death he was made Surveyor. In Wren his contemporaries believed they had found the universal genius. Evelyn, writing in 1668, was convinced that Wren like Bernini could build the theatre, "cut the figures," paint the scenes, write the play, and compose the music for an opera[1]. At any rate, it was Wren who built the theatres, for in 1671 the Duke's company moved to a great new theatre in Dorset Garden, and in 1674 the King's company moved to the new Drury Lane Theatre, both of which theatres were built by Wren.

In 1668 Davenant, in fulfilment of his plan which had been maturing for thirty years, engaged Wren to design a new theatre. A few months later Davenant died, but the theatre was completed under the management of Betterton, Harris, and Dr Charles Davenant, and in it the dreams of Davenant were at last realized. The great spectacles of the succeeding years to be seen in this playhouse were said to surpass in luxury those presented in the Continental theatres. Betterton, tradition has it, was sent to Paris to find the latest inventions by which the new house in Dorset Garden might be adorned. Wright records the fact that he improved the machines, as we have already noted. But Wren was given a free hand in all matters pertaining to the architecture of the theatre. Five thousand pounds were spent on its construction. Grinling Gibbons carved the de-

[1] Cf. "To the Reader" prefixed to his translation of Freart's *Perfection of Painting* in 1668, published in his *Miscellaneous Writings* (1825), pp. 561, 562.

corations of the house, the great gilded proscenium arch of which was the most noted feature[1].

Of the theatre in Dorset Garden we have definite knowledge from the "sculptures" which adorned the first edition of *The Empress of Morocco*, four of which show the great carved proscenium arch, while another pictures the exterior of the theatre.

In 1674 the new theatre of the King's company in Drury Lane was opened. Their old theatre having been destroyed by fire in January 1671–2, they had in the meanwhile occupied the theatre vacated by the Duke's company when they moved to Dorset Garden. The prologue written by Dryden and spoken on the opening night in the new Drury Lane made comparison of this theatre with the new house of the other company:

> A Plain built House after so long a stay,
> Will send you half unsatisfy'd away;
> When, fall'n from your expected Pomp, you find
> A bare convenience only is design'd.
> You who each Day can Theatres behold,
> Like *Nero's* Palace, shining all with Gold,
> Our mean ungilded Stage will scorn, we fear,
> And for the homely Room, disdain the Chear[2].

[1] Cf. especially W. J. Lawrence, "The Old Duke's Theatre in Dorset Garden," in the London *Architectural Review*, vol. XLVI, pp. 112–15. An interesting record of Gibbons's work taken from Vertue's note-book is to be found in H. A. Tipping, *Grinling Gibbons and the Wood-Work of his Age* (1914), p. 45.

[2] Professor Odell, *op. cit.* vol. I, p. 10, quotes the passage but interprets: "'the theatres...shining all with gold' I take to refer to the stage set with scenes; the line in contrast, 'Our mean ungilded stage,' would seem to substantiate the belief." Such an interpretation seems unnecessarily strained in view of the fact that the great gilded proscenium arch of Dorset Garden was its most striking feature and the one most apt to be commented on. Furthermore in view of the fact that the Drury Lane stage was also set with scenes, there would seem to be little point in such a comparison. And Professor Odell accepts the evidence offered by Mr Bell as to the identity of the section drawing of a theatre

That the theatre was in fact a magnificent theatre for the period is shown, however, by adequate evidence. It is said to have cost £4000. In the *Shakespeare Society Papers* Collier has preserved a deed of March 23, 1673–4, which shows how the actors combined to raise money to erect for this new playhouse a scene-house

for the makeing and providing of Scenes, Machines, Cloathes, apparell, and other things to be used in or relating to the acting of Comedies, Tragedies, and other Interludes at the said Theatre, or in any other place where the Company...shall act[1].

The most important evidence concerning this theatre is that contributed by Mr Hamilton Bell in an article in the *Architectural Record* for 1913 concerning "Three Plans by Sir Christopher Wren[2]." Mr Bell has in this article succeeded in establishing at least the probability if not the certainty that one of the drawings which he has described is that of the 1674 theatre in Drury Lane. The section which is reproduced shows a stage divided into two parts, the whole stage being built with an incline from front to back. The front part of the stage is flanked by two proscenium doors; the back part is arranged for flat scenes or shutters in the usual fashion.

supposed to be Drury Lane, a section which clearly shows the arrangement for scenes on the stage. Mr Bell gives further evidence on this point, for he says that the section drawing seems to indicate that the upper part of the proscenium was "left bare to be supplied by a temporary drapery or painted valence." He notes that in the frontispiece to *Ariane* (a performance of which opened the house) there are pilasters represented, "but the strip of cornice which connects them has no visible thickness and might easily represent a canvas valence." If such a conclusion as to the Drury Lane proscenium is the true one, there was good reason for commenting on the contrast with Dorset Garden.

[1] *Shakespeare Society Papers*, vol. IV, pp. 147 *sq.* The article, "Dryden, Killigrew, and the First Company which Acted at Drury Lane Theatre," gives a good account of the known facts concerning the wanderings of the King's company.

[2] *The Architectural Record*, vol. XXXIII, pp. 359 *sq.*

PLATE VI

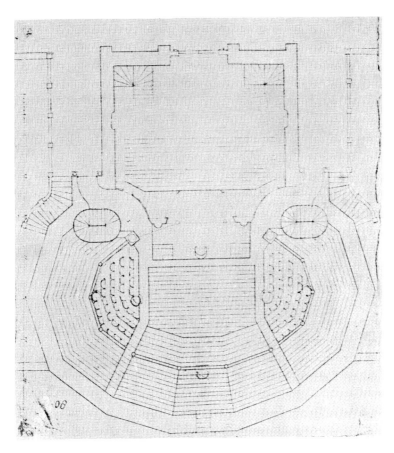

PLAN 80
Reproduced by kind permission of the Warden and Fellows of All Souls
College, Oxford, and by courtesy of the *Architectural Record*

PLATE VII

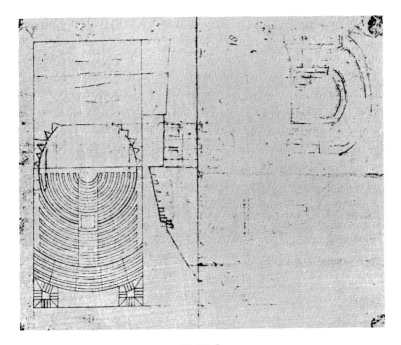

PLAN 81

PLAN 82

From the original drawings by Sir Christopher Wren

The back shutters, it would seem, could be opened up to reveal the further recesses of the stage when it was desired to do so. Whether or not the theatre represented was the Theatre Royal, the group of drawings of which this section forms a part is of great importance, for they show that Wren was experimenting both with the rectangular theatre and with the shell-shaped or modified circular theatre, his experiments being exactly of the type based on the Vitruvian models long since familiar.

The contest for popularity between the two new theatres now rapidly developed. Mr Lawrence in his discussion of the question "Did Shadwell Write an Opera on 'The Tempest'?[1]" quotes Shadwell's "Prologue and Epilogue to the Tempest," in which Shadwell made reply to Dryden's prologue on the occasion of the opening of Drury Lane. The prologue taunted the opposing company, probably with some reason:

> To splendid things they follow in, but late:
> They n're invent, but they can imitate:
> Had we not, for yr. pleasure found new wayes
> You still had rusty arras had, and thred-bare playes;
> Nor scenes nor Woomen, had they had their will.

And the epilogue chronicled with evident truthfulness:

> When you of witt and sence were weary growne,
> Romantick, riming, fustian Playes were showne,
> We then to flying Witches did advance,
> And for your pleasures traffic'd into ffrance.
> From thence new acts to please you, we have sought
> We have machines to some perfection brought,
> And above 30 Warbling voyces gott.
> Many a God and Goddesse you will heare
> And we have Singing, Dancing, Devils here
> And Devils, and such gods, are very Deare.
> We, in all ornaments, are lavish growne.

---

[1] Lawrence, *Elizabethan Playhouse*, vol. I, pp. 200–3.

Indeed the inventiveness of the whole theatrical world was drawn upon during the ensuing years when the two houses were in competition. Gregorio Leti in his *Teatro Britanico* in 1683 commented:

our splendid and magnificent theatres deserve to be seen by foreigners...for all that concerns the scenes of the comedians, the skill of the actors, the inventions and designs and everything else; they are in advance of the other theatres of Europe[1].

But the companies were at last forced to unite in 1682. The magnificent theatre in Dorset Garden was abandoned, and the united companies acted at Drury Lane until 1695, when part of the actors seceded. Meanwhile the stage of the theatre was remodelled in 1693, at which time, according to Cibber, the projecting apron was cut off four feet, and stage boxes were introduced instead of the lower doors of entrance, which were then moved back to take the place of two side wings.

In 1705 a new theatre designed by Vanbrugh[2] was

---

[1] Quoted by Lacy Collison-Morley, *Shakespeare in Italy* (1916), p. 2.

[2] This theatre, the Queen's Theatre in the Haymarket, became the home of opera, and is generally known as Vanbrugh's opera-house. Like everything that Vanbrugh did it was subject to much ridicule. Swift's lines in "The History of Vanbrugh's House" are typical of the taunts flung at all his architectural efforts (*The Works of Dr Jonathan Swift*, 1754–68, vol. VI, pp. 83–5):

> Van's genius, without thought or lecture,
> Is hugely turn'd to architecture:
>
> * * * *
>
> Van is become by due degrees
> For building fam'd, and justly reckon'd
> At court *Vitruvius* the *second*.
>
> * * * *
>
> We might expect to see next year
> A *mouse-trap* man chief engineer.

His appointment as Surveyor to succeed Wren was, therefore, not a popular one.

opened with an Italian opera[1]. To the difficulties not yet conquered in the other houses of arranging the stage and the auditorium so that all the audience could with ease obtain a view of the stage, Vanbrugh's opera-house added with its great size a new difficulty in regard to acoustics. The next century of theatre-building was a century of experiments in making the actors on the stage both visible and audible to those in all parts of the auditorium, and with the history of the solution of that problem we are not concerned in this study. The theatres of the seventeenth century fixed the principles of the representation of spectacle as they remained well into the nineteenth century, and it is because of this fact that they are of supreme importance in the history of the stage. The modifications by which succeeding theatres were adapted to the solution of a new problem form a new chapter in the history of the theatre.

The technique of the stage of the latter years of the seventeenth century may be studied in its most available records in the editions of Vitruvius by Claude Perrault published in 1673[2] and 1684 at Paris and universally accepted then and thereafter as the great editions of Vitruvius, and in a work on perspective by Andrea Pozzo, *Prospettiva de' Pittori ed Architetti*, published in Rome and later translated into English.

The comment of Perrault in regard to the nature of the dependence of modern architects on the utterances

[1] The opera was Greber's *Loves of Ergasto*, said to have been a melodrama with Italian music. Cf. *Dictionary of National Biography*, article on "Vanbrugh." For a history of the house, cf. R. Wilkinson, *Londina Illustrata* (1825), vol. ii, "The King's Theatre, or the Italian Opera, Haymarket."

[2] *Les dix livres d'architecture de Vitruve*, corrigez et traduits nouvellement en Francois, avec des notes & des figures, a Paris, chez Jean Baptiste Coignard, 1673. Republished 1684.

of Vitruvius makes an interesting contribution to the study of classical theory, for he says:

On a estimé que les preceptes de cet excellent Auteur, que les Critiques mettent au premier rang des grands esprits de l'antiquité, étoient absolument necessaires pour conduire ceux qui desirent de se perfectionner dans cet Art, en établissant par la grande autorité que ses écrits ont toûjours euë, les veritables regles du beau & du parfait dans les Edifices: car la Beauté n'ayant guere d'autre fondement que la fantasie, qui fait que les choses plaisent selon qu'elles sont conformes à l'idée que chacun a de leur perfection, on a besoin de regles qui forment & qui rectifient cette Idée: & il est certain que ces regles sont tellement necessaires en toutes choses, que si la Nature les refuse à quelques-unes, ainsi qu'elle a fait au langage, aux caracteres de l'écriture, aux habits & a tout ce qui dépend du hazard, de la volonté, & de l'accoutumance; il faut que l'institution des hommes en fournisse, & que pour cela on convienne d'une certaine autorité qui tienne lieu de raison positive[1].

This work of Perrault is, however, otherwise important than as it reveals the attitude of architects in the period of classicism toward the sole architectural authority, for it furnishes us a record of the interpretations of Vitruvian precepts. From the translation of Perrault we know that the placing of the *periaktoi* back of the doors of entrance on the stage was still accepted as the Vitruvian arrangement. Also we know that the entrance of the gods on the stage was to be heralded by thunder if the method of Vitruvius were to be followed[2].

[1] Quoted from the preface. I have consulted both editions, but the text quoted is that of the 1684 edition.

[2] Vitruvius, V, vii, "Dans chaque machine il doit y des ornemens de trois especes, qui serviront aux changemens qui se font en tournant leur differentes faces: Car cela est necessaire dans la representation des Fables; comme quand il faut faire paroistre des Dieux avec des tonnerres surprenans."

Perrault gives us also an interesting account of the varying interpretations of the methods which should be used in presenting the satyric play. Incidentally he gives us convincing evidence of the desire to follow classical tradition in the modern theatre in his note on the passage in Book V, chapter VIII, which follows:

LES PAÏSAGES DES TAPISSERIES. Les Auteurs sont peu d'accord sur la signification de *Topiarium opus*. La plus grande partie estime que c'est la representation qui se fait avec du buis, du cypre, de l'if, & d'autres tels arbrisseaux verds, taillez de plusieurs sortes de figures pour l'ornement des Jardins. D'autres croyent avec plus de raison que ce sont des païsages representez ou en peinture, ou dans des Tapisseries. Car soit qu'on fasse venir ce mot du Grec *Topion*, qui signifie une ficelle, ou de *Topos* qui signifie un lieu ou un païs, il exprime toujours fort-bien ou un paysage qui est la representation des lieux, comme des eaux, des bois, des montages; ou une Tapisserie qui est faite par l'entrelacement de la soye, de la laine & de l'or dans de petites ficelles qui font la chaisne de l'ouvrage de Tapisserie.

Of far greater interest, however, is the note in regard to effecting changes of scene, a note on the passage in Book V, chapter VII, of Vitruvius:

LES DECORATIONS QUE LES GRECS APELLENT PERIACTOUS. Nostre mot François de decorations de Theatres rend hereusement celuy de Vitruve, qui est *ornatus*. Ces decorations estoient de deux sortes, selon Servius sur les Georgiques de Virgile. Car outre ces machines faites en triangle, que les Grecs apelloient *Periactous*, c'est-à-dire tournantes, & qui fournissoient chacune trois differens changemens, chacune de leurs faces ayant des peintres differentes; les Anciens en avoient d'autres qui sont encore en usage dans nos Theatres, dont l'artifice consistoit à faire paroistre des faces differentes, lorsqu'on les faisoit couler, en sorte que lorsque l'on en tiroit une, elle en découvroit une autre, qui estoit cachée derriere elle. Celle-cy éstoit appellée *ductilis* & l'autre *versatilis*. Il est neanmoins difficile de croire que ces changemens fussent aussi prompts que ceux de nos

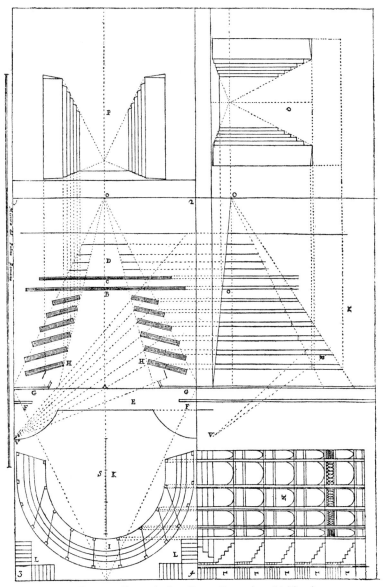

FIG. 15. From Andrea Pozzo, *Prospettiva de' Pittori ed Architetti*, 1693

[*Explanation opposite*

Theatres, qui se font presque en un moment & sans qu'on s'en apperçoive; car nous lisons que lorsque les Anciens vouloient changer les ornemens de leur Scene, ils tiroient un rideau qui estoit appellé *Siparium*, derriere lequel ils faisoient à loisir ce qui estoit necessaire au changement.

In this note we find the idea of scenes as decoration recognized as having a classical origin, and we find too the acceptance of the classical origin of the *scena ductilis* in use on the contemporary stage. It is significant also that instead of apologizing for the contemporary habit of changing the scenes before the eyes of the spectators, Perrault speaks with pride of the swift changes which made a concealing curtain unnecessary.

More informative concerning the technique of the stage during the latter part of the seventeenth century is the work of Pozzo already referred to. This work was published in England as *Rules and Examples of Perspective Proper for Painters and Architects*, both a Latin and an English text being included. The translation was made by John James, while the engraving of the "105 ample folio Plates" which adorned the work was done by John Sturt. That which gives the work its peculiar significance and authority as a

---

Explanation of Fig. 15, showing stage arrangement by Pozzo.

"*D* is the Place of those things that are to appear most remote. *BC* is the Place of the Poscene. *HH* are the Oblique Grooves, whose length are double the Breadth of the Scenes. *FG* is the Front of the Stage. *AO* is its Depth or Length. *E* is the Place for the Musick. *K* is the Room for Spectators. *I* is the Place of the Galleries, *L* the Stairs to the same. *N* is the Elevation of the Galleries. *M* shews the Declivity of the Floor, with the Section and Elevation of the Stage and Scenes view'd on the Side; answering their respective Grooves, as the occult Lines demonstrate....In this Profile *M*, part of the Height belongs to the Scenes, and part to their Soffites, or Ceilings, *R*; where each Pair of these Frames are join'd. *VV* are the Lines by which is espy'd what Vacancy there is either between the Scenes and the Ceilings, between the Scenes themselves, or between their respective Ceilings; tho in some Scenes the Place of these last is supply'd by painting therin the Air with Clouds, etc."

record of the English stage is "The Approbation of this Edition" printed with the English edition and signed with the names of "Chr. Wren," "J. Vanbrugh," and "N. Hawksmoor." This approbation attests that,

At the Request of the Engraver, We have perus'd this Volume of Perspective; and judge it a Work that deserves Encouragement, and very proper for Instruction in that Art.

An accurate description of stage scenery as it was conceived of in the late seventeenth century is contained in the words of the prefatory statement:

The Manner of Designing, where the Perspective is drawn on several Ranges of Frames one behind the other, and such Scenes of Theatres whose Grooves lie oblique to the middle line, is also here laid down.

Pozzo tells us that the scenes in most of the theatres of his day were arranged to run in grooves which were thus laid "oblique to the middle line" after the manner first practised by the Italians, though the Germans generally kept them parallel to the "poscene." The advantages gained by the use of the scenes in the oblique grooves were, he pointed out, "That those who are employ'd to prompt the Actors, and shift the Scenes, &c. are less expos'd to Sight, in the Performance of their Business."

The work contains the usual instructions for theatrical perspective, explaining how to find the point of sight, how to fix the horizon on the level of the eye, how to determine the rise of the stage floor toward the horizon, and how to conceal the spaces between pairs of scene flats and pairs of ceiling flats. The stage arrangement is most clearly seen in the illustration (Fig. 15, p. 248).

But as theatrical technique reached a stage of comparative perfection, dramatic theory was also attaining more definite formulation. Clash and compromise were the inevitable results. On the one hand, the study of

Vitruvius and Pollux and other classical writers had inspired the architects and the scholars of the Renaissance to research and experiment which resulted in scenery painted in perspective, movable scenery, and machines. Meanwhile the new interest in the science of the ancients had impelled the scholars of the Renaissance likewise to experiments in applied mathematics and in optics. The final result was, as we have seen, a perfecting of the *scena ductilis* into the movable flat, on which scientific and artistic experiment had made it possible to represent objects in perspective, and also a perfecting of the machines of the ancients into elaborate spectacular devices.

Yet spectacle was luxury, and only gradually was the right of the public accepted to possess in full the glories of the theatre. The steps by which scenery was advanced from the court to the public theatre, and the steps by which the sovereign progressed from having a spectacular drama enacted for his pleasure to becoming a part of the audience in the public theatre to which spectacular performances of the drama had been transferred, form records of no small significance in the history of the political evolution of Europe and of England[1]. But our concern here is with these steps not as they represented political progress but as they indicated artistic advancement. The essential fact to be remembered is that spectacle was perfected on the English stage previous to the Commonwealth, but that its luxurious incorporation in the public theatre was the attainment of the period after the Restoration. And the public liked

[1] As a matter of course, the sovereign did not give up private performances when the public theatres became more luxurious. But after the Restoration the history of theatrical spectacle is transferred to the public theatres. Thenceforth the public performances established the standards of the theatrical world. That the Cockpit-in-Court continued to serve the royal household is shown by the evidence gathered by Professor Adams, *Shakespearean Playhouses*, pp. 405–9.

spectacle and demanded it. Movable scenery having been achieved, changing scenes were necessary to the popularity of a play. Machines having been perfected, gods and ghosts and devils were not to be omitted, and the thunder must roar and the lightning flash if the public were to be satisfied. Excitement of every kind was necessary for dramatic success.

On the other hand, dramatic theory, which had for a time been modified from its original classicism by the genius of Shakespeare, was now, chiefly through the influence of the French Academy, coming to crystallize its classicism into the formalism of rules. The authority of classical precept and example was invoked at the same time that critics were engaged in an effort to prove the supreme authority of the rules which they had derived from the classics to consist in their conformity to nature or probability. The ancient rules for the drama were thus newly formulated on the basis of the demand for verisimilitude.

The critics insisted upon keeping pure each ancient dramatic type, upon the observance of the unities, upon decorum, upon the strict adherence to stage decencies. They decried the love of spectacle, the confusion of dramatic types, the lack of decorum, the bloody and the noisy stage. But the theatres were then as now run with a deeper concern for the purses of the managers than for the theories of the critics. Spectacle paid, and the dramatist had to have an audience if he continued to write. Inevitably the result was compromise, compromise made possible by the interpretation of the ancient rules on the basis of their demand for verisimilitude. It is, therefore, my purpose to show how the representation of the drama was affected by the clash between dramatic theory and popular demand for spectacle on the stage.

CHAPTER XV

THE JUSTIFICATION OF DRAMATIC
SPECTACLE

AS a matter of course the foundation struggle of the conservatives, who usually call themselves classicists, has in every period of dramatic progress been concerned with the legitimacy of theatrical spectacle. Scenery, incorporated at the Renaissance in the revived presentations of classical drama as an integral part of the ancient art which scholars were emulating, had later to meet the attacks of those who quoted Aristotle to prove that decoration was an inferior and unnecessary part of drama, even while their opponents cited Aristotle to prove that spectacle was one of the six parts of tragedy, and that the tragic emotions of pity and terror might be roused by spectacle.

The Abbé d'Aubignac in his *Pratique du théâtre* gave the foundation arguments of the compromise[1]. He admitted ornament to dramatic representation but demanded that the decorations be necessary to the action, agreeable to the sight, modest, and easy of execution. They must be probable and must not violate the principle of unity of place. Also he insisted that "out of

[1] The French works of criticism were during the post-Restoration period accepted as authoritative in England to a surprising degree. They were translated into English and furnished the basis of English critical doctrine. I have quoted from the English translation rather than from the original French wherever it has been practicable to do so. This work of the Abbé d'Aubignac (Monsieur Hedelin) was first published in French in 1657, having been undertaken in 1640 by the command of Cardinal Richelieu; it was translated into English in 1684 as *The Whole Art of the Stage*.

this Shew and Decoration some notable event may result in the Body of the Play[1]." Things and actions may be complementary, as when an actor falls from a rock, or when a sea-fight occurs. Thus decoration may justify itself.

Dacier likewise wrote as an apologist for spectacle in his notes on Aristotle's *Poetics*[2], explaining:

The Greek word which I have translated Decoration, is a general term, which properly signifies Sight, and Comprehends all, that makes the Beauty of the Shows as the Scene, the Ornaments, the Machines, the Habits of the Actors, &c. The Decoration was a Piece of Magnificence, never to be equal'd, and always proportion'd, to the Subject; nevertheless *Aristotle* makes it the last part of Tragedy....We ought not however, to desist from improving it; for besides the Service it does in the representation, it excites the Poets, and elevates their Spirits[3].

Dacier further justified the use of scenes by a more significant appeal to probability in his note to the *Poetics*, vi. 4:

For truly there is no Action, which doth not suppose a Place where it was done, and Actors dress'd after one certain Fashion, rather than another, for this Decoration seems not only for Pomp and Show, but to express the Nature of the things which are represented. But as Tragedy will bear reading without being Acted, it follows that the Decoration is not one of its Essential Parts, which made *Aristotle* say, *That it is in some sort a Part*; we manage Decoration now adays, as if it was in no respect a Part of Tragedy, and our Theatre is (if I dare say it) no more than the Skeleton of the *Greek* and *Latin* ones[4].

---

[1] Cf. Bk III, pp. 97, 98.

[2] André Dacier's *Aristotle: La poétique* was published in 1692. The English "*Aristotle's Art of Poetry*, translated from the Original Greek, according to Mr Theodore Goulston's edition. Together with Mr. D'Acier's notes. Translated from the French" was published in 1705.

[3] Cf. p. 102.   [4] Cf. p. 81.

Yet the English stage was always being attacked for its use of spectacle. The words of Sidney seem particularly to have lingered in the minds of foreigners, and we find them frequently echoed in the supposedly original criticisms of travellers. Samuel de Sorbière wrote in 1663 of the English theatres and their love of spectacle[1], to which attack Dr Sprat replied:

By their full Stage, they prevent men's being continually tyr'd with the same Objects; and so they make the Doctrine of the Scene to be more lively, and diverting, than the precepts of Philosophers, or the grave delight of *Heroick Poetry*: which the *French Tragedies* do resemble[2].

Chappuzeau, writing in 1674, also described the crowded English stage with its processions, its heralds of royalty, and its general confusion[3].

Dryden defied those who objected to his use of drums and trumpets and his presentation of battles on the stage, insisting that these things were "no more than necessary to produce the effects of an heroic play[4]." However, no one has so frequently or aptly expressed the need which constantly exists that the dramatist persist in providing those things which the audience demands. In the dedication to the *Examen Poeticum* of 1693 he wrote:

However it be, I dare establish it for a rule of practice on the stage, that we are bound to please those whom we pretend to entertain; and that at any price, religion and good manners only excepted.... There is a sort of merit in delighting the spectators,

[1] Sorbière, *op. cit.* pp. 129, 130.

[2] Thomas Sprat, *A Letter Containing some Observations on Monsieur de Sorbier's Voyage into England.* Written to Dr Wren, Professor of Astronomy in Oxford, 1665, p. 252.

[3] Chappuzeau, *Le théâtre François* (1674). Reprinted at Bruxelles (1861). Cf. pp. 43, 44.

[4] Dryden, "Of Heroic Plays," prefixed to *The Conquest of Granada, Works,* vol. iv, p. 25.

which is a name more proper for them, than that of auditors; or else Horace is in the wrong, when he commends Lucilius for it[1].

In 1711 we find the *Spectator* still apologizing for the battles and processions of the English stage and yet forced to the conclusion:

The tailor and the painter often contribute to the success of a tragedy more than the poet. Scenes affect ordinary minds as much as speeches; and our actors are very sensible that a well-dressed play has sometimes brought them as full audiences as a well-written one. The Italians have a very good phrase to express this sort of imposing upon the spectators by appearances; they call it the *Fourberia della scena,* "the knavery, or trickish part of the drama." But however the show and outside of the tragedy may work upon the vulgar, the more understanding part of the audience immediately see through it, and despise it[2].

[1] Cf. W. P. Ker, *Essays of John Dryden* (1900), vol. II, p. 7. Similarly Edward Howard, writing in the preface to his *Six Days Adventure* (1671) of the state of comedy, said: "And though the ear be the principal sense to receive satisfaction from the Stage, yet we find, that of seeing has not a seldome a greater predominancy, whilst scenes, habits, dances, or perhaps an Actress take more with Spectators, than the best Dramatick Wit, or contrivance of the Age...."

[2] No. 42, for April 18, 1711.

CHAPTER XVI

THE INFLUENCE OF OPERA
ON DRAMATIC GENRE

ONE of the basic doctrines of dramatic criticism during the Renaissance was that dealing with dramatic genre. This doctrine as applied by Vitruvius to the scenic representation of the drama furnished the foundation upon which the rules and practices of dramatists and architects were built up. Modifications crept in, indulgence was of necessity granted the public, compromises were inevitable. But the rules grew more minute as their exponents grew more philosophical concerning them; they grew more rigid even as their apologists grew more eloquent in their interpretation.

The fundamental distinction between tragedy and comedy, persisting throughout the Renaissance, was one of elevation and luxury. Tragedy was concerned with princely characters, and its setting was magnificence. Dryden in his "Essay on the Grounds of Criticism in Tragedy" prefixed to *Troilus and Cressida* described tragedy: "It ought to be great, and to consist of great Persons, to distinguish it from Comedy; where the Action is trivial, and the persons of inferior rank[1]." The first result of such a distinction was to permit greater luxury in the presentation of tragedy than

---

[1] Dryden, *Works*, vol. vi, pp. 261, 262. Cf. the *Prologue* to the *Monk's Tale* of Chaucer:

> Tragedie is to seyn a certeyn storie,
> As olde bokes maken us memorie,
> Of him that stood in greet prosperitee
> And is y-fallen out of heigh degree
> Into miserie, and endeth wrecchedly.

in that of comedy and to insist upon a differentiation of palaces and humbler houses in the scene in the manner described by Vitruvius.

Another distinction came to be made as a sort of corollary to this primary distinction. Remoteness of time and place enhanced the illusion of tragic greatness; hence tragedy must find its setting in places far removed from seventeenth-century England. Thus Davenant wrote in "The Author's Preface to his Much Honour'd Friend Mr Hobbs" affixed to *Gondibert*:

> As in the choice of time, so of place, I have comply'd with the weakness of the generalitie of men; who think the best objects of their own countrey so little to the size of those abroad, as if they were shew'd them by the wrong end of a Prospective.... This leads us to observe the craftiness of the *Comicks*, who are onely willing when they describe humor...to lay the Scaene in their own Country...: yet when they wo'ld set forth the greatness and excellent vertue (which is the Theme of Tragedie) publickly to the people; they wisely...remove the Scaene from home. And by their example I travell'd too; and Italie (which was once the Stage of the World) I have made the Theatre....

To which prefatory remarks "An Answer of Mr Hobbes to Sr William Davenant's Preface before Gondibert" made reply in metaphysical arguments:

> As Philosophers have divided the Universe...into three Regions, Celestial, Aerial, and Terrestrial, so the Poets...have lodg'd themselves in the three Regions of mankind, *Court*, *Citie*, and *Countrey*.

And he further explained:

> From hence have proceeded three sorts of Poesie, *Heroique*, *Scommatique*, and *Pastorall*. Every one of these is distinguished again in the manner of *Representation*, which sometimes is *Narrative*...and sometimes *Dramatique*.

Accordingly there are listed the epic poem, tragedy, satire, comedy, pastoral, and pastoral comedy as the six types of poetry, each of which must be appropriately presented[1].

Davenant's statement as to the remoteness of place desired for tragedy represented the attitude of most of the critics of the period. Rymer in his *Short View of Tragedy* ventured to suggest a possible tragedy dealing with the time of Elizabeth and the coming of the Spanish Armada, though placing the scene in Madrid and working out the play on the lines of classical tragedy[2]. To which suggestion Dennis made ironic reply in *The Impartial Critick*, ridiculing the idea by imagining the scene in England and picturing a chorus of ladies dancing a saraband while Queen Elizabeth bewailed the landing of the Spanish[3].

Yet defence of the English scene as a possible setting for tragedy was also made on the grounds of classical precedent. The prologue to John Caryll's *English Princess* expressed the usual arguments:

> You must to day your Appetite prepare
> For a plain English Treat of homely Fare:
>
> * * * *
>
> But to plain Hollinshead, and down right Stow
> We the coarse web of our Contrivance owe.
>
> * * * *
>
> Greece, the first Mistress of the Tragick Muse,
> To grace her Stage did her own Heroes chuse;
>
> * * * *
>
> On us our Country the same duty lays,
> And English Wit should English Valour raise[4].

In spite of such appeals, however, the remote setting was usually chosen for tragedy, and conversely, the contemporary English setting was as a rule adopted for

[1] Printed with *Gondibert: an Heroic Poem* (1651). Cf. pp. 11, 12, 52, 53.

[2] Reprinted by Spingarn, *op. cit.* Cf. vol. II, pp. 216, 217.

[3] *Ibid.* vol. III, pp. 148, 149.   [4] Text of 1674 used.

comedy. Such settings were, of course, inherent in the heroic tragedy and the comedy of manners as dramatic necessities, but the fact remains that they were justified on the basis of classical authority.

Because tragedy occasionally admitted of supernatural intervention, "machines" were also a possible feature of the representation of tragedy as distinguished from comedy. Aristotle said that the unravelling of the plot should arise out of the plot itself and should not be brought about by the *deus ex machina*. The *deus ex machina* should, indeed, according to Aristotelian precept, be used only when events which are antecedent or subsequent to the action of the play must be related or foretold; since the gods can see all things, they may be brought to the stage to tell that which lies beyond the possible knowledge of men. But within the action of the drama there must be nothing irrational.

Concerning this classical prohibition Dryden wrote in his essay "Of Heroic Plays" that

an heroic poet is not tied to a bare representation of what is true, or exceeding probable; but that he may let himself loose to visionary objects, and to the representation of such things, as, depending not on sense, and therefore not to be comprehended by knowledge, may give him a freer scope for imagination[1].

The most elaborate piece of quibbling on the subject, however, is that contained in Dacier's notes on the passage. While condemning the use of machines in general, Dacier yet admits the possibility of their use on certain occasions, and he adds:

But to return to *Aristotle*, I can't tell whether he be not too severe, when he would have no Machines employ'd, but only to explain those things which are out of the action. 'Tis out of doubt, that this Law is made for Pieces of the first Rank, and I believe this rigor must and ought to be moderated, and Machines

[1] Cf. *Works*, vol. iv, p. 23.

suffered in the unravelling of the subject, provided it cannot be well done, any other way. It seems *Horace* mitigated this precept, when he is content, to say in general

> Nec Deus intersit, nisi dignus vindice nodus
> Inciderit:
> Let great occasion make the Gods attend,
> And no slight cause oblige them to descend.

And if we take due notice, the practice of the antients is conformable to this Opinion....I put into the number of the Machines, which *Aristotle* speaks of, that furious storm, which makes the unravelling of the *Second Oedipus*...for altho' *Jupiter* does not appear, 'tis he who sends the Tempest, during which *Oedipus* is buried. We see then, that Machines may be employed, not only out of, but also in the action of Tragedy, provided there be an absolute necessity for them....The poets ought not to be prodigal of their Miracles, and their Gods.

Yet Dacier continues in the strain of Dryden to argue that "the Gods can see all things, and take care of men." Hence they may appear at times. They are not so much out of reason as above reason, incomprehensible and uncomprehended[1].

Thus on the basis of such reasonable interpretation the gods were brought to the stage by the most devout classicists. But other divine agencies were also recognized on the tragic stage of the period as the arbiters of human destiny; angels and spirits visibly participated in human affairs. Furthermore pity and terror were roused in the audience and the participants in the dramatic action alike by other manifestations of the supernatural on the stage. Ghosts and furies and devils rose from beneath the stage, while the thunder roared, the lightning flashed, and strange wonders were performed. The full spectacular equipment of an heroic

---

[1] Cf. pp. 253–5. Cf. also D'Aubignac, *op. cit.* Bk iii, pp. 93–6, for the citing of classical precedent.

tragedy was well ridiculed in Duffet's *Empress of Morocco* with its constant "Scene opens," its recurring thunder and lightning, its ghost, its dancing, its machines which include witches flying over the stage and Hecate descending in a basket[1].

The grafting of pagan rules for the conduct of the gods on to plays written under the shadow of a Christian Puritanism which threatened the existence of the theatre brought curious results. Pagan gods were interpreted in the terms of the hierarchies of the heaven and hell of Christian theology. Pity and terror were roused by the thunderbolts which expressed still the power of divine justice. But to these older means of manifesting the supernatural were added those which were derived from the practice of magic.

Thus the Aristotelian discussion of "machines" which might introduce the gods to effect the unravelling of the plot became confused with his discussion of the use of spectacle to rouse pity and terror, for the seventeenth-century audience invariably associated machines and spectacle[2], and the critics were prone to do likewise. In this they found a certain justification in the fact that machines were most often used to represent some supernatural agency, and the audience was moved to pity

[1] Published 1674.

[2] The history of the use of machines on the English stage is interwoven with that of their use on the French stage. The French wonder-workers in spectacle, Torelli, and Gaspare and Carlo Vigarani, were brought to France from Italy. The history of their work and of the *Salle des Machines* in the Tuileries is given by Mr W. J. Lawrence in his "Louis XIV's Scene Painters," in his *Elizabethan Playhouse*, Second Series, pp. 203 *sq*. The influence of the *Salle des Machines*, which was opened February 7, 1662, constitutes a chapter in the history of the English theatre which has as yet been by no means adequately written, for practically all of the great spectacles of the period were adapted from those originally produced in the *Salle des Machines* or were indebted for ideas of spectacle to those produced there.

and terror by the presence of the supernatural. However, the two possible functions of the agents of divine justice in unravelling the plot and in inspiring pity and terror were never clearly differentiated in the drama of the period.

Writing in the *Spectator* for April 20, 1711, Addison said:

Among the several artifices which are put in practice by the poets to fill the minds of an audience with terror, the first place is due to thunder and lightning, which are often made use of at the descending of a god, or the rising of a ghost, at the vanishing of a devil, or at the death of a tyrant. I have known a bell introduced into several tragedies with good effect; and have seen the whole assembly in a very great alarm all the while it has been ringing. But there is nothing which delights and terrifies our English theater so much as a ghost, especially when he appears in a bloody shirt. A specter has very often saved a play....

And he adds, "For the moving of pity, our principal machine is the handkerchief[1]."

An excess of spectacle designed to rouse pity and terror came to distinguish heroic tragedy as a type. The bloody cloud, the flashes of fire from the altar, the hand appearing to write fearful words upon the wall, were common variations from the older forms of such spectacle. Gradually the gentler spirits from above descended to music rather than thunder when they came to afford peace and protection to the hectored heroes of the stage, while thunder and lightning, tolling bells, and similar devices were reserved for the terrifying manifestations of the supernatural.

In comedy the use of machines save that of the *exostra* was generally unnecessary. With the rise of the comedy of manners and the presentation of interior

[1] No. 44.

scenes on the stage[1] as dramatic setting for plays the need for any such machine rapidly disappeared[2]. Though instances of its use are still to be found, it was no longer essential.

The difficulty of maintaining any rigid distinctions between dramatic types in the face of the popular demand for spectacle was also enhanced by the introduction of opera during this period. Dryden in his preface to *Albion and Albanius* gives us the most complete definition

[1] Professor Odell, *op. cit.* vol. I, pp. 113, 114, discusses the question of the presentation of interior scenes by means of the *chambre-à-quatre-portes*. He bases his belief on the words of the prologue to the Duke of Newcastle's *Country Captaine*, produced at Blackfriars in 1640, and as Professor Odell says, taking "a fling at certain plays recently using scenery at the 'private' houses." The prologue says:

> Gallants, I'le tell you what we not meane
> To shew you here, a glorious painted Scene,
> With various doores, to stand instead of wit,

which Professor Odell says "speaks conclusively for the age before Davenant's and Killigrew's theatres." The uncertainty that applied to the use of the word *scene*, the undisputed presence of proscenium doors, and the lack of appropriateness of "a glorious painted scene" as a phrase to describe the *chambre-à-quatre-portes* are considerations which tend to make this reference seem to me anything but conclusive. The other piece of evidence, which Professor Odell refers to as "the rarest 'find' conceivable," is Flecknoe's description in the *Damoiselles à la Mode* (quoted by Malone, *op. cit.* vol. III, p. 92, note, and by Lawrence, *Elizabethan Playhouse*, p. 167): "the Scaenes & Cloaths being the least Considerable in it, any *Italian* Scaenes with four Doors serving for the one...." Whether this can be made to constitute absolute proof of the use of the French *chambre-à-quatre-portes* or its equivalent seems dubitable, but Professor Odell makes it serve to substantiate not only his acceptance of this method of staging interior scenes but also his belief in the reality of the unbroken side scenes which the "sculptures" of *The Empress of Morocco* and the frontispiece of *Ariane* depict, so that he accepts also the use of lateral scenes on the stage.

[2] A very interesting scene of this sort is introduced in Killigrew's *The Princess: or, Love at First Sight,* published in 1663, where in Act III. Scene ii, the technique follows definitely that used in Aristophanes's *Acharnians*.

of an opera as it was conceived in the seventeenth century:

An opera is a poetical tale, or fiction, represented by vocal and instrumental music, adorned with scenes, machines, and dancing. The supposed persons of this musical drama are generally supernatural, as gods, and goddesses, and heroes, which at least are descended from them, and are in due time to be adopted into their number.

He adds, however, that meaner persons may be introduced if they are of the Golden Age, such as shepherds, innocent and happy, "who, by reason of the spare time they had, in their almost idle employment, had most leisure to make verses, and to be in love[1]." In this statement is seen the essentially close relation between opera and tragedy on the one hand, and opera and pastoral on the other.

Of the confused notion which resulted concerning the representation of pastoral the most specific account with which I am familiar is that contained in the author's complaint over the failure of *The Constant Nymph: or, The Rambling Shepherd*:

As for Adornments, in Habit, Musick, and Scene-Work, it was Vacation-time, and the Company would not venture the Charge: Though they could not be ignorant, that without such Embellishments, they might, with as much hope to have it take, have presented a Masque as a Pastoral. For, as well the one as the other receives it's Grace, more from Show then Plot; from Novel, and Sprightly Aires and Dances, then curious and busy Intrigues borrowing more indeed of the Opera then Comedy. Wherefore, in regard of the great Cost in the Presentation of them, they are both of them made almost the peculiar divertisement of Courts, at the Celebration of Marriages, and the like Splendid Entertainments[2].

---

[1] *Works*, vol. VII, pp. 228, 229, 232.
[2] "Written by a Person of Quality," and published in 1678.

But the close relation between opera and tragedy was still more influential in the stage representations of the period. The participation of gods and goddesses in the action of opera made the use of machines a matter of course. The exalted station of the characters made luxurious presentation necessary. Thus the popular idea of opera came to be chiefly concerned with music, machines, and spectacle[1]. Downes wrote of Davenant's *Macbeth* as "being drest in all it's Finery, as new Cloath's, new Scenes, Machines, as flyings for the Witches; with all the Singing and Dancing in it[2]." And he added, "it being all Excellently perform'd, being in the nature of an Opera, it Recompenc'd double the Expence; it proves still a lasting Play." Of Shadwell's *The Lancashire Witches*, he wrote also as "a kind of Opera, having several *Machines* of Flyings for the Witches, and other Diverting Contrivances in't[3]."

Dryden wrote of his *Albion and Albanius* as intended for a prologue to

a play in the nature of "The Tempest"; which is a tragedy mixed with opera, or a drama, written in blank verse, adorned with scenes, machines, songs, and dances....It cannot properly be called a play, because the action of it is supposed to be conducted sometimes by supernatural means, or magic; nor an opera, because the story of it is not sung[4].

These operas, or "dramatic operas" as they came to be called, were the spectacular achievements of the age, but they are too familiar to every student of the stage to need description here. Yet it is necessary to recall that they were arranged, according to the evidence of their stage directions, to use the full stage of the theatres, the back flats being opened up for the great scenes; that they used the same lateral division of the stage

---

[1] Cf. Lowe, *Betterton*, p. 168.   [2] Downes, *op. cit.* p. 33.
[3] *Ibid.* p. 38.   [4] *Works*, vol. VII, pp. 237, 238.

used in the later masques, so that the heavens could be separately opened up; that they used machines of all sorts, both infernal and heavenly spirits being brought to the stage in most spectacular fashion. The contribution of these operas to stage spectacle must not be minimized, for *The Tempest*, *Psyche*, *The Lancashire Witches*, *Circe*, *King Arthur*, *Albion and Albanius*, and the other operas brought a famous array of painting and machinery to the English stage and greatly increased the demand for spectacle[1].

Yet always the madness of operatic spectacle was decried by the conservatives, and always classical autho-

[1] That there was a reaction against the use of French scenery is evidenced in many ways in the last decade of the century. One of the most significant bits of evidence is that contained in Settle's *The World in the Moon* (printed 1697). In the dedicatory letter to Christopher Rich, Settle says "That never was such a Pile of Painting rais'd upon so Generous a Foundation." And he adds, "I have remov'd a long Heap of Rubbish, and thrown away all our old *French* Lumber, our Clouds of Clouts, and set the Theatrical Paintings at a much fairer Light." In his epilogue to the opera he goes further in suggesting the native origin of operatic spectacle:

> 'tis all home-spun Cloth;
> All from an *English Web*, and *English Growth*.
> But if we'd let it make a costly Dance
> To Paris, and bring home some Scenes from France,
> I'm sure 'twould take: For you, Gadzooks, are civil;
> And wish them well, that wish you at the Devil.

The italicizing here makes it evident that the play on the word *Web* was based on the name of a man, and since John Webb was in fact the designer of the first English operatic scenery, the reference seems unmistakably to him. However, the coarse farce interwoven with the opera gives further opportunity for ridiculing Jo Haynes and his search in France for machines for the King's House, which journey he is supposed to have taken with the engineer for the Duke's House. The "machine" which he has brought home is a bed which lets down under the stage, "and this Machine," he is made to say, "and a few Clouds of Clouts, was all we brought over for Two Thousand Guineas."

rity was invoked in the *pro* and *con* of the argument. Rymer's *Short View of Tragedy* protested:

> *Horace* was very angry with these empty *Shows* and Vanity, which the Gentlemen of his time ran like mad after.
>
> > *Insanos oculos, et gaudia vana.*
>
> What would he have said to the *French Opera*, of late so much in vogue? there it is for you to bewitch your *eyes* and to charm your *ears*. There is a cup of Enchantment, there is Musick and Machine; *Circe* and *Calipso* in conspiracy against Nature and good Sense. 'Tis a Debauch the most insinuating and the most pernicious, none would think an *Opera* and Civil Reason should be the growth of one and the same Climate[1].

Nevertheless opera was justified by the usual appeal to Aristotle and his inclusion of music and decoration as two parts of tragedy. Dacier railed at opera as "the Grotesque of Poetry," even while he used *Operas* and *Tragedies in Music* as equivalent terms. He suggested that Aristotle might have referred to the inclusion of the music of the chorus between acts when he included music as one of the parts of tragedy[2].

But the influence of operatic spectacle went far beyond its own bounds. Both tragedy and comedy were influenced by it. E. Howard in his preface to *The Woman's Conquest* commented:

> Nor do I find that the serious Plays (now in use) wholly relie upon the Heroick foundation, why else are we diverted by Scenes, Machines, Habits, Jiggs, and Dances; but to give more variety of entertainment to the Spectators?[3]

And Shadwell in his preface to *The Lancashire Witches* explained:

> The Bounds being then so narrow, I saw there was no scope for the writing of an intire Comedy (wherein the Poet must have a relish of the present time;) and therefore I resolved to

---

[1] Reprinted in Spingarn, *op. cit.* Cf. vol. II, p. 214.
[2] *Op. cit.* pp. 81–3.   [3] Quoted from text of 1671 ed.

make as good an entertainment as I could, without tying myself up to the strict rules of Comedy; which was the Reason of my introducing of Witches[1].

The result of the desire to conform to the rules and at the same time to satisfy the public taste for spectacle was again compromise. Strict adherence to dramatic type could be maintained even while elasticity was secured through the introduction of extraneous episodes of spectacle into the play. The play within the play, the masquerade, the dream, the traffic with the super-natural in magic and witchcraft were devices familiar from their use by the Elizabethans, but they had been used to make their contribution to the plot. Now these devices were used for spectacle's sake alone. Only rarely did they advance the action of the play or con-tribute to the understanding of plot or character. Almost uniformly, too, they were reminiscent of the method of masque and opera.

In Settle's *Cambyses* a typical dream scene is intro-duced. In the directions for Act IV, Scene i, we read:

The scene drawn, Cambyses is discover'd seated in a chair sleeping: The Scene representing a steep Rock, from the top of which descends a large Cloud, which opening, appear various shapes of Spirits seated in form of a Councel, to whom a more glorious Spirit descends half way, seated on a Throne; at which, the former Spirits rise and Dance: In the midst of the Dance arises a Woman with a Dagger in her hand at which the Scene shuts[2].

The technique is that of the present-day cinema, but our interest here is in the use of the spectacular devices made familiar in the masque and opera of the seven-teenth century.

In the Earl of Orrery's *Black Prince* (II, i) a masque

[1] Quoted from text of 1691 ed.
[2] Text used, 1672 ed. Date of first performance, 1667 (Genest).

is shown while a royal audience sits on the stage to witness it.

The Scene opens; two Scenes of Clouds appear, the one within the other; in the hollow of each Cloud are Women and Men richly apparell'd, who sing in Dialogue and Chorus, as the Clouds descend to the Stage; then the Women and Men enter upon the Theater, and dance; afterwards return into the Clouds, which insensibly rise, all of them singing until the Clouds are ascended to their full height; then onely the Scene of the King's magnificent Palace does appear, all the Company arise[1].

Magic may be used to bring spectacle to the stage also, as in Crowne's *Charles the Eighth of France* (Act v), where as the magician exercises his power,

There arises a Spirit, and immediately the Scene is drawn, and the supposed shapes of Charles and Julia are presented; royally habited, and seated on Chairs of State, at their feet several Masquers; and near the Chairs the Music in White Robes, and Laurels on their heads. A Chorus of Voices and loud Music heard. The Duchess seems much disturb'd at the Vision, and with a naked poynard moves towards the shapes, but is stopt by the Magician, whilst at the same time one of the Masquers touches her with a White Wand, at which she seems to fall into a slumber, and is plac'd on a Chair by the Magician. Then the Masquers rise and dance; after a dance the Spirit descends, and the Scene closes[2].

In comedy both masque and masquerade were introduced, and magic also was resorted to for the sake of spectacle. But in both comedy and tragedy diversion was frequently attained by the less costly method of introducing musicians and dancers to perform in the scene.

Mr Lawrence has indicated the tendency of these

[1] Text used, 1669 ed. Date of first performance 1667 (Genest).

[2] Cf. *The Dramatic Works of John Crowne* (Maidment and Logan ed. *Dramatists of the Restoration*), vol. I, pp. 117–218. Produced 1671 (Genest).

introduced spectacles to develop into intermedia, and he cites the instance of Ravenscroft's *The Anatomist,* which was adorned with Motteux's *The Loves of Mars and Venus* given in instalments between the acts[1]. However, it must be remembered that the intermedia had probably antedated the period of the introduced masque and should probably be considered as cause as well as effect for this phenomenon. But underneath all the changing aspects of introduced spectacle we find the constant clash between the classical demand for purity of dramatic type and popular demand for variety and spectacle. As a result, during this post-Restoration period, the introduced spectacle was of the type made familiar in masque and opera.

[1] Cf. W. J. Lawrence, "The Persistence of Elizabethan Conventionalisms," in *Elizabethan Playhouse,* Second Series, pp. 151 *sq.,* for a very interesting discussion of the whole question of introduced spectacle.

CHAPTER XVII

"DISCOVERIES"

THE chief contemporary criticism of the English stage of the seventeenth century was directed to the bloody scenes which were enacted on it. Chappuzeau, writing in 1674 on *Le Théâtre François*, said:

> Estant à Londres il y a six ans, j'y vis deux fort belles troupes de comédiens, l'une du roy, et l'autre du duc d'York, et je fus à deux représentations, à la Mort de Montezuma, roy de Mexique, et à celle de Mustapha, qui se défendoit vigoureusement sur le théâtre contre les muets qui le vouloient étrangler; ce qui faisoit rire, et ce que les François n'auroient représenté que dans un récit[1].

Rapin in his Reflections on Aristotle's *Treatise of Poesie*, which was translated into English in 1674 by Thomas Rymer, said: "The English, our Neighbors, love Blood in their Sports, by the quality of their Temperament. These are Insularies, separated from the rest of men; we are more humane[2]."

To this comment Rymer in his preface to the translation added:

> And, perhaps, it may be true, that on our Stage are more Murders than on all the Theatres in Europe. And they who have not time to learn our Language, or be acquainted with our Conversation, may there in three hours time behold so much blood-shed as may affright them from the inhospitable shore, as from the Cyclops Den. Let our Tragedy-makers consider this, and examine whether it be the disposition of the People, or their own *Caprice* that brings this Censure on the best natur'd Nation under the Sun[3].

[1] Cf. p. 44.　　　　　[2] Edition of 1694, p. 117.
[3] Cf. "The Preface of the Translator."

The complaint was a constant one from critics at home and abroad. Addison commented in the *Spectator* for April 20, 1711:

But among all our methods of moving pity or terror, there is none so absurd and barbarous, and which more exposes us to the contempt and ridicule of our neighbours then that dreadful butchering of one another, which is so very frequent upon the English stage. To delight in seeing men stabbed, poisoned, racked, or impaled, is certainly the sign of a cruel temper: and as this is often practiced before the British audience, several French critics, who think these are grateful spectacles to us, take occasion from them to represent us as a people that delight in blood. It is indeed very odd, to see our stage strewed with carcasses in the last scenes of a tragedy, and to observe in the wardrobe of the playhouse several daggers, poinards, wheels, bowls for poison, and many other instruments of death.

Yet Addison adds that the French custom of enacting all murders and executions behind the scenes likewise gives rise to ludicrous situations. He argues that Horace did not intend to prohibit all deaths on the stage, "but only such as had too much horror in them, and which would have a better effect upon the audience when transacted behind the scenes." Furthermore he finds the custom of the ancient dramatists on which the rule is based to have sprung from the fact that violent deaths were improbable when represented on the stage rather than from any abhorrence of the sight of death itself. This interpretation of the rule Addison justified by citing the ancient custom of exposing to the view of the audience the bodies of those who had met death behind the scenes but a short time before[1].

The French attitude toward the rule had been explained by D'Aubignac:

The Decoration of the Stage, is the Image of those places where the thing is suppos'd to be transacted....'Tis to arrive to

[1] *Spectator*, No. 44.

this Representation of the thing, that the Poet causes sometimes one, sometimes another Actor to appear, and discourse upon the Stage: making recitals of things that ought to be known, and yet ought not to appear; and employing Machines, and other Contrivances, for the appearance of those things which are to be shew'd to the Audience[1].

Furthermore he had explained the method of the classical dramatists in representing death:

Eschylus causes *Agamemnon* to be murder'd in his Palace; but the Audience must know this, and how does he inform them of it? He makes the Unfortunate Prince cry out like a man that expires under the violence of those who murder him. *Sophocles* observes the same thing in the murder of *Clitemnestra* by the hand of *Orestes*. And I cannot but admire at some who tax both those Poets of having defil'd the Stage with blood, when 'tis apparent that they are kill'd in the Houses represented upon the Stage, and out of sight of the Spectators, who only hear their cries and lamentations, and see the body afterwards when 'tis dead[2].

Dacier commented on this same subject:

A Poet has need of a great deal of Judgment, and Ingenuity, not to leave any of those Incidents behind the Scene, which will affect the Audience by being seen: And to hide those which might offend by reason of their Cruelty, or be found fault with for the want of probability[3].

While it is thus evident that the custom of having death take place behind the scenes was being defended on the grounds both of the offence given by representing cruelty on the stage and of the sense of improbability which clung to such representations, it is also evident that the critics were concerned with the various methods of making death known effectively. In general, the French relied upon "narrations" or

[1] D'Aubignac, *op. cit.* Bk i, p. 34.   [2] *Ibid.* Bk i, p. 40.
[3] Dacier, *op. cit.* p. 276.

"recitals." But the English stage made persistent use of "discoveries." The flat scene easily drawn on or off to conceal or reveal what had taken place within the scene made the use of the *exostra* no longer necessary to these discoveries, and the drama of the period is crowded with stage directions explaining "Scene draws to discover" or "Scene draws to reveal" some event transacted behind the scenes. Such stage customs are significant, for they reveal a definite and conscious imitation of classical precedent as it was interpreted at the time.

In 1665 Sir Robert Howard in the preface to *Four New Plays* commented on the French custom of "presenting the business in Relations" and on the English imitations of this custom. He insisted that while many old plays would be ridiculous if presented in their full horror, and while they consequently demanded the method of narration, the use of such a subject as enforced this method was undesirable, for representation is always more effective than narration[1].

Dryden argued the question at length in the *Essay on Poesy*, repeating the familiar arguments of classical authority and French precedent, and opposing them by those concerning the unnaturalness of "narrations" and the demand of the English public for battle and blood and tumult on the stage[2].

It must always be remembered that the classicists could cite Aristotle in justifying the presentation of death, for death could be used to move pity and terror. Therefore the "discovery" came to be regarded as the means of rousing pity and terror, while the classical prohibition of death on the stage was also observed. But it must also be remembered that the "discovery" was in reality a compromise between the French method

[1] Reprinted in Spingarn, *op. cit.* Cf. vol. II, p. 99.
[2] *Works*, vol. xv, pp. 323–38.

of narrations and the method of representing horror demanded by the English public. It was, too, a compromise which found defenders among those who cited classical precedent as justification.

The method of presenting these discoveries can most easily be understood from certain typical instances of their use. For example, at the close of Act v of Thomas Porter's *The Villain*[1], Malignii enters "gag'd and blinded with a Handkerchief 'twixt two servants." Then he is led off, his cries are heard from within, and "Malig[nii] discover'd pierct with a stake."

Settle was among those most habitually addicted to the use of the discovery, and a typical discovery is represented in one of the "sculptures" of *The Empress of Morocco*. In his *The Conquest of China by the Tartars*[2] he expresses all the horror of which his imagination was capable. The king has almost decided to let his queens live to see him die when he is told that it is too late. As Lagoque exclaims,

See there the Ruins of your sinking State,

The Scene opens, and is discovered a Number of Murdered Women, some with Daggers in their Breasts, some thrust through with Swords, some Strangled, and others Poyson'd; with several other Forms of Death.

Very often the discovery is used to connote the happening which it was impossible to present on the stage. Thus in Banks's *The Destruction of Troy*[3], though Achilles kills Troilus on the stage, in Act iv "The Scene draws, and discovers Polyxana weeping over the dragg'd Body of Troilus," the last indignity being thus suggested.

Durfey likewise used the discovery to reveal cruelty

---

[1] Text used, 1670 ed. Produced 1662 (Genest).
[2] Text used, 1676 ed. Produced 1674 (Genest).
[3] Text used, 1679 ed. Produced 1678 (Genest).

PLATE VIII

A "DISCOVERY" AS REPRESENTED BY ONE OF THE "SCULPTURES"
IN *THE EMPRESS OF MOROCCO*
Reproduced through the courtesy of Professor F. C. Brown

impossible to enact on the stage. *The Famous History of the Rise and Fall of Massaniello*[1] presented as a final scene a discovery thus described in the stage directions:

The Scene opens and discovers the Trunk of Massaniello Headless and Handless, dragg'd by Horses, his Head and Hands fastened to a Pole, with an Inscription, and behind these the Bodies of Blonzabella, Pedro and Pietro Hanging upon Gibbets.

The prohibition of death on the stage resulted in other curious compromises also. Ravenscroft's *The Italian Husband*[2] offers a particularly interesting study of devices thus resorted to. Though scorning the plays which are "all Talk and no business[3]," he accepted the necessity of concealing death from the sight of the audience. Therefore when in Act III, Alfonso is murdered as he sits at the banquet, "A little Silk Curtain falls to screen him, that hung ruffled above his Head." Then "They draw up the Curtain. Alfonso appears murder'd, one Dagger in his Breast, with the Picture, another in his Forehead, all bloody." When the body of Alfonso has been subsequently shown lying in a bed, and when the duchess has been summoned by the duke to view it, the duke "Pulls the Bed-Curtains over her Face, and strangles her, sitting in the chair." After an interval he "Throws the Curtains off and looks on her." The demand for the observance of the stage decencies has again been heeded.

[1] Text used, date lacking. Printed 1699 (Genest).
[2] Text used, 1698 ed. Produced 1697 and probably earlier (Genest).
[3] Cf. the Poet's defence in "The Praelude" to the play.

CHAPTER XVIII

MOVABLE SCENES AND THE
UNITY OF PLACE

THE final stand of the classicists was always made on the matter of the unities[1], and at this period the unity of place was definitely accepted as authorized by ancient precept and example. The English were again accused of non-conformity. Sorbière, after commenting on the beauty of the theatres and the stage spectacle, added:

> Les Poëtes se mocquent de l'uniformité du lieu, & de regle des vingt-quatre heures. Ils sont des comedies de vingt-cinq ans, & apres avoir representé au premier acte le mariage d'un Prince, ils representent tout d'une suite les belles Actions de son fils, & luy sont voir bien du pays[2].

To these charges Dr Sprat made excited reply:

> He grants *our Stage to be handsom, our Musick tolerable,* better I suppose, then that of the *Polack Gentleman.* But yet he says that *our Poets laugh at the Rules of Time, and Place: that all our Playes contain the Actions of Five and Twenty years: that we Marry a Prince in the First Act, and bring in his Son fighting in the Second, and his Grand-child in the Third.* But here, Sir, he has committed a greater disorder of time, then that whereof he accuses our Stage: For he has confounded the Reign of King *Charles the Second,* with that of Q. *Elizabeth.* 'Tis true, about an hundred years ago, the *English Poets* were not very exact in such decencies; But no more then were the *Dramatists* of any other Countries. The *English* themselves did laugh away

---

[1] An illuminating discussion of this question in its relation to the critical doctrines of the time is contained in Professor C. H. C. Wright's chapter on "The Drama," in his *French Classicism* (1920), pp. 116–36.

[2] Sorbière, *op. cit.* pp. 129, 130.

such absurdities as soon as any, and for these last *Fifty* yeares, our Stage has been as Regular in those Circumstances, as the best in *Europe*. Seeing he thinks fit to upbraid our present Poets, with the errors of which their predecessors were guilty so long since: I might as justly impute the vile absurdities that are to be found in *Amadis de Gaul*, to *Monsieur de Corneille*, *de Scudery*, *de Chapelaine*, *de Voiture*, and the rest of the famous Modern *French* Wits[1].

The question which the dramatists and critics and managers were alike facing was that of satisfying the public and at the same time observing the rule in regard to unity of place. Ultimately the question resolved itself into a search for methods by which changes of scene could be secured without violation of the unity of place[2]. The first definite and considerable attack was made on the problem by D'Aubignac, who explained the omission of any reference to the unity of place on the part of Aristotle by the fact that "this Rule was in his time too well known." Furthermore, he affirmed, the chorus on the stage throughout the performance would make unity of place obvious and necessary.

At the outset D'Aubignac recognized the identity of the scene and the place of dramatic action. To him the scenes were no longer decorations or illustrations; their function was to represent the place of the action. Yet he did not fail to recognize their attractiveness for the public. Accordingly he advised:

That when the Spectacles are of *Things*, that is of Permanent Objects, they must, if possible, appear at the first opening of the

---

[1] Sprat, *op. cit.* pp. 243, 244.

[2] Cf. D. C. Stuart, "Stage Decoration and Unity of Place in France in the Seventeenth Century," in *Modern Philology*, vol. x, pp. 393–406, for a study of the compromises on the French stage which resulted from the clash of the desire for conformity and the desire for variety on the stage. To Professor Stuart's analysis I am indebted for suggestions in regard to certain types of staging thus effected.

Stage, to the end that the Surprise and Applause of the People, which generally attends such Sights, may be over, before the Actors begin to speak: or that if there be any necessity of changing the Decorations, let it be done in the Interval of an Act, that the Workmen may have the time necessary for their Machines moving, and the Actor that is to appear, that of dressing himself at leisure. But if, by the necessity of his Subject, some great Change is to be in the middle of an Act, let him contrive his Actors Part so, as he have but little to say at that time, and those too Words of Admiration, Grief, or Astonishment, to give some time to the Murmur of the Spectators, which is always rais'd upon some such new Appearance[1].

All rules for the management of scenes were based on the fundamental demand for verisimilitude. Thus he argued:

Let it be allowed for a certain truth, that the Place, where the first Actor, who opens the Play, is suppos'd to be, ought to be the same place to the end of the Play; and that, it not being in the ordinary course of Nature, that the Place can receive any change, there can be none likewise in the Representation; and by consequent, that all your other Actors cannot rationally appear in any other place.

But we must remember, that the Place, which cannot be suppos'd to change, is the *Area* or floor of the Stage, upon which the Actors walk, and which the Ancients call'd by the name of *Proscenium*....

'Tis not the same with the sides and end of the Theatre, for as they do but represent those things which did actually environ the Persons acting, and which might receive some change, they may likewise receive some in the Representation, and 'tis in that that consists the changing of Scenes, and other Ornaments of Decoration which always ravish the People, and please the best Judges, when they are well done....

It is, he added, legitimate to open up the scene of a temple to reveal the interior of the temple. To show

[1] D'Aubignac, *op. cit.* Bk II, p. 98, and Bk III, pp. 98, 99.

of how great variety this interpretation of the rule
admits, he gave a curious illustration:

So for Example, he might feign a Palace upon the Sea side,
forsaken, and left to be inhabited by poor Fishermen; a Prince
landing, or being cast away there, might adorn it with all the
rich Furniture fit for it; after this by some Accident it might
be set on fire; and then behind it the Sea might appear, upon
which one might represent a Sea Fight; so that in all the five
changes of the Stage, the unity of Place would still be ingeniously
preserv'd; not but that the very floor or *Proscenium* may change
too, provided it be superficially, as if some River should overflow
it, as the *Tyber* did in the time of Augustus; or if Flames came
out of the Earth and cover'd the face of it, in all those cases the
unity of place would not be broke.

The place presented on the stage must be large
enough to make it probable that an actor at one end
of the stage would be unable to identify another whom
he saw at the other end of the stage, for many plays
are dependent on such circumstances. Furthermore it
is necessary to choose certain rooms or certain houses
for representation on the stage, for it is impossible to
represent all the rooms or all the houses of a city, in
which case someone would be somewhere on the stage
all the time. Yet it is impossible to represent a place
with too many intervening objects removed. The *Louvre*
at one side of the stage and the *Place Royale* at the other
are improbable, for one cannot imagine away all the
intervening objects.

That such a compromise was not to be interpreted
too indulgently was indicated, however, by the dictum:

Let it then be setled for a constant Maxim, That the *Proscenium*, or floor of the Stage, can represent nothing but some open
place of an ordinary extent, where those, that are represented
by the Actors, might naturally be in the truth of the Action;
and when we see it written, The Scene is at *Aulis, Eleusis,* or
Argos, 'tis not that the place, where the Actors appear, is all that

Town or Province, but onely that all the Intrigues of the Play, as well what passes out of the sight of the Spectators, as what they see, are treated in that Town, of which the Stage takes up but the least part[1].

The great compromise concerning changes of scene and unity of place, however, was that of Corneille in his *Troisième Discours*, published in 1660 and dealing with the three unities. Corneille recognized the fact that neither Aristotle nor Horace had said anything about the unity of place; yet he felt that the rule might have been established as the result of the acceptance of the rule of unity of time. Since in modern times kings and princes do not come into public places to discuss their secrets, and since it is likewise improbable that they who act in a tragedy will all find their confidants in the same room, Corneille suggested:

je voudrais, a leur exemple, introduire des fictions de théâtre, pour établir à lieu théâtral...une salle sur laquelle ouvrent ces divers appartemens, a qui j'attribuerois deux privileges: l'un, que chacun de ceux qui parleroient fut presumé y parler avec le même secret que s'il étoit dans sa chambre; l'autre, qu'au lieu que dans l'ordre comme il est quelquefois de la bienseance que ceux qui occupent le théâtre aillent trouver ceux qui sont dans leur cabinet pour parler a eux, ceux-ci pussent les venir trouver sur le théâtre sans choquer cette bienseance, afin de conserver l'unité de lieu et la liaison de scenes[2].

Corneille suggested also that unity of place might still be preserved if the place was conceived to be a single house or a single village or city. The whole village need not, however, be shown, but only two or three selected parts of the village or city. The unity of the whole could be indicated by the use of the place name.

[1] D'Aubignac, *op. cit.* Bk ii, pp. 100 *sq.*

[2] *Théâtre de Corneille*, avec les commentaires de Voltaire (1797), vol. i, pp. 185 *sq.*

In this case the scene must not be changed within the act.

I have quoted these two interpreters of unity of place because it was to their influence that the English stage was largely indebted for the compromises which were evident in the staging of plays throughout the succeeding period. The dramas themselves give ample evidence that the methods thus suggested were tried and to a certain extent adopted on the English stage.

Among English critics Dryden gives the arguments concerning unity of place that were most influential in regard to the stage presentation of plays. Always an apologist for compromises, Dryden was forever insisting "how much in vain it is for you to strive against the stream of people's inclination." In the *Essay of Dramatic Poesy* the dialogue form gave opportunity for the presentation of various points of view in regard to the critical matters discussed. Two points in the discussion of unity of place are of importance here, however. First and most important was Dryden's recognition of the fact that painted scenes were aids to illusion such as would make change of place seem more probable. The second was the suggestion in line with that of the French critics that near-by places could be perceived and accepted by the spectators as one place[1].

To the arguments contained in this essay Sir Robert Howard replied in his preface to *The Great Favourite, or, The Duke of Lerma*:

To shew therefore upon what ill grounds they dictate *Lawes* for *Dramatick Poesie*, I shall endeavor to make it evident that there's no such thing as what they all pretend; for, if strictly and duely weigh'd, 'tis as impossible for one stage to present two Houses or two Roomes truely as two Countreys or Kingdomes,

[1] Cf. Dryden, *Works*, vol. xv, pp. 297, 298. For a study of the critical work of the period in England as it touched the matter of the unities, cf. Friedland, *op. cit.* concluding chapter.

and as impossible that five houres, or four and twenty houres should be two houres and a halfe as that a thousand houres or yeares should be less then what they are...for Impossibilities are all equal, and admit no degrees[1].

In 1668 Dryden in his *Defence of an Essay of Dramatic Poesy* again commented on the fact that the audience might by the aid of the imagination be led to regard a change of place as effected by a change of scene. He also emphasized the suggestion previously made in regard to the inclusiveness of the single place represented:

for 'tis proved that a stage may properly represent two rooms or houses; for the imagination being judge of what is represented, will in reason be less shocked with the appearance of two rooms in the same house, or two houses in the same city, than with two distant cities in the same country, or two remote countries in the same universe[2].

The experiments evident in the dramas of the period afford us our clearest proof of the acceptance of the idea of unity of place in theory at least. Perhaps the most curious adherence to the rule was in such plays as pictured two far distant places united in a single scene as background for the action. Thus Stapylton's *Hero and Leander* is written for a scene described as "The Towers and Towns of Sestos and Abydos, the Hellespont flowing between them," and the entrances are arranged for Sestos and Abydos as the action demands[3]. Hopkins's *Pyrrhus King of Epirus* was supposed to be enacted in a scene which represented "The City of Argos besieged by King Pyrrhus; the Camp of the Epirotes on the one side, and that of the Macedonians, who came to the Relief of it, on the other." Only one change in the scene is described: "The Scene Draws,

---

[1] Cf. Spingarn, *op. cit.* vol. II, pp. 108, 109.

[2] Ker, *op. cit.* vol. I, p. 127. Cf. also p. 129.

[3] Whether or not this play was ever acted is uncertain. Its title-page indicates that it was licensed in 1668 and printed in 1669.

and Discovers the Image of a Bull and Wolf Engraven in Copper, and placed at the Entrance of the Forum," which was the recognized omen of disaster[1].

Though the unchanging scene might thus be accepted as the equivalent of unity of place, the audience was not in this way satisfied in its demand for variety and excitement. The most frequent compromise therefore resorted to by those who would serve both public and critics was that suggested by Corneille—a general unity of place incorporating a variety of scenes within it. The great majority of the plays of the period were arranged in this fashion to include both unity and variety. The place was indicated—usually at the close of the record of the *dramatis personae* in the printed play—as "London" or "Paris," while the scene was allowed to move about within the anything but narrow confines thus established. The comedies were generally indicated as having London for their place of action. Yet Wycherley's *Plain-Dealer*, for instance, while having London for its place of action, presented scenes in Captain Manly's lodging, in Olivia's lodging, in Westminster Hall, in Eliza's lodging, and in the Cock in Bon-street[2]. The expectation of more elaborate settings for tragedy than for comedy was generally fulfilled by a greater variety of scenes, but the same principle prevailed in their arrangement. Thus in Crowne's *The History of Charles the Eighth of France*, while the place is Naples, the scenes represent "a fair country before the walls of Naples," a room in the palace, a grove, etc., a variety sufficient to prove the rule of unity of place as working no hardship to the dramatist.

That such changes of scene were regarded as conforming to the classical demand for unity of place is

[1] Text used, 1695 ed. Produced 1695 (Genest).
[2] Text used, *William Wycherley*, ed. by W. C. Ward (1888), pp. 363 *sq*.

seen in Dryden's preface to *Secret Love*: "I would tell the Reader that it is regular, according to the strictest of Dramatick Laws[1]." Yet the scene of action varies from the walks near the court, to the queen's apartment, and to the court gallery, even while the place remains "Sicily."

But in his preface to *Don Sebastian*, where the action moves from place to place within the castle, Dryden apologized:

> I must further declare freely, that I have not exactly kept to the three mechanic rules of unity. I knew them, and had them in my eye, but followed them only at a distance; for the genius of the English cannot bear too regular a play: we are given to variety, even to a debauchery of pleasure. My scenes are therefore sometimes broken, because my under-plot required them so to be, though the general scene remains,—of the same castle[2]....

The scenes here represented are within the Castle of Alcazar, but they include a market-place under the castle, a terrace walk on the side of the castle, a garden, a "night scene of the Mufti's garden," Benducai's palace in the castle, the castle yard, and a room of state. Certainly variety was not lacking.

A town or village was sometimes represented, according to the suggestion of Corneille, by two or three houses. Tuke's *Adventures of Five Hours* devoted prologue and epilogue to extolling the new interest to be found in its limiting of the time to five hours and the place to three houses of Seville[3]. Mrs Behn's *Sir Patient Fancy* placed its scene in "London, in two houses," the adjacent houses of Lady Knowell and Sir Patient Fancy[4].

---

[1] *Works*, vol. II, p. 418.   [2] *Ibid.* vol. VII, p. 313.

[3] Text used, 1663 ed. Produced 1663 (Genest).

[4] Produced 1678. Cf. *The Works of Aphra Behn*, ed. by Montague Summers (1915) for text.

Experiments were also made with Corneille's *lieu théâtral*, which was closely approximated in Congreve's *Double-Dealer*. In this play the author declared he was "resolved to preserve the three unities of the drama[1]." The scene was laid in "A gallery in the Lord Touchwood's house, with chambers adjoining," and was varied only in the fourth act, when the scene opened to show Lady Touchwood's chamber. Mrs Mary Pix in *The False Friend* also worked out an interesting experiment, the scene being "a Hall," which furnished a common meeting-ground for the characters of the play. Here the scene apparently is drawn three times during the play to reveal interior rooms[2]. The idea of the *lieu théâtral* was most commonly used, however, in the street scenes which were habitually used in the drama of the period.

Dryden's suggestion that two places could be conceived of as one was evidently popularly accepted. Thus, to mention but a few instances taken at random, the scene of Crowne's *Darius* was "The Plains, and Town of Arbela in Persia"; of Caryll's *English Princess*, "the Head Quarters of King *Richard* and the Earl of *Richmond*, when they are in sight of one another"; of Pordage's *Siege of Babylon*, "Babylon and the Fields adjacent"; and in Banks's *The Destruction of Troy*, "Troy and before the Walls."

That changes of scene should be made between acts was a principle recognized if not always observed. The old idea of the chorus wafting the audience over sea and land by the appeal to the imagination was still influential. Also the intervals between acts made disconnected scenes less startling. Dryden explained one of the improvements he had wrought in Shakespeare's

[1] Cf. *The Comedies of William Congreve* (1895), for text. Intro. by G. E. Street.
[2] Text used, 1699 ed. Produced 1699 (Genest).

Troilus and Cressida: there is now "no leaping from Troy to the Grecian tents, and thence back again in the same act; but a due proportion of time allow'd for every motion[1]." And in the latter part of the century this relation between the lapse of time and the overcoming of space was, indeed, generally considered.

The complete recognition of the principles involved in the discussion of this question came in Farquhar's *Dissertation upon Comedy*[2], which brought to the study a sturdy good sense and incisive irony which have made it persist as one of the most interesting of critical documents. Though concluding, "I am as little a friend to those rambling plays as anybody, nor have I ever espous'd their party by my own practice; yet I cou'd not forbear saying some thing in vindication of our great Shakespear," Farquhar wrote:

So much for the decorum of Time; now for the regularity of Place. I might make one a consequence of t'other, and alledge that by allowing me any extent of time, you must grant me change of place, for the one depends upon t'other; and having five or six years for the action of a play, I may travel from Constantinople to Denmark, so to France, and home to England, and rest long enough in each country besides. But you'll say: How can you carry us with you? Very easily, sir, if you be willing to go. As for example, here is a new play; the house is throng'd, the prologue's spoken, and the curtain drawn represents you the scene of Grand Cairo. Whereabouts are you now, sir? Were you not the very minute before in the pit in the English playhouse talking to a wench, and now, *presto pass*, you are spirited away to the banks of the river Nile. Surely, sir, this is a most intolerable improbability; yet this you must allow me, or else you destroy the very constitution of representation. Then, in the second act, with a flourish of fiddles, I change the scene

[1] *Works*, vol. VI, p. 256.

[2] *A Discourse upon Comedy, The Recruiting Officer, The Beaux Stratagem*, ed. L. A. Straus (1914), pp. 1–32.

to Astrachan. *O, this is intolerable!* Look 'ee, sir, 'tis not a jot more intolerable than the other; for you'll find that 'tis much about the same distance between Egypt and Astrachan, as it is between Drury-Lane and Grand Cairo; and if you please to let your fancy take post, it will perform the journey in the same moment of time, without any disturbance in the world to your person. You can follow Quintus Curtius all over Asia in the time of Alexander, and trudge after Hannibal, like a cadet, through all Italy, Spain, and Afric, in the space of four or five hours; yet the devil a one you will stir....

Farquhar thus made concrete the principle which he enunciated as the principle of all art: "We can expect no more decorum or regularity in any business than the nature of the thing will bear...."

It is, of course, true that all the dramatists of the post-Restoration period gave more definite acceptance to the rules for unity in their critical writings than in their dramas. It is likewise true that the dramas of the transition period immediately after the Restoration were for the most part written without much heed to their regularity. But it is true also that there was in England as elsewhere a growing tendency to conformity, that this tendency to conformity was in direct conflict with the love of spectacle newly perfected and popularized on the public stage, and that the result of these conflicting desires was seen in the formulation of minute rules of conduct for the stage. These minute rules were based on the interpretation of classical principles in terms of verisimilitude or probability, and in them were expressed the compromises which established the traditions of modern stage mounting.

CHAPTER XIX

CONCLUSIONS

THE history of stage spectacle during the sixteenth and seventeenth centuries appears as fundamentally a history of the Renaissance conceptions of the ancient classical stage as these conceptions were modified by the conditions of the age into which they were projected, and as they were developed to meet a steadily increasing demand for variety and novelty in stage representations of the drama. The rapid development of stage spectacle was, however, made possible by the growing interest in and knowledge of the mathematical sciences.

As we have seen, the beginnings of the modern stage are to be traced to the dramatic performances of the Roman Academy, which showed the first scenery painted in perspective on the modern stage, and which sponsored the first edition of Vitruvius's *De Architectura*, the work which established the principles of stage mounting. From these beginnings we have seen the theory of stage spectacle elaborated and standardized by Italian artists of the Renaissance and gradually adopted throughout the whole of western Europe. Meanwhile the dramatic theories of Aristotle and other ancient writers were also extending their influence, so that they were finally applied to the presentation as well as to the construction of the drama.

Certain characteristic ideas concerning the scenic representation of the drama persisted throughout the period under observation, and it is about these ideas that the history of spectacle on the Renaissance stage centres. First among these ideas was the idea of stage spectacle as the concern of the architect (who was also the engineer), rather than of the dramatist. This idea persisted throughout the period, and because of it we find scenery developed primarily for its own sake rather than for the sake of its contribution to dramatic effectiveness. We find also the history of stage spectacle inevitably interwoven with the history of theatrical architecture.

The idea of the spectacular representation of the drama as serving especially the royal pleasure is also one of the fundamental Renaissance ideas which led to the rapid development of spectacle for its own sake. The demand for new satisfactions of the princely taste for spectacle was complemented by comparative freedom from financial worries on the part of the architect who was called upon to provide the satisfying spectacle. The result was free experimenting and rapid progress. The transference of spectacle to the public playhouse constitutes one of the interesting signs of the rise of modern democratic ideas.

The conception of scenes as the ornaments of the drama, essential to dramatic presentation in the manner of the ancients, was accepted by the early Italian academies and persisted well into the seventeenth century under the influence of the study of Vitruvius and Aristotle. That this conception became finally a conception of scenes as setting for dramatic action, as symbols or representations of dramatic place, was due largely to the transition of Aristotle's demand for probability into the demand of the French Academy for detailed verisimilitude.

The supreme artistic interest of the Renaissance was an interest in the rediscovery and development of perspective. This interest was reflected in the primary requisite for stage scenery,—that it be painted in perspective. This requirement demanded that the constituent elements of the scene, the "houses," be painted in perspective, and that they be arranged on the stage according to the rules established by perspective. The increased knowledge of mathematics gradually made possible the change from the two-sided or angle-shaped houses of the sixteenth century to the flats of the seventeenth century, the arrangement of the houses and that of the flats remaining in all essentials the same, however.

Experiments with the two types of changing scene ascribed by Servius to the ancients were to a certain extent dependent upon the development of the perspective painting of scenes on flats. When the flat scene became adequate to the representation of the drama, the *scena versatilis*, which had been the subject of early experiments, was finally discarded in favour of the *scena ductilis*, which reached its highest development through the experiments of Inigo Jones.

The "machines" of the stage seem chiefly to have been known to the Renaissance through the descriptions of Pollux and the scholia of the ancient dramas, though they were also partially described by Vitruvius. In direct imitation of the ancient stage devices the Renaissance drama introduced these machines, those most freely adopted by the English stage being the *deus ex machina*, the *exostra*, the steps and trap-doors by which the ghosts and furies were brought to the stage after the manner of the Charon's steps and the *anapeismata*, and machines for representing thunder and lightning patterned after the *bronteion* and the device used for lightning by the ancients. These machines have persisted on the stage with necessary modifications to the present day except for the *exostra*, which became an anachronism when the presentation of interior scenes was finally accepted on the stage, and when the *scena ductilis* had made possible the discovery of scenes of horror in another fashion.

Finally, in the so-called period of classicism the inevitable clash of conflicting theories and practices came about. Dramatic theories fostered by the followers of the French Academy and demanding rigid conformity to Aristotelian and Horatian precepts in their modern interpretation came into direct conflict with the popular demand for spectacle made possible through the developing art of the theatre. The result was, as we have seen, compromise and temporizing rules in regard to the admission of spectacle to the stage, in regard to the presentation of the different dramatic types, in regard to the change of scene and the change of place, in regard to the presentation of death on the stage, in regard to the introduction of heavenly and infernal beings on the stage, and in regard to the use of thunder and other devices by which terror was to be aroused. The conflict did much to cause dramatic spectacle to come to be regarded as the concern of the dramatist, to make the stage-artist subservient to the dramatist and the stage-manager. But it also did much to break down the authority of classical tradition as such, causing it to seek new justification as expressing the rules of verisimilitude, and verisimilitude led inevitably to realism on the stage as elsewhere.

Thus the Renaissance treatment of spectacle on the stage stands out as the result of the conscious and imitative re-creation of the classical stage. It was the result of scholarship. In its purpose it was aristocratic. In matters of spectacle, at least, the public stage followed after the academic stage and the court stage, which pioneered the way in the scenic representation of the drama.

INDEX

Academies, English, 162
— French, 200, 252, 291, 293
— Italian, Accademia della Virtù, 22, 23; influenced stage decoration, 10, 19, 47, 291; Olympic, 42, 55, 117; plays acted by, 11, 12, 14, 44, 46, 47; of Pomponius, 10, 84, 290
Accolti, Pietro, 150
Adams, J. Q., 3, 117, 149 n. 1, 163 n. 2, 191–3, 200 n. 1, 201, 202 n. 1, 203, 205, 211 n. 1, 231 n. 3, 251 n. 1
Addison, 263, 273
Ady, Julia C., 13 n. 2, 45 n. 1, 48 n. 2, 49, 50 n. 2, 60 n. 1
Aeschylus, 66, 67, 274
Ajax Flagellifer, 89
Alberti, Leon Battista, 28, 54, 75, 81, 145
Albion's Triumph, 176, 177
Albright, V. E., 2
Amadis de Gaul, 279
Amsterdam, 62
d'Ancona, A., 48 n. 1, 53 n. 1
Angelo, Michael, 81 n. 1
Apius and Virginia, 94
Aragon, Eleanor of, 11
Architecture, 16, 18, 32, 44, 47, 52, 56, 57, 67, 79–81, 90, 105, 118, 119, 145, 146, 159, 160, 167, 176, 177, 184, 185, 202, 204–9, 239, 240, 291; study of Roman, 23, 28, 29, 55
Aretino, Pittore, 80
Ariosto, 14, 77; *Cassaria*, 48, 49; comedies of, 14; *Suppositi*, 46, 52; theatre of, 14, 54
Aristophanes, 139, 220; *Acharnians*, 139; *Pax*, 87; *Plutus*, 86; *Thesmophoriazousae*, 139
Aristotle, 19, 66–9, 75, 81 n. 1, 127, 128, 134, 141, 253, 254, 260–2, 268, 272, 275, 279, 282, 290, 291, 293
Ascham, Roger, 87, 88, 123
d'Aubignac, 253, 261 n. 1, 273, 274, 279–281
Aubrey, 194, 218 n. 1

Augsburg, 62
Austria, Empress Maria of, 56

Bacon, Sir Francis, 146; *Essays*, 182; *New Atlantis*, 147
Bacon, Roger, 146 n. 2
Baldi, Bernardino, 145, 146
Baldwin Brown, G., 12 n. 2
Bale, Bishop, 85
Bang, W., 130 n. 1
Banks, 276, 287
Bapst, G., 45 n. 1, 53 n. 1, 59 n. 1, 198 n. 1, n. 2, 199 n. 1
Barbaro, Daniello, 25, 26, 31, 55, 57, 62, 65, 75, 119 n. 3, 135 n. 1, 145, 206
Baskervill, C. R., 76 n. 2
Basle, 62
Beaumont, 174 n. 2
Behn, Aphra, 286
Bell, Hamilton, 202, 204, 207, 241 n. 2, 242
Bellini, Niccolo, 78
Bentivogli, Giovanni Battista, 77
Bereblock, J., 90
Bernini, 197, 240
Betterton, 230, 232, 234, 240
Bibbiena, Cardinal, 77; *La Calandria*, 49–51, 61
Bigio, 15
Billingsley, Sir H., 80
Birth of Hercules, The, 134, 135
Blomfield, R., 75 n. 3, 77, 79 n. 1, n. 2, 163 n. 1, 164, 165 n. 1
Boas, F. S., 4, 86, 87 n. 1, 88, 105, 106, 127
Bologna, 77
Bond, R. W., 4, 41 n. 1, 49 n. 1, 93 n. 4, 127 n. 1
Borgo, Piero dal, 29–31
Bramante, of Milan, 20 n. 1, 28, 29, 33, 52
— of Urbino, 28
Brotanek, R., 4
Brunelleschi, 28, 59
Buckingham, Duke of, 161
Burbage, 118, 119
Burckhardt, J., 10 n. 2, 59 n. 1
Butcher, S. H., 66 n. 1

Caesariano, 21, 29, 60, 117
Cajori, Florian, 146 n. 1
Campion, 169; *Lords' Masque*, 174
Campori, G., 52, 53
Canossa, Ludovico, 49
Cantelmo, Sigismondo, 45
Caporali, 22
Carew, 214; *Coelum Britannicum*, 178
Carleton, Sir Dudley, 187
Carmellion, Alice, 78
Carnival plays, 45
Carow, John, 111
Cartwright, *Royal Slave*, 189–191, 193, 210
Caryll, John, 259, 287
Cassiodorus, 24, 125, 141
Castelvetro, 69, 70
Castiglione, 49–51, 77
de Caus, Salomon, 150
Cavallari, Antonio, 78
Cawarden, Sir T., 104
Cecca, 60
Chalmers, 191
Chambers, E. K., 3, 54, 85 n. 2, n. 3, n. 6, 93 n. 1, n. 3, 104, 118 n. 1, 177 n. 1, 178 n. 1
Chapelain, 200, 201
Chappuzeau, 255, 272
Charles I, 161, 162, 188, 190, 194, 200, 225, 226
— II, 191, 226, 229
— Emperor, 99
Charlton, 69
Charon's ladder, 65, 91, 94
Chassang, A., 9 n. 1, 10 n. 2, 11 n. 1, n. 2, 12 n. 1, n. 2, 13 n. 1, n. 2, 14 n. 1, 28 n. 2
Chaucer, 257 n. 1
Cibber, 234 n. 2, 244
Circe, 267
Clement VII, 84
Cleodora, 192, 193, 209
Cloetta, W., 9 n. 1
del Cogo, Niccolo, 13
Colet, 76, 83
Collier, 1 n. 2, 242
Collison-Morley, 244 n. 1
Comedy, 66, 86, 87, 93, 123, 124, 135, 257–260, 263, 265, 268, 270, 285; type of scenery for, 17, 36, 42, 48, 49, 52, 53, 63, 64, 104, 110
Como, 20
Congreve, *Double-Dealer*, 287

Constant Nymph, The, 265
Consuetudinary, 85
Corneille, 218, 282, 285–7; *Le Cid*, 200, 201
Coryat, *Crudities*, 55, 209
Courts, dramatic patronage of, English, 73, 82, 84–92, 96, 97, 99–116, 118, 140, 158, 162, 165–194, 202, 203, 251, 291; Italian, 13, 14, 18, 19, 23, 33, 38, 43, 44, 48–51, 53, 54, 77, 119, 167, 190, 291
Cousin, J., 31 n. 2
Creighton, M., 11 n. 1
Cromwell, 85, 229
Crowne, John, 270, 285, 287
Cunliffe, J. W., 4, 13 n. 2, 14 n. 1, 48 n. 1, 94, 95–8, 127, 133, 135, 138 n. 1
Cunningham, P., 163 n. 1, 164 n. 2

Dacier, André, 254, 260, 261, 268, 274
Daniel, Samuel, *Tethys' Festival*, 172, 184; *Vision of Twelve Goddesses*, 165, 184
Davenant, C., 240
Davenant, W., 180, 184, 210, 211, 217–234, 237, 238, 240, 259, 264 n. 1; *Gondibert*, 258; *History of Sir Francis Drake*, 227–9; *History of the Spaniards in Peru*, 226, 227; *Just Italian*, 213; *Love and Honour*, 222; *Macbeth*, 266; *Playhouse to be Let*, 238; *Salmacida Spolia*, 165, 182, 189, 223; *Siege of Rhodes*, 2, 218, 220–7, 231–3, 238
De Critz, J., 159, 161
De Laet, 23, 62, 145
De Rayssiguier, 201
De Witt, 208
Death, on stage, 135, 136, 272–7, 293
Dee, Dr John, 75 n. 3, 80, 87, 88
Denham, Sir John, 226, 238, 240
Denmark, Anne of, 162
— Court of, 162
Dennis, 259
Dido, 85, 89, 91, 92
Diogenes, 220
"Discovery," 68, 138, 212, 228, 275–7
Downes, John, *Roscius Anglicanus*, 232, 233, 266

Drama, Greek, 56, 66–9, 86, 87, 95; influence of, 10, 43, 44, 47, 58, 135, 136, 139, 199; scenery used for, 17, 18, 24, 44, 63, 65
— Roman, 12, 13, 48, 84, 86, 89; influence of, 10, 43, 44, 47, 58, 199; scenery used in, 17, 18, 24, 32, 44, 58
Drama, theory of, English, 122–141, 250, 252–289; influence of classics on, 125–7, 132, 135, 136, 139–141, 252–6, 259–261, 278, 279, 282, 293
— French, 252–4, 260–2, 273–5, 279–282, 285–7
— Italian, 66–70
Dryden, 218, 241, 242 n. 1, 243, 255, 260, 261, 275, 283, 284, 287; *Albion and Albanius*, 264, 266, 267; *Don Sebastian*, 286; *King Arthur*, 267; *Secret Love*, 286; *Troilus and Cressida*, 257
Du Breuil, 150
Du Cerceau, 31 n. 2
Du Jon, *Nomenclator*, 62
Duffet, *Empress of Morocco*, 241, 262, 264 n. 1, 276
Durand, W. Y., 91 n. 1
Dürer, Albert, 30
Durfey, 276, 277

Edward VI, 147, 191
Einstein, Lewis, 74 n. 2, 77
Elizabeth, Queen, 34, 78, 79, 85, 88, 89–92, 96, 106, 110, 114, 115, 191, 192, 194, 259
Erasmus, 76
d'Este, Duke Ercole, 11, 45; his painter, 49; patron of drama, 13
— Isabella, 48, 49, 59
Euclid, 29, 31, 80
Euripides, 69; *Medea*, 68
Evans, H. A., 174 n. 2, 175 n. 2
Evelyn, John, 62, 146, 148, 197, 217, 229, 239, 240

Farquhar, 288, 289
Ferrara, 11, 13, 14, 48, 59, 76
— Duke of, 52
Ferrari, G., 15 n. 2
Festivals, sacred, 59–61, 65
Feuillerat, A., 2, 3, 104–116, 120, 191

Fiddes, Richard, 76 n. 1
Fielding, T. H., 150 n. 1
Fisher, 76
— D. C., 200 n. 1
— John, 203
Flechsig, E., 54
Flecknoe, R., 236, 264 n. 1
Fleming, Robert, 76
Fletcher, *Faithful Shepherdess*, 192, 193
Flickinger, R. C., 136, 137
Florence, 14, 19, 59–61
Florimène, 164, 179, 189, 192, 193
Florio, 95
Francis I, 23
Franco, Battista, 15
Frankfurt, 62
Freart, 239, 240 n. 1
Friedland, 68, 69, 75 n. 4, 127, 129, 283 n. 1

Gager, W., 88
Gardner, E. G., 49 n. 1, 54 n. 3
Gascoygne, *Jocasta*, 95
Gauricus, Pomponius, 80
Genest, J., 233 n. 1
Genga, 15, 33, 38, 77
Gentileschi, 161
Gerbier, Balthazar, 162, 239
Ghirlandajo, 15
Gibbons, Grinling, 240
Gloucester, Humphrey, Duke of, 74
Gorboduc, 93, 128
Gotch, J. A., 226 n. 1
Graves, T. A., 3, 116, 120, 208 n. 1, 209 n. 4
Gray, William, 76
Greber, *Loves of Ergasto*, 245 n. 1
Greg, W. W., 3, 97 n. 1, 209 n. 1, n. 2
Grimald, Nicholas, 127
Grocyn, 76
Grynaeus, 62
Guarino, 48 n. 1

Haddington, Viscount, 170
Haigh, A. E., 64, 65, 137 n. 1
Hall, *Chronicle*, 78, 84 n. 2, 93, 99
Halliwell-Phillips, J., 231 n. 3
Hampton Court, 77
Harrington, 123
Harris, Henry, 230, 231, 240
Harvey, Gabriel, 209

Hawksmoor, N., 250
Haydocke, R., 81
Hayes, Lord, 169
Hemsterhuys, 62
Henry VII, 77, 99, 100
— VIII, 77, 100–102
— Prince, 159, 160, 173
Hentzner, P., 148 n. 1
Herbert, Sir H., 3, 191, 192
Heron, 64
Heywood, 203, 211; *Love's Mistress*, 179, 180; *The Royal King and the Loyal Subject*, 212
Higgins, *Nomenclator*, 62, 75, 94, 124, 133, 137
Historia Betica, 69
History of the Emperor Constantine, The, 11
Holbein, 78
Holinshed, 77 n. 1, 99, 101, 102, 259
Holt, John, 104
Hopkins, W., 213, 284
Horace, 75, 125, 132, 135, 141, 256, 261, 268, 273, 282, 293
Howard, Edward, 256 n. 1, 268
— Sir R., 275, 283
Hughes, *The Misfortunes of Arthur*, 96, 138
Hymenaeus, 88

Indaco, Francesca, 15
Innocent VIII, 12
Inns of Court, drama at, 82, 92–9, 118, 140
Izarde, John, 111

James I, 51, 106, 115, 159, 161, 162, 164, 165, 186–194
James, John, 249
Jason, 51
Jocundus, 19–21, 43, 52, 75, 117
Jones, Inigo, 2, 56, 57, 74, 81, 103, 106, 161–194, 202, 204, 205, 207, 223, 225, 226, 292; influences on, 5 n. 1, 163, 164, 187
Jonson, Ben, 2, 75 n. 3, 129, 131 n. 1, 132, 133, 147, 148, 163, 165, 170, 214; *Chloridia*, 176; *Every Man in his Humour*, 130, 135; *Expostulation with Inigo Jones*, 163, 183; *Fortunate Isles*, 175; *Hue and Cry after Cupid*, 170; *Masque of Augurs*, 149; *Masque of Beauty*, 169; *Masque of Blackness*, 162, 165, 185, 186; *Masque of Hymen*, 168; *Masque of Queens*, 171, 187; *Neptune's Triumph*, 175; *News from the New World*, 149; *Oberon*, 173; *Staple of News*, 83; *Tale of a Tub*, 163; *Vision of Delight*, 175
Juno, 51

Keith, W. G., 4, 5 n., 28 n. 1, 50 n. 2, 56, 164, 204, 205, 207, 223, 224
Kempe, A. J., 85 n. 5
Ker, W. P., 256 n. 1, 284 n. 2
Killigrew, Thomas, 229, 230, 234, 235, 242 n. 1, 264 n. 1
Knight, Joseph, *Roscius Anglicanus*, 2
Koeck, Pieter, 159
Kristeller, P., 14 n. 2, 45

Lancaster, H. C., 198, 199, 201
Lanier, Nicholas, 161, 174 n. 2
Laurent, 199
Laurentius Valla, 10
Lawrence, W. J., 4, 109 n. 1, 114 n. 1, 165 n. 1, 206, 210, 211 n. 1, 218, 241 n. 1, 243, 262 n. 2, 264 n. 1, 270, 271 n. 1
Leach, A. F., 83 n. 1
Leo X, 10, 46, 51, 52 n. 1
Leonardo da Vinci, 30, 59 n. 1
Leti, Gregorio, 244
Lightning, presentation of, 39, 42, 64, 92, 111, 130, 135, 157, 212, 252, 261–3, 292
Lily, 83, 84
Linacre, 62, 75, 76, 140
Lindsay, T. M., 76 n. 1
Lodge, 123
Lomatius, 81, 167 n. 2
Lowe, R. W., 2, 231, 266 n. 1
Lyzard, W., 110

Machines, 18, 19, 24, 26, 41, 51, 59–65, 67, 68, 100, 120, 136, 157, 168–176, 178, 180, 185, 187, 188, 197, 211, 212, 217, 234, 235, 237, 240, 242, 251, 252, 260–7, 274, 292; *deus ex machina*, 26, 64, 67, 68, 87, 92, 130, 132–4, 212, 260, 292; *eccyclema* and *exostra*, 24, 25, 63, 137–9, 212, 263, 275, 292; *Salle des Machines*, 237, 262 n. 2

Mahelot, 168, 198, 199
de Majona, John, 77
Malone, 1, 99 n. 1, 151, 191, 230 n. 1, 231 n. 1, 264 n. 1
Mantegna, 15, 45, 46
Mantua, 14, 45, 48
— Duke of, 161
Manutius, Aldus, 61
Marcus Geminus, 90
Mariano, Father, 46, 52
Martin, J., 27, 145
Mary, Queen, 85, 191
Masques, 51, 99, 103, 106, 112, 114, 158, 161, 162, 165–194, 202, 219, 223, 225, 265, 267, 269, 271
Matthews, Brander, 198 n. 1
Mayne, Jasper, 132, 214
Mazarin, Cardinal, 198, 211
Medici, Cardinal Ippolito dei, 22
Milan, 14
Minerva Museum, 162
Miracle plays, 94
Molmenti, P. G., 195, 197 n. 1
de Monconys, 235
Montenari, C., 56 n. 2, 57
— Giovanni, 55 n. 1
Moore-Smith, G. C., 88 n. 2
Moralities, 94
More, Sir T , 76
Morgan, Appleton, 138
Motteux, 271
Mountjoy, Charles, 75
Müntz, E., 11 n. 1, 15, 20 n. 1, 22 n. 2, 28, 32 n. 2, 53 n. 1
Mustapha, 238

Nabbes, *Covent Garden*, 207 n. 1; *Hannibal and Scipio*, 222 n. 1; *Microcosmos*, 179, 180, 209
Naples, 14
Neptune, 51
Neuendorff, B., 2
Newcastle, Duke of, 264 n. 1
Nicholas V, 54
Nichols, J. G., 78 n. 1, 89 n. 1, 91 n. 1, 92 n. 1, n. 2, 187 n. 1, 188 n. 1
Northumberland, Duke of, 79

Odell, G. C. D., 4, 218 n. 2, 241 n. 2, 264 n. 1
Opera, 195, 197, 198, 210, 211, 217–229, 231–5, 245, 264–271
Orrery, Earl of, 269

Pageants, 99, 103
Palamon and Arcyte, 90, 91
Palatine, Count, 174
Palladio, Andrea, 14, 26, 47, 54–6, 117, 164, 195, 203, 204, 239
Paris, 32, 240, 245
Parma, 195, 205, 207
Paul II, 10
Pauluzzi, 52, 53
Peake, R., 115, 159, 160
Penni, Bartholomew, 78
Pepys, 148, 233, 234, 238 n. 3
Perrault, 27, 245–9
Perspective, theory of, 16, 17, 18, 28–45, 47, 58, 80, 89, 105, 146–150, 152, 250; use of, 44–58, 110, 165–7, 172, 173, 175, 180, 195, 197, 204, 207, 220, 226, 227, 238, 239, 251, 290, 291
Peruzzi, Baldassare, 15, 29, 30, 32, 33, 51, 52 n. 1, 77
Philander, 23, 24, 62, 79, 119 n. 3, 125 n. 1, 145
Pix, Mrs M., 287
Plautus, 11, 102; *Amphitruo*, 139 n. 2; *Aulularia*, 89; *Menaechmi*, 13, 48, 103
Players, 101, 103, 107–9, 118, 179, 190, 191, 203, 229–234, 240–4
Pliny, 75, 81 n. 1, 125, 126, 141, 147
Poggio, 28, 74
Pollard, A. W., 76 n. 2
Pollux, *Onomasticon*, 15 n. 2, 17 n. 4, 24, 61–5, 75, 87, 91, 135, 136, 139–141, 207, 292
Pomponius Laetus, academy of, 10–13, 83
Pordage, 287
Porter, Thomas, 276
Poudra, M., 29 n. 3, 30 n. 1, 31, 32 n. 1, 149, 150
Pozzo, Andrea, 245, 249, 250
Progne, 90, 91
"Properties," spectacular, 39–42, 51, 53, 59–61, 64, 65, 67, 68, 91, 92, 97, 111–14, 156, 166, 169, 180, 232, 261–3, 293
Prosperi, Bernardino, 49
Psyche, 267
Ptolemy, 31
Puttenham, 123–5

Radcliffe, R., 85

Raffaello, 15, 20 n. 1, 33, 46, 52, 53, 77, 78
Rainolds, J., 88
Rapin, 272
Rastell, John, 76 n. 2
Ravenna, 151
Ravenscroft, 271, 277
Reeves, 148
von Reinhardstöttner, K., 9 n. 1
Reresby, Sir John, 217
Revels, Master of, 85, 101, 104, 149, 163, 192, 193; Office of, 3, 34, 88, 108, 109, 120, 231 n. 3, n. 4; records of, 85, 101, 103–115, 120, 191
Reyher, P., 4, 77, 99 n. 1, 103, 161 n. 1, n. 3, 162 n. 1, n. 2, 165, 170, 172 n. 1, 177 n. 1, 178, 179 n. 1, 185 n. 1, 202 n. 1
Reynolds, G. F., 2, 111, 120, 133
Riario, Cardinal Piero, 11
— Cardinal Raffaelle, 11–13
Richelieu, Cardinal, 198, 200, 211, 253 n. 1
Ritwise, John, 83, 84
Rivales, 91
Rivius, Gualther, 27, 79, 145
Robortello, 69
Romano, Giulio, 33
Rome, 10–12, 20 n. 1, 22, 23, 28, 29, 48, 52, 54, 69, 83, 197, 245
Ross, John, 112
della Rovere, Cardinal, 11
da Rovezzano, Benedetto, 77
Rubens, 161
Rye, W. B., 148 n. 1
Rymer, 259, 268, 272

Sabbatini, Nicola, 61, 149–158, 172, 173, 197
Saintsbury, G., 75 n. 4
Salmasius, 145
San Angelo, 52
San Gallo, 15
Sandys, J. E., 10 n. 2, 12 n. 2, 20 n. 1, 22 n. 2, 29 n. 2, 75 n. 4
Satirical plays, 123; type of scenery for, 17, 37, 42, 110, 164, 247
Scaliger, 62, 69, 87, 119 n. 3, 136, 137, 139
Scamozzi, Ottavio, 56, 58, 117, 164, 207, 239
Scene-painting, 15, 30–3, 35, 40, 44–7, 49–53, 57, 66, 104, 105,

107, 108, 110, 152, 153, 156, 166–8, 170–194
Scharf, G., 78 n. 1, n. 2
Schools, grammar, 82–6, 99, 118, 140
Scott, L., 28 n. 1
Seberius, 62
Seneca, 133, 135
Serlio, Sebastiano, Architettura, 29–42, 53–5, 57, 61, 79, 80, 91, 105, 110–15, 117, 119 n. 3, 135, 150, 152, 159, 164, 168, 169, 204, 207
de' Servi, Constantino, 161
Servius, 24 n. 1, 187, 292
Settle, Cambyses, 269; Conquest of China, 276; World in the Moon, 267 n. 1
Shadwell, 243; Lancashire Witches, 266–8
Shakespeare, 2, 130, 252, 288; Henry V, 131, 132; 2 Henry VI, 138; King Lear, 134; Richard III, 138; Troilus and Cressida, 287
Shute, John, 75 n. 3, 79–81
Sidney, Apology, 123, 128, 129, 237, 255
Siradia, Palatine of, 91
Sixtus IV, 10, 11
Smith, Gilbert, 127
— Gregory, 124 n. 1, 128 n. 1, 129 n. 1, n. 2, 132 n. 3, 135 n. 2
Somers, 173 n. 1
Sophocles, 66, 67, 69, 274; Oedipus, 56, 139 n. 2
de Sorbière, 236, 255, 278
Spectator, 256, 263, 273
Spinelli, Gasparo, 102
— Ludovico, 102
Spingarn, J. E., 10, 66 n. 1, 69, 75 n. 4, 200, 201, 237 n. 1, 259 n. 2, 268 n. 1, 275 n. 1, 284 n. 1
Sprat, Thomas, 255, 278
Stage, 'apron,' 119, 244; lighting of, 157, 158, 168, 171–3, 178, 237
Stage Decoration, in England, 70, 140, 141; cost of, 88, 102, 105, 106, 187, 193; at Court, 100, 101–115, 120, 165–185, 189, 191–4, 225, 238, 251; at Grammar-schools, 84 n. 2; influence of classics on, 73–87, 90, 98, 121, 140, 141, 290, 293; influence of France on, 200, 201; influence of Germany

on, 79; influence of Italy on, 42, 74–84, 90–2, 103, 105, 111–15, 140, 141, 200; at Inns of Court, 93–8; in Theatres, 116, 120, 121, 179, 193, 195, 205, 206, 208–214, 217, 221–239, 250–2; theory of, 122–141, 151–8, 252–6, 260–271, 274–289; at Universities, 87–91, 185–192

Stage Decoration, in France, 32, 197–201; influence of Italy on, 42, 198–200

— in Greece and Rome, 16–18, 24, 32, 44, 58, 63, 65

— in Italy, 32–5, 43–53, 56–8, 195, 197; accessories of, 39–42, 51, 52, 59–65, 67; classed as architecture, 16, 32, 42, 44, 47, 67, 291; corresponding to type of drama 17, 19, 26, 35–8, 42, 48, 49, 52, 53, 63; cost of, 41, 42, 50; influence of Academies on, see Academies; influence of Courts on, see Courts; influence of Greece and Rome on, 9, 12, 18, 43, 44, 47, 48, 69; influence of Vitruvius on, see Vitruvius; theory of, 18, 30, 32–8, 41–4, 47, 53, 58, 66–70

Stapylton, 284
Steevens, 1
Stenwyck, 148
Stocket, Lewis, 106
Stockwood, J., 119
Stopes, Mrs C. C., 3 n. 5, 118 n. 3, 119 n. 2, 193 n. 4
Stringer, 186, 187
Stuart, D. C., 279 n. 2
Sturt, John, 249
Suckling, Sir J., Aglaura, 193, 194, 209
Sullivan, M., 175 n. 2, 184
Sulpitius Verulamus, 12, 13, 44, 47, 48, 83, 117
Swift, Dean, 244 n. 2
Symmachus, 125
Symonds, J. A., 10 n. 2, 14 n. 1, 22 n. 2, 28 n. 1, 59, 60 n. 2

Tancred and Gismund, 97, 98
Tasso, Aminta, 201
Tatham, John, The Rump, 232
Taylor, Brook, 150
— H. C., 75 n. 4

Tempe Restored, 176, 178
Tempest, The, 267
Terence, Phormio, 84
Teuffel, 125 n. 1
Theatres, English, 116–121, 140, 179, 201–8, 210, 232, 233, 236–8; architecture of, 117–19, 202, 204–9, 240–3, 245, 246; Blackfriars, 193, 206; Cockpit, 179, 202, 206, 226–8; Cockpit-in-Court, 201–3, 205; Dorset-Garden, 234, 240–4; Drury Lane, 234, 240–4; Duke's House, 233, 235; King's, 233, 235, 236; Queen's, 244, 245; Red Bull, 230, 234; Rutland House, 219–225; Salisbury Court, 179, 206, 230, 232; Swan, 119, 208; Vere Street, 230, 234

— French, 197–9, 201, 211

— Greek, 16, 17, 20, 24, 32, 43, 44, 61–3, 65, 206

— Italian, 43, 44, 54, 117, 206, 207; of Ariosto, 54; at Ferrara, 14, 48; mural decorations in, 45–7, 56; at Parma, 195, 205, 207; at Rome, 54, 124, 126; at San Angelo, 52, 53; in Vatican, 54; at Venice, 195, 211, 217; at Vicenza, 5 n. 1, 14, 42, 54–8, 117, 164, 203, 204, 206

— origin of, 123–5

— Roman, 16, 17, 21, 24, 32, 43, 44, 55, 58, 206

Thorndike, A. H., 4, 84 n. 2, 85 n. 7, 139 n. 1, 180 n. 2, 185 n. 1, 191, 207 n. 1, 213 n. 1
Thunder, presentation of, 17, 19, 21, 22, 39, 42, 60, 64, 65, 67, 91, 92, 111, 120, 130, 133–5, 157, 212, 246, 252, 261–3, 292, 293
Thynne, 92 n. 3
Tipping, H. A., 241 n. 1
Tiraboschi, G., 11 n. 2, 14 n. 3, 22 n. 2
Torelli, Giacomo, 197, 198, 262 n. 2
Torresany, Peter, 77
Toto, Anthony, 77
Townshend, Aurelian, 167 n. 2, 176, 177 n. 1, 178 n. 1
— D., 161 n. 3
— Heywood, 78 n. 2
Tragedy, 66–9, 86, 93, 123, 124,

127–9, 135–8, 253–263, 266, 268, 270, 273, 285; type of scenery for, 17, 36, 42, 56, 63, 64, 104, 110
de Treviso, Girolamo, 77
Trissino, Giorgio, 55; *Sofonisba*, 55 n. 2, 69
Triumph of Caesar, The, 45, 46
Troilus and Pandor, 101
Tuke, 286
Tupper, J. W., 4, 5 n., 219 n. 1, 220 n. 1, 222, 223, 235 n. 1
Tuscany, Prince Don Francesca of, 53, 61

Ubaldi, Guido, 149–151
Udall, Nicholas, 85; *Ezechias*, 89; *Ralph Roister Doister*, 85
Unity, of place, 68–70, 126–132, 151, 252, 253, 278–289; of time, 69, 128, 129, 200, 252, 278, 282, 284
Universities, drama at, 73, 82, 86–92, 99, 106, 118, 140, 192; Cambridge, 86, 87–92, 106, 187; Oxford, 74, 86, 87–92, 106, 179, 185, 186, 188–191, 193, 210
Upham, A. H., 200 n. 1
Urbino, 14, 38, 76, 114
— Duke of, 49, 50, 112

Valla, Georgius, 69
Van Dyck, 161
Vanbrugh, 206, 244, 245, 250
Varchiese, Antonio Francesco, 62
Vasari, 21, 22 n. 2, 28, 29 n. 3, 32 n. 2, 41 n. 1, 44, 46, 47 n. 1, 51, 52 n. 1, 53, 55 n. 2, 59, 60, 77, 78 n. 1, 80, 159
Venice, 14, 19, 29, 31, 61, 75, 195, 197, 209, 211, 217
Venus, 51
Viator, 30
Vicenza, 14, 29, 42, 54–8
Vickers, K. H., 74 n. 3
Vigarani, Carlo, 262 n. 2
— Gaspare, 262 n. 2

Vignola, 23, 31, 32, 164
Vitruvius, *De Architectura*, 12–35, 37, 42–4, 47–9, 52–5, 57, 61–3, 65–7, 74, 75, 79–81, 84, 91, 111, 116–121, 133, 136, 140, 141, 145–7, 150, 167, 195, 202, 206, 207, 243, 245–7, 251, 257, 258, 290, 291
Vives, 75, 76
Voigt, G., 10 n. 2

Wallace, C. W., 3, 73, 74, 84 n. 2, 85 n. 2, n. 7, 99, 101, 115, 185 n. 1
Walton, Izaak, 147 n. 1
Ward, Sir A. W., 73, 94
Warton, T., 84 n. 1, 85 n. 4, 93 n. 3
Watson, Edmund, 87
— Foster, 75 n. 1, n. 2, 83 n. 1
Webb, John, 5 n. 1, 163, 164, 202, 205–7, 222, 223, 225, 226, 238, 267 n. 1
Webbe, 123, 132
Wegener, R., 213 n. 1
Wheatley, H. B., 208 n. 2
Whetstone, *Promos and Cassandra*, 127, 128, 132
Wilkinson, R., 245 n. 1
Withington, R., 99 n. 1
Wits, The, 233
Wolsey, Cardinal, 77, 84, 85, 93, 102
Wood, Anthony à, 84 n. 1, 85 n. 1, 188–191, 193
Woodward, W. H., 83 n. 1
Works, Office of, 105, 106; Surveyor of, 162, 163, 185, 206, 226, 238, 240, 244 n. 2
Wotton, Henry, 145–7
Wren, Christopher, 146, 205, 206, 240, 242, 250
Wright, *Historia Histrionica*, 206, 234, 240
— C. H. C., 278 n. 1
Wycherley, *Gentleman Dancing-Master*, 239; *Plain-Dealer*, 285

Zucchero, Federigo, 47